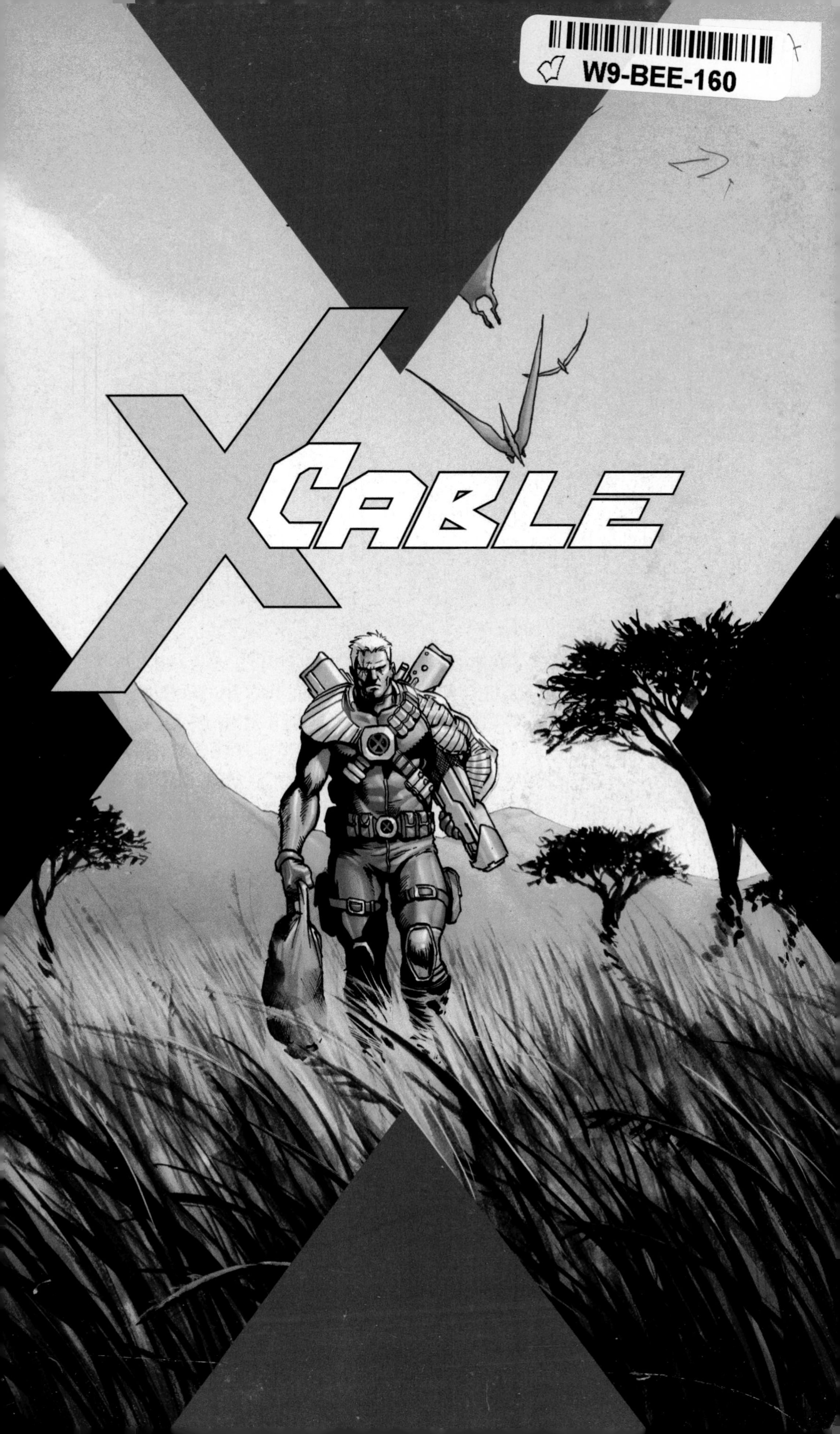
CABLE

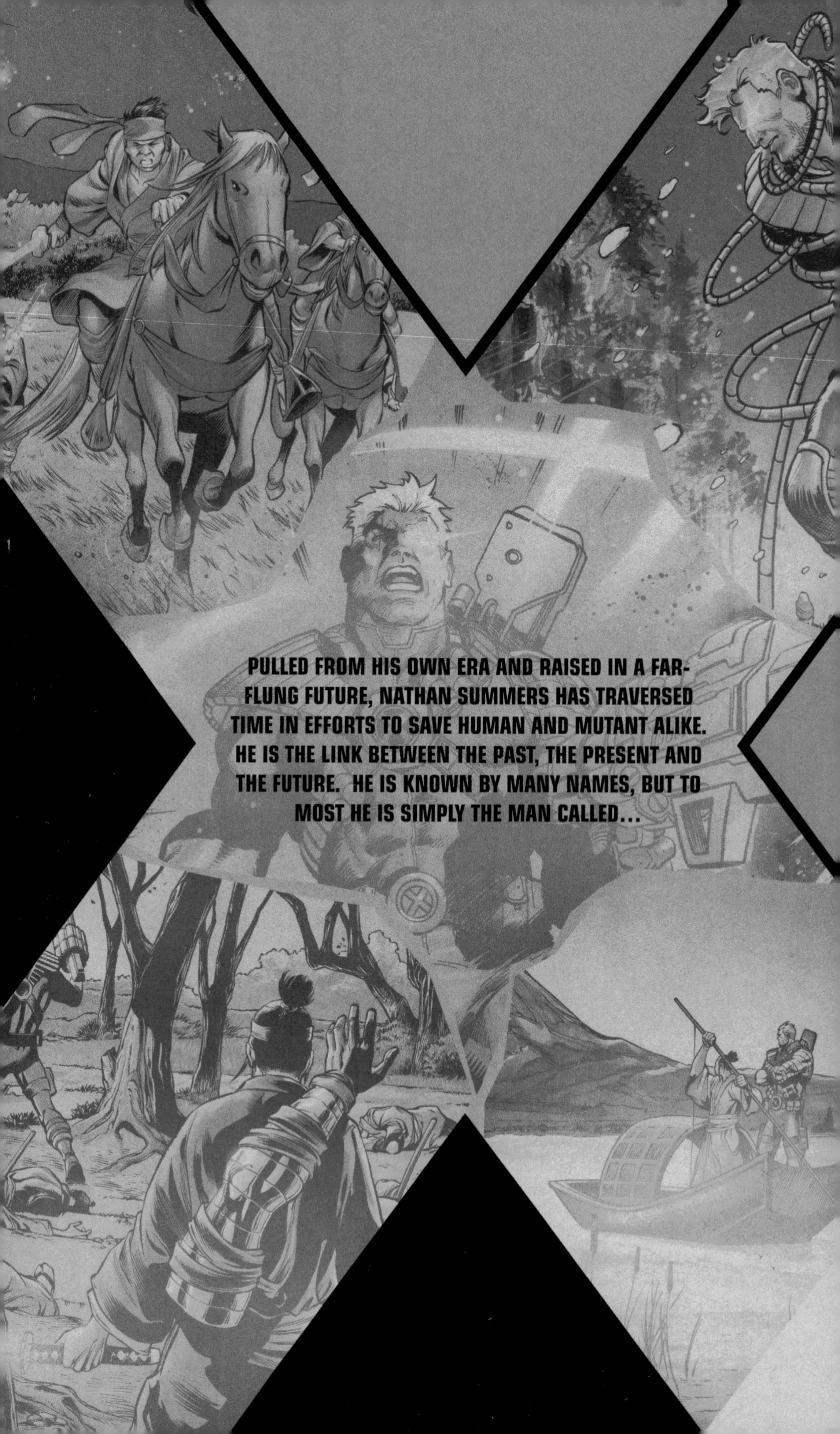
PULLED FROM HIS OWN ERA AND RAISED IN A FAR-FLUNG FUTURE, NATHAN SUMMERS HAS TRAVERSED TIME IN EFFORTS TO SAVE HUMAN AND MUTANT ALIKE. HE IS THE LINK BETWEEN THE PAST, THE PRESENT AND THE FUTURE. HE IS KNOWN BY MANY NAMES, BUT TO MOST HE IS SIMPLY THE MAN CALLED...

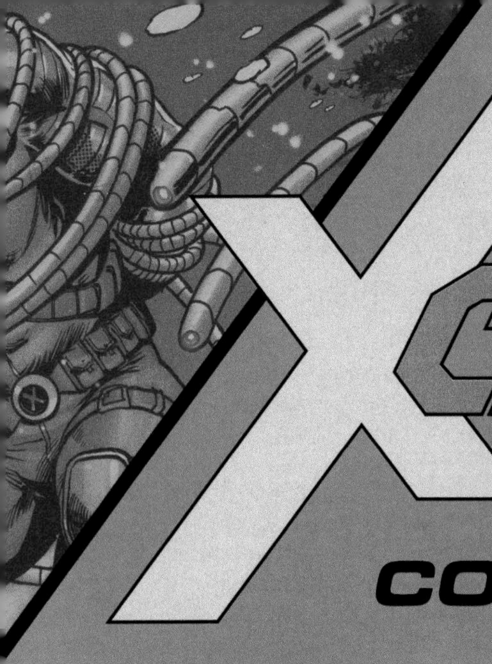

CABLE

CONQUEST

Writer/**JAMES ROBINSON**

ISSUES #1-3

Pencilers/**CARLOS PACHECO** with **THONY SILAS** (#3)

Inkers/**RAFAEL FONTERIZ** with **THONY SILAS** (#3)

Colorists/**JESUS ABURTOV** with **FEDERICO BLEE** (#2-3) & **DONO SÁNCHEZ-ALMARA** (#3)

ISSUES #4-5

Artist/**YILDIRAY CINAR**

Colorists/**JESUS ABURTOV** with **FEDERICO BLEE** (#4)

Letterers/**VC's CORY PETIT** with **JOE SABINO** (#5)

Cover Art/**DALE KEOWN** & **JASON KEITH**

Assistant Editor/**CHRIS ROBINSON**
Associate Editor/**MARK BASSO**
Editor/**MARK PANICCIA**

Collection Editor/**JENNIFER GRÜNWALD** • Assistant Editor/**CAITLIN O'CONNELL**
Associate Managing Editor/**KATERI WOODY** • Editor, Special Projects/**MARK D. BEAZLEY**
VP Production & Special Projects/**JEFF YOUNGQUIST** • SVP Print, Sales & Marketing/**DAVID GABRIEL**
Book Designer/**JAY BOWEN**

Editor in Chief/**AXEL ALONSO** • Chief Creative Officer/**JOE QUESADA**
President/**DAN BUCKLEY** • Executive Producer/**ALAN FINE**

CABLE VOL. 1: CONQUEST. Contains material originally published in magazine form as CABLE #1-5. First printing 2017. ISBN# 978-1-302-90482-1. Published by MARVEL WORLDWIDE, INC., a subsidiary of MARVEL ENTERTAINMENT, LLC. OFFICE OF PUBLICATION: 135 West 50th Street, New York, NY 10020. **Printed in the U.S.A.** DAN BUCKLEY, President, Marvel Entertainment; JOE QUESADA, Chief Creative Officer; TOM BREVOORT, SVP of Publishing; DAVID BOGART, SVP of Business Affairs & Operations, Publishing & Partnership; C.B. CEBULSKI, VP of Brand Management & Development, Asia; DAVID GABRIEL, SVP of Sales & Marketing, Publishing; JEFF YOUNGQUIST, VP of Production & Special Projects; DAN CARR, Executive Director of Publishing Technology; ALEX MORALES, Director of Publishing Operations; SUSAN CRESPI, Production Manager; STAN LEE, Chairman Emeritus. For information regarding advertising in Marvel Comics or on Marvel.com, please contact Vit DeBellis, Integrated Sales Manager, at vdebellis@marvel.com. For Marvel subscription inquiries, please call 888-511-5480. **Manufactured between 10/13/2017 and 11/13/2017 by QUAD/GRAPHICS WASECA, WASECA, MN, USA.**

10 9 8 7 6 5 4 3 2 1

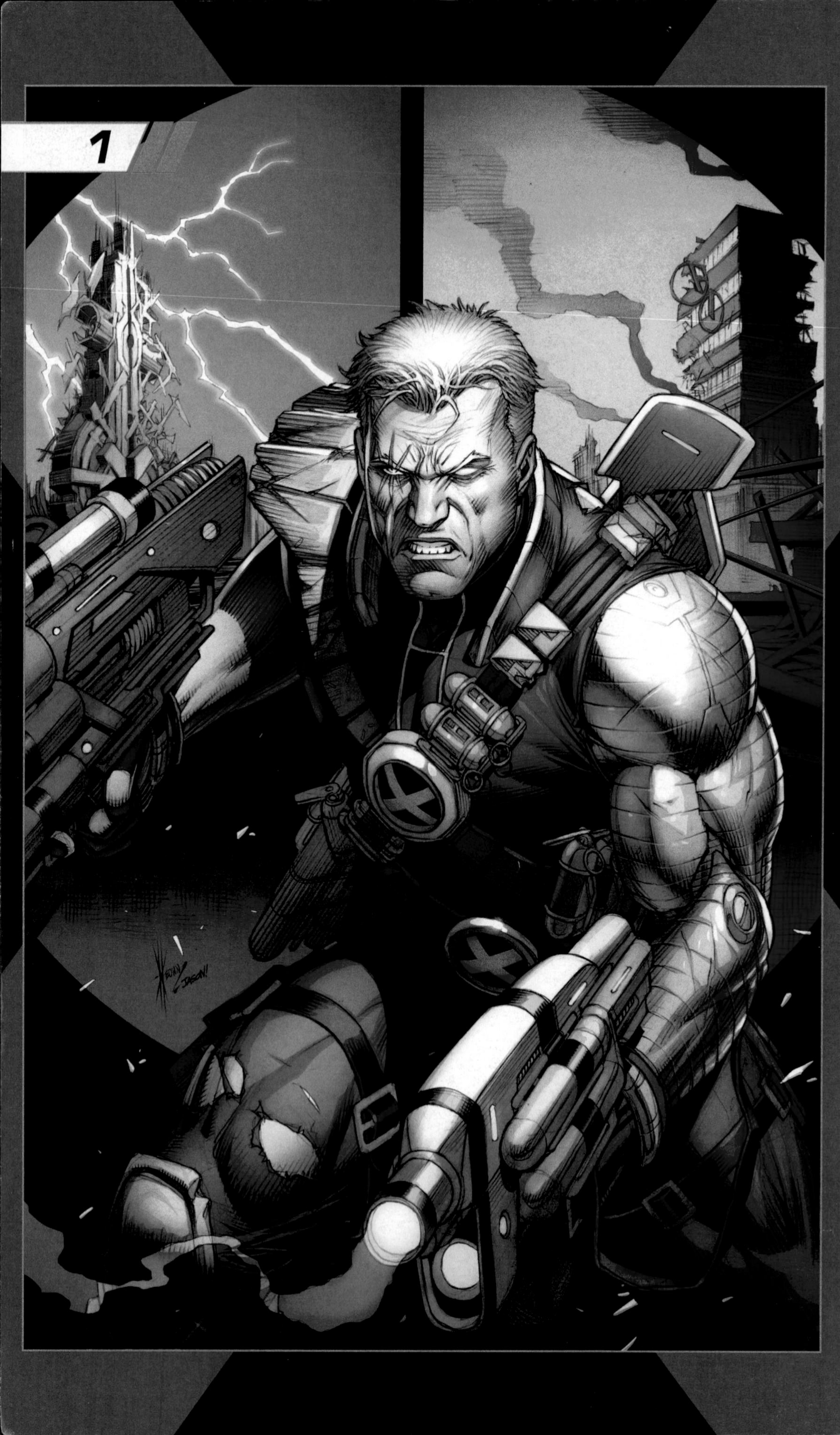
1

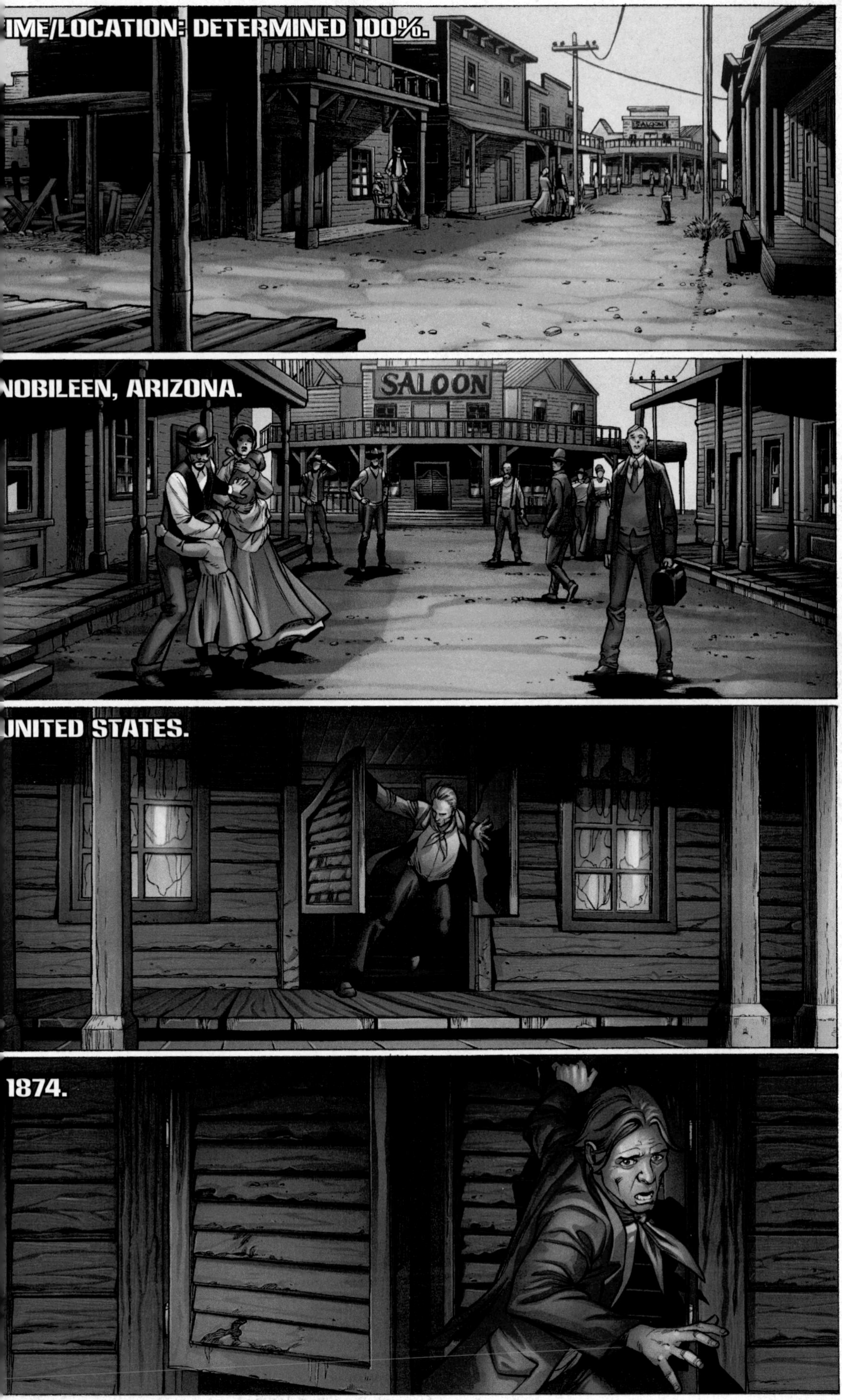
IME/LOCATION: DETERMINED 100%.
SALOON
NOBILEEN, ARIZONA.
SALOON
UNITED STATES.
1874.

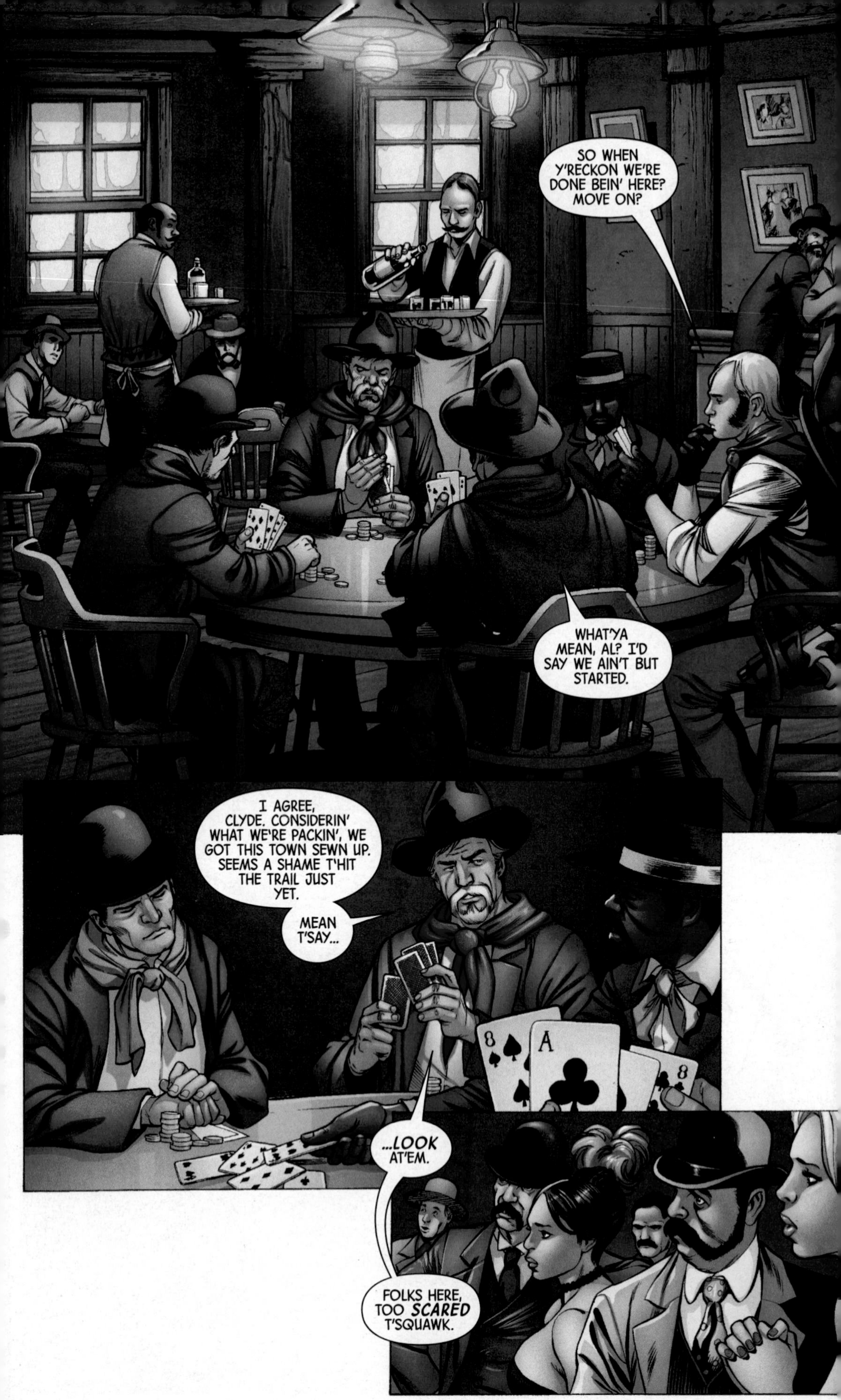
SO WHEN Y'RECKON WE'RE DONE BEIN' HERE? MOVE ON?
WHAT'YA MEAN, AL? I'D SAY WE AIN'T BUT STARTED.
I AGREE, CLYDE. CONSIDERIN' WHAT WE'RE PACKIN', WE GOT THIS TOWN SEWN UP. SEEMS A SHAME T'HIT THE TRAIL JUST YET.
MEAN T'SAY...
...*LOOK* AT'EM.
FOLKS HERE, TOO *SCARED* T'SQUAWK.

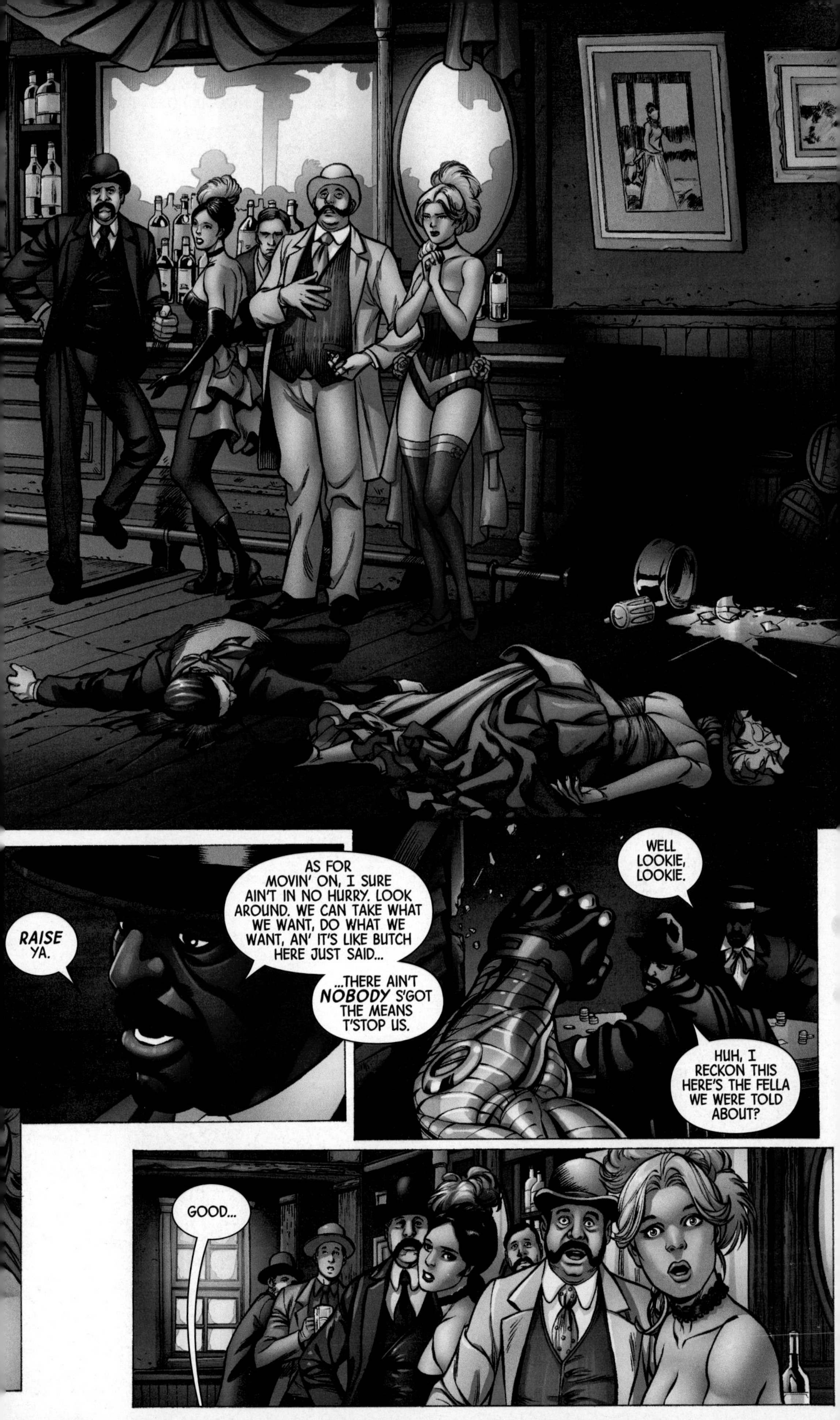

RAISE YA.
AS FOR MOVIN' ON, I SURE AIN'T IN NO HURRY. LOOK AROUND. WE CAN TAKE WHAT WE WANT, DO WHAT WE WANT, AN' IT'S LIKE BUTCH HERE JUST SAID...
...THERE AIN'T NOBODY S'GOT THE MEANS T'STOP US.
WELL LOOKIE, LOOKIE.
HUH, I RECKON THIS HERE'S THE FELLA WE WERE TOLD ABOUT?
GOOD...

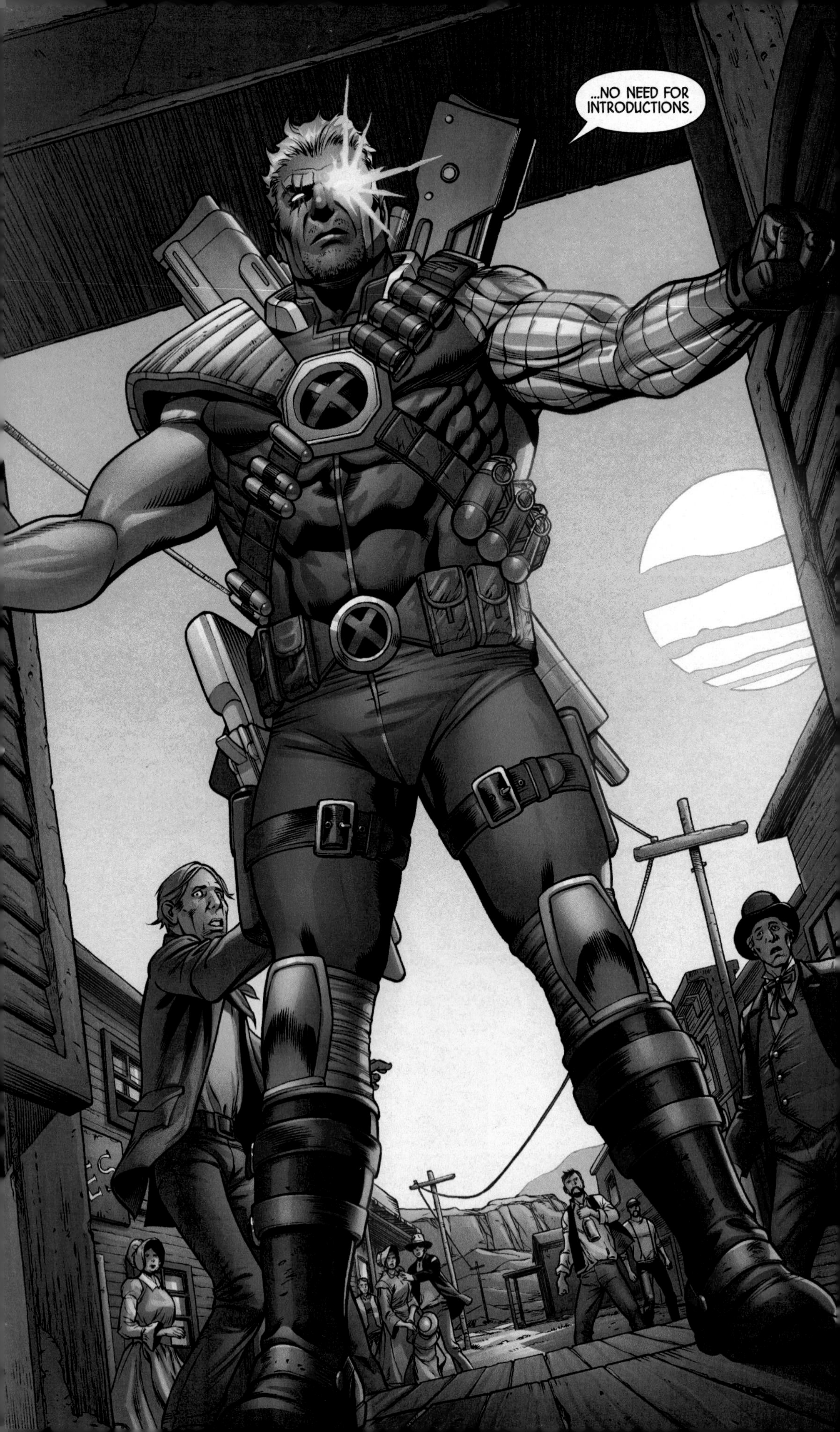
...NO NEED FOR INTRODUCTIONS.

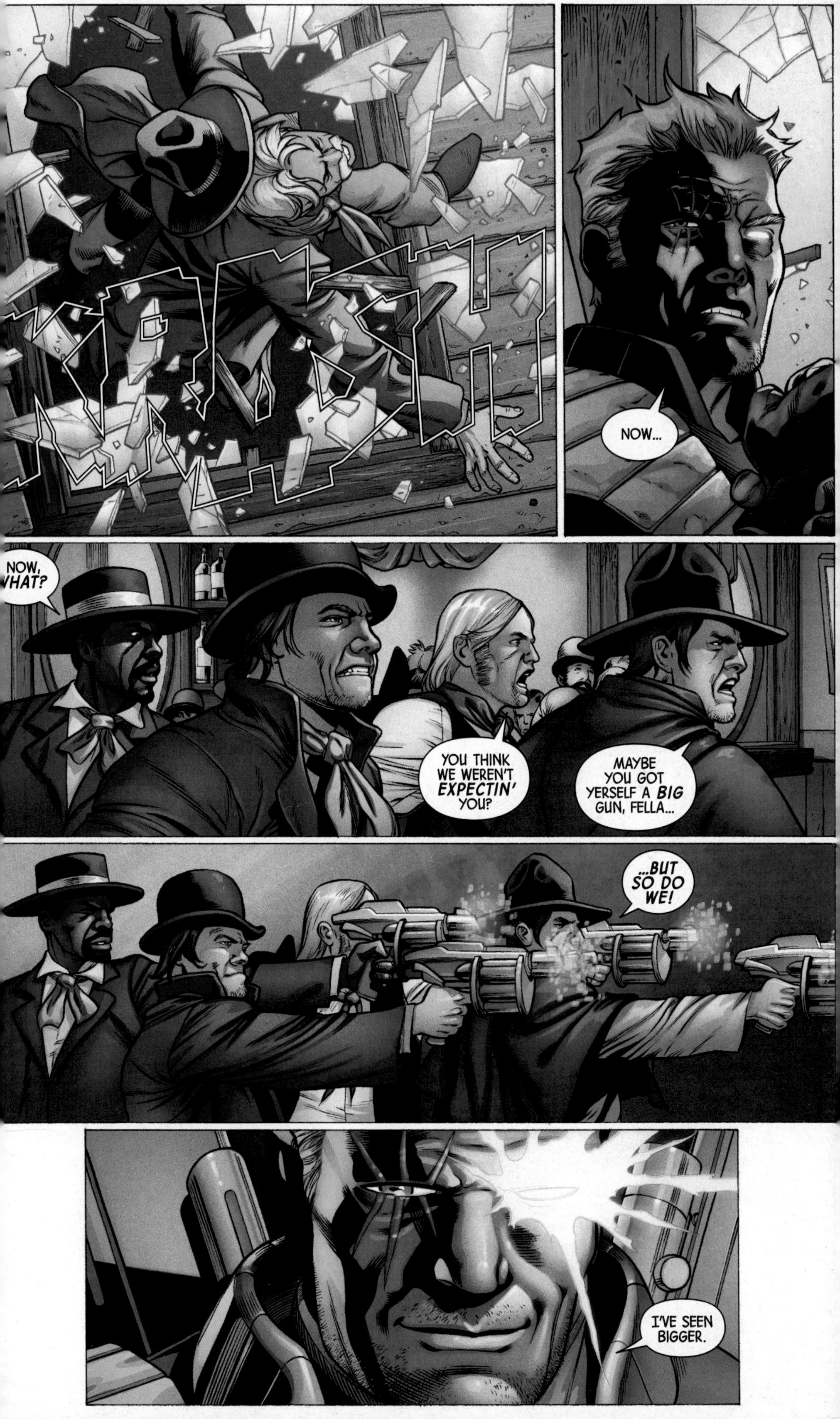
KRASH
NOW...
NOW, WHAT?
YOU THINK WE WEREN'T EXPECTIN' YOU?
MAYBE YOU GOT YERSELF A BIG GUN, FELLA...
...BUT SO DO WE!
I'VE SEEN BIGGER.

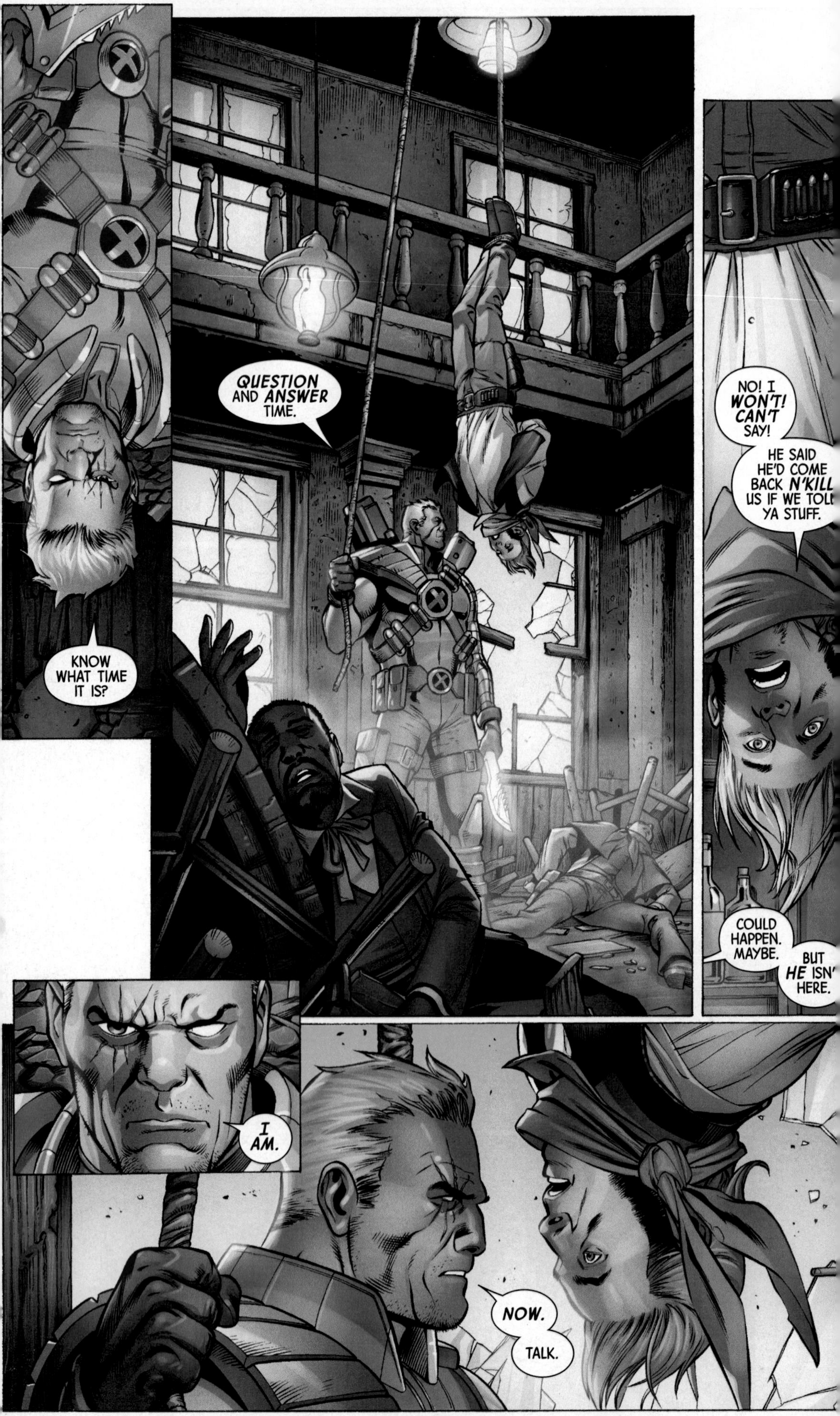

KNOW WHAT TIME IT IS?
QUESTION AND ANSWER TIME.
NO! I WON'T! CAN'T SAY!
HE SAID HE'D COME BACK N'KILL US IF WE TOLD YA STUFF.
COULD HAPPEN. MAYBE.
BUT HE ISN'T HERE.
I AM.
NOW.
TALK.

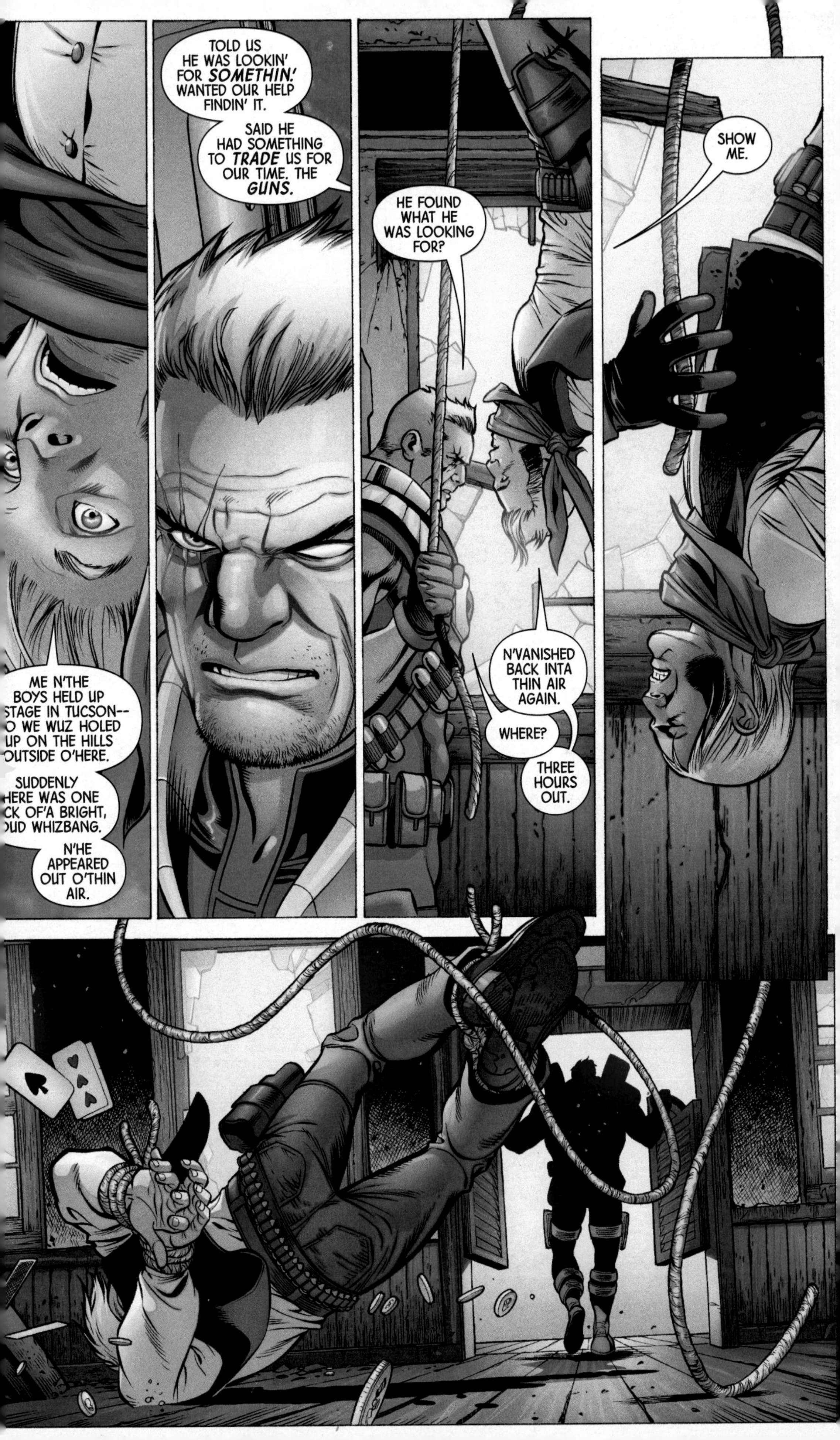
ME N'THE BOYS HELD UP STAGE IN TUCSON-- O WE WUZ HOLED UP ON THE HILLS OUTSIDE O'HERE.
SUDDENLY HERE WAS ONE CK OF'A BRIGHT, OUD WHIZBANG.
N'HE APPEARED OUT O'THIN AIR.
TOLD US HE WAS LOOKIN' FOR SOMETHIN.' WANTED OUR HELP FINDIN' IT.
SAID HE HAD SOMETHING TO TRADE US FOR OUR TIME. THE GUNS.
HE FOUND WHAT HE WAS LOOKING FOR?
N'VANISHED BACK INTA THIN AIR AGAIN.
WHERE?
THREE HOURS OUT.
SHOW ME.

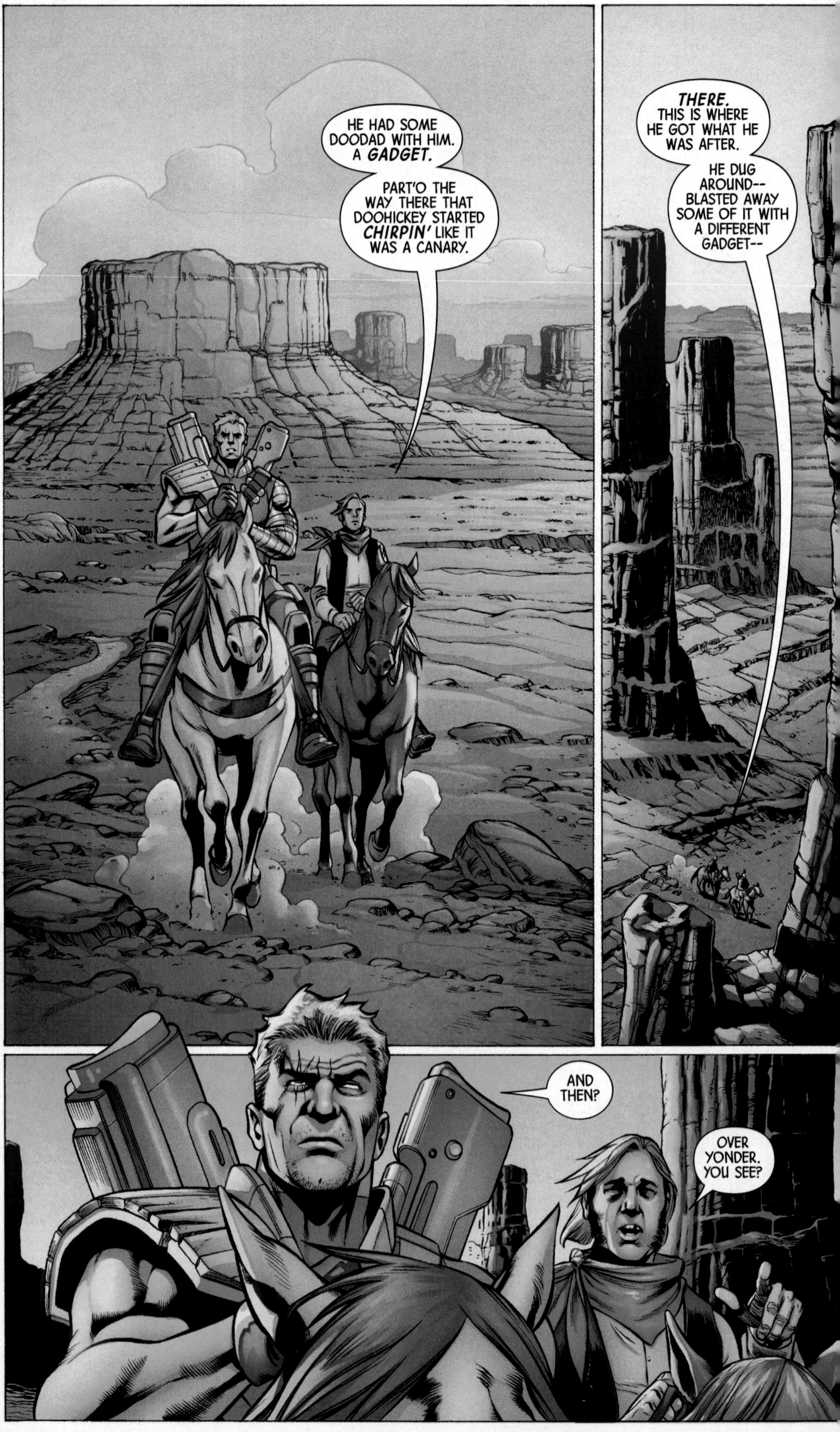
HE HAD SOME DOODAD WITH HIM. A GADGET.
PART'O THE WAY THERE THAT DOOHICKEY STARTED CHIRPIN' LIKE IT WAS A CANARY.
THERE. THIS IS WHERE HE GOT WHAT HE WAS AFTER.
HE DUG AROUND-- BLASTED AWAY SOME OF IT WITH A DIFFERENT GADGET--
AND THEN?
OVER YONDER. YOU SEE?

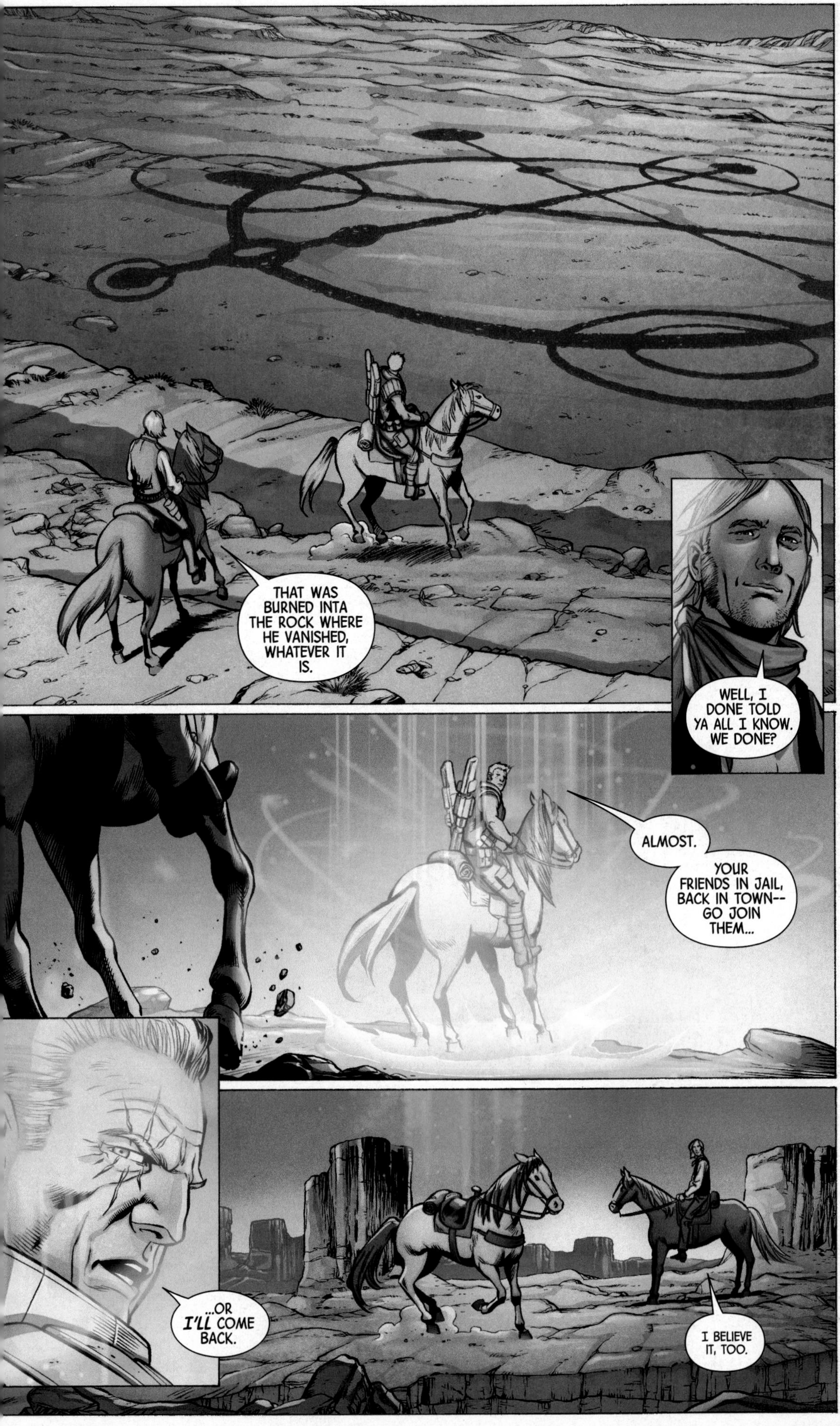
THAT WAS BURNED INTA THE ROCK WHERE HE VANISHED, WHATEVER IT IS.
WELL, I DONE TOLD YA ALL I KNOW. WE DONE?
ALMOST.
YOUR FRIENDS IN JAIL, BACK IN TOWN-- GO JOIN THEM...
...OR I'LL COME BACK.
I BELIEVE IT, TOO.

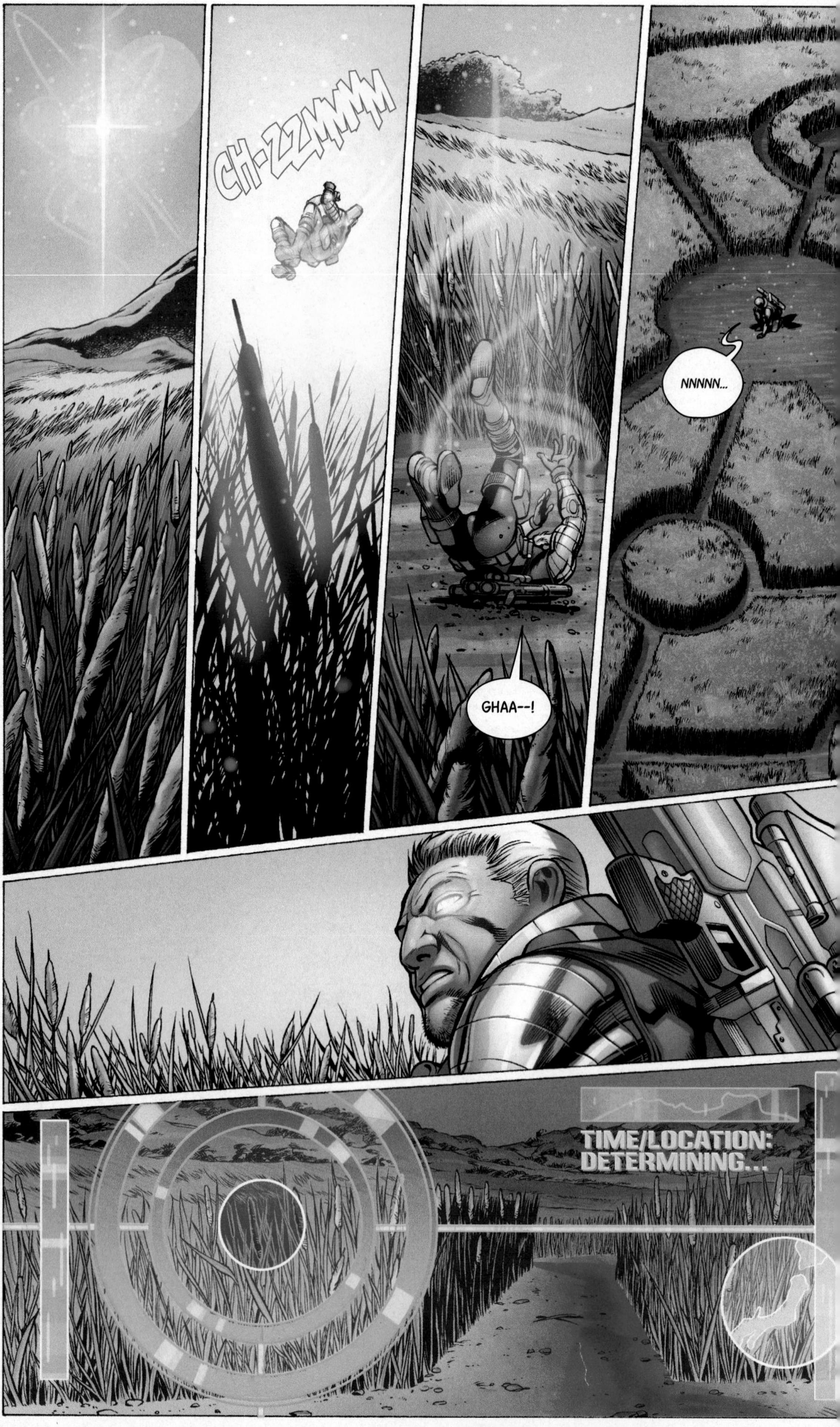
CH-ZZMMM
GHAA--!
NNNNN...
TIME/LOCATION:
DETERMINING...

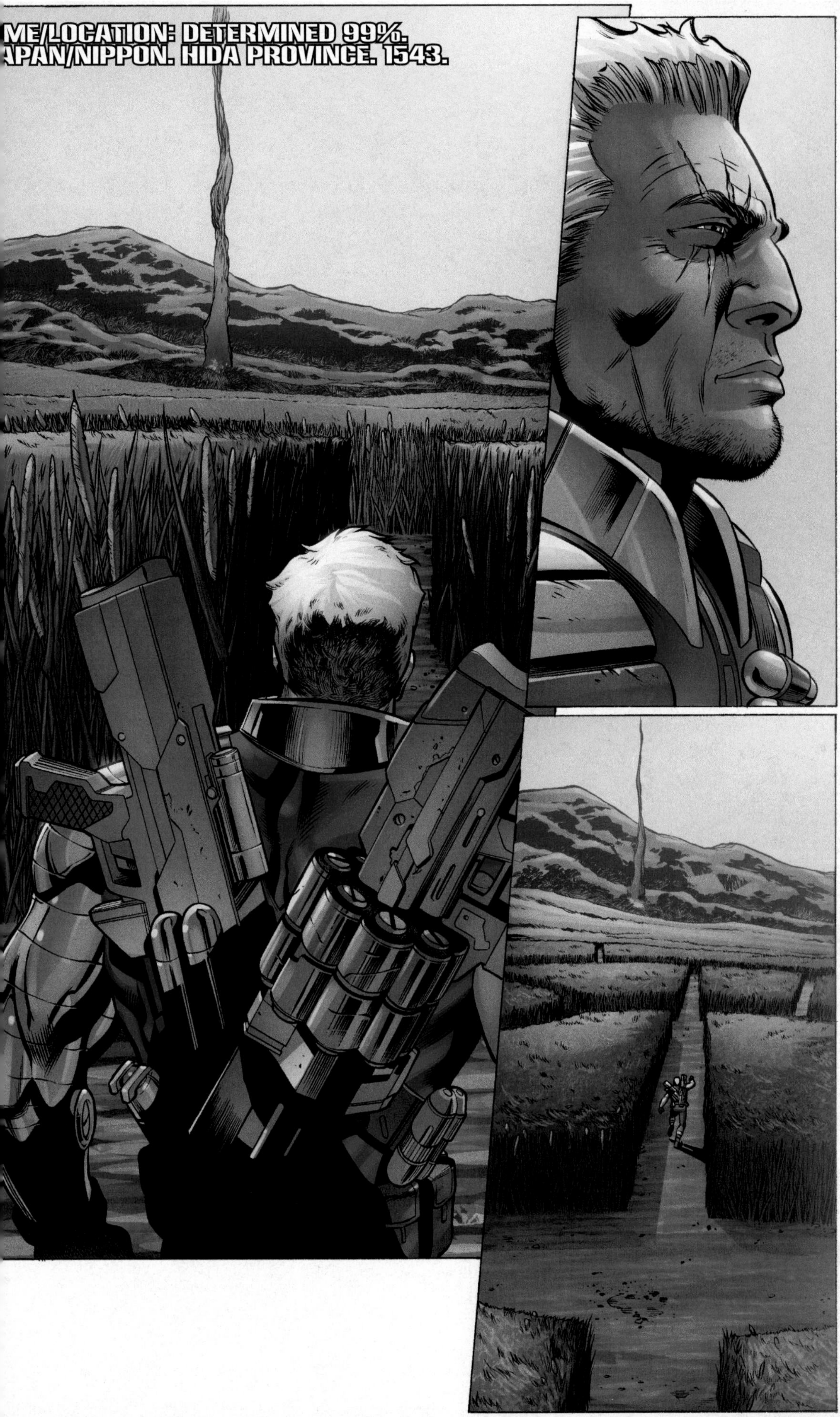
ME/LOCATION: DETERMINED 99%.
APAN/NIPPON. HIDA PROVINCE. 1543.

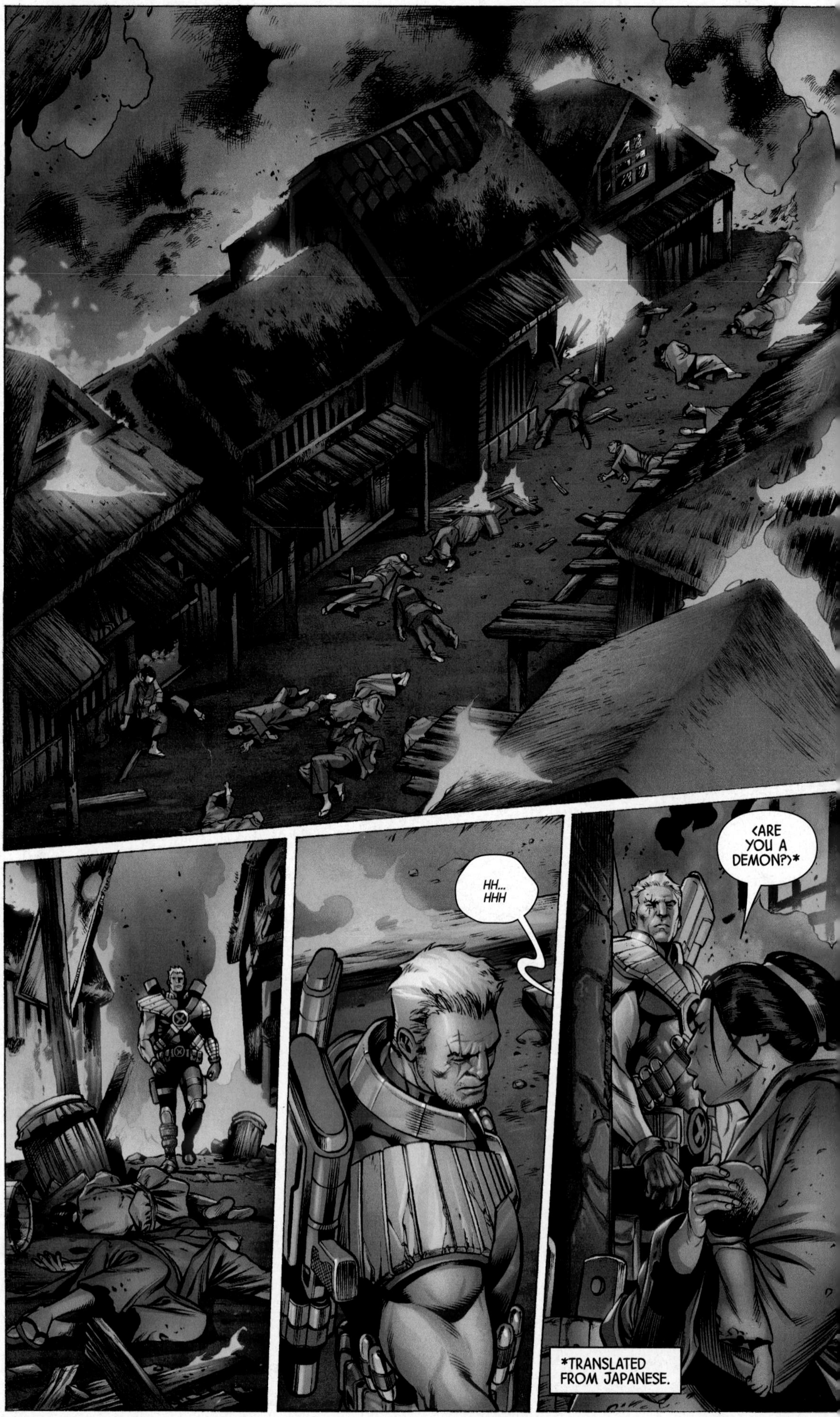
HH... HHH
<ARE YOU A DEMON?>*
*TRANSLATED FROM JAPANESE.

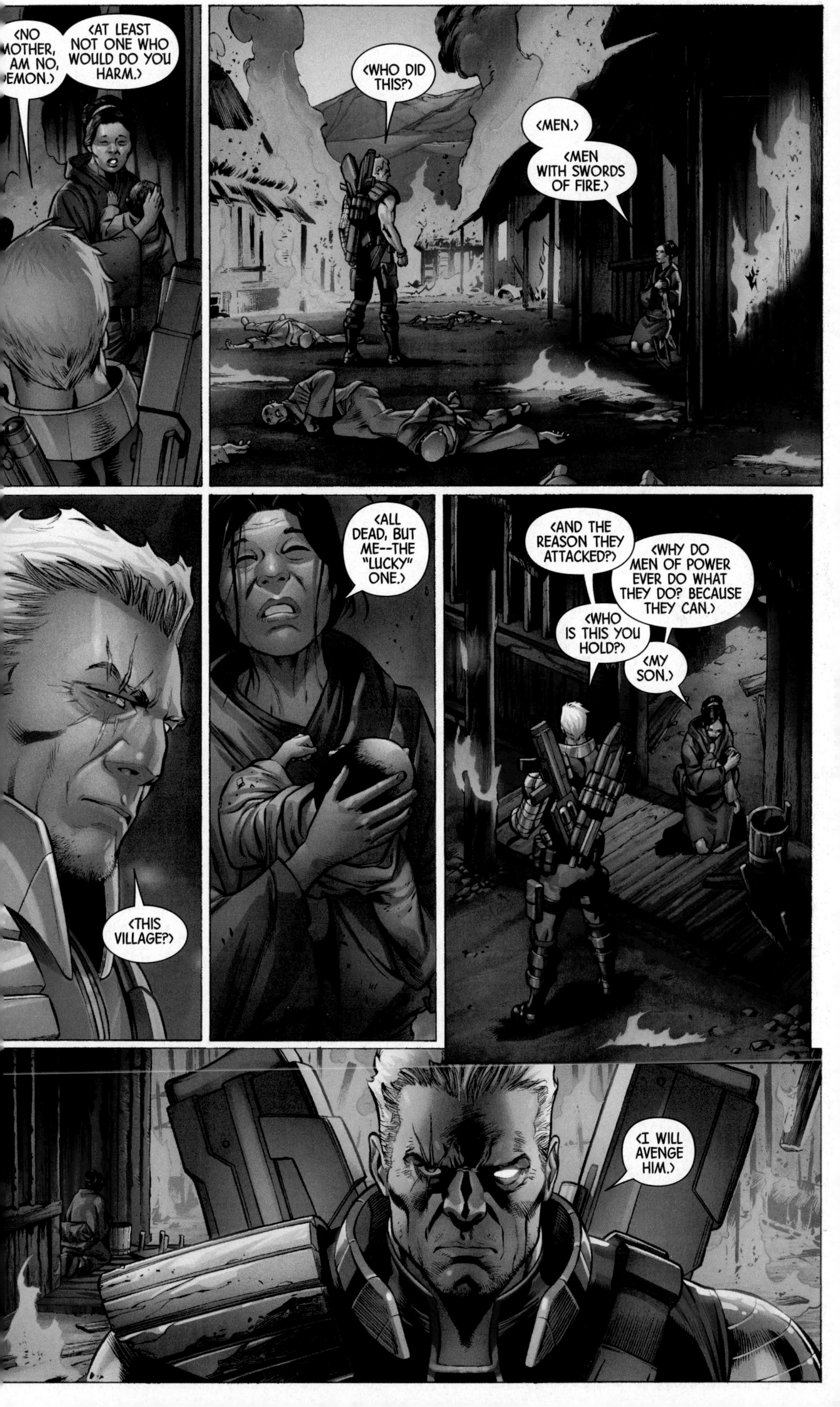

<NO MOTHER, I AM NO DEMON.>
<AT LEAST NOT ONE WHO WOULD DO YOU HARM.>
<WHO DID THIS?>
<MEN.>
<MEN WITH SWORDS OF FIRE.>
<THIS VILLAGE?>
<ALL DEAD, BUT ME--THE "LUCKY" ONE.>
<AND THE REASON THEY ATTACKED?>
<WHY DO MEN OF POWER EVER DO WHAT THEY DO? BECAUSE THEY CAN.>
<WHO IS THIS YOU HOLD?>
<MY SON.>
<I WILL AVENGE HIM.>

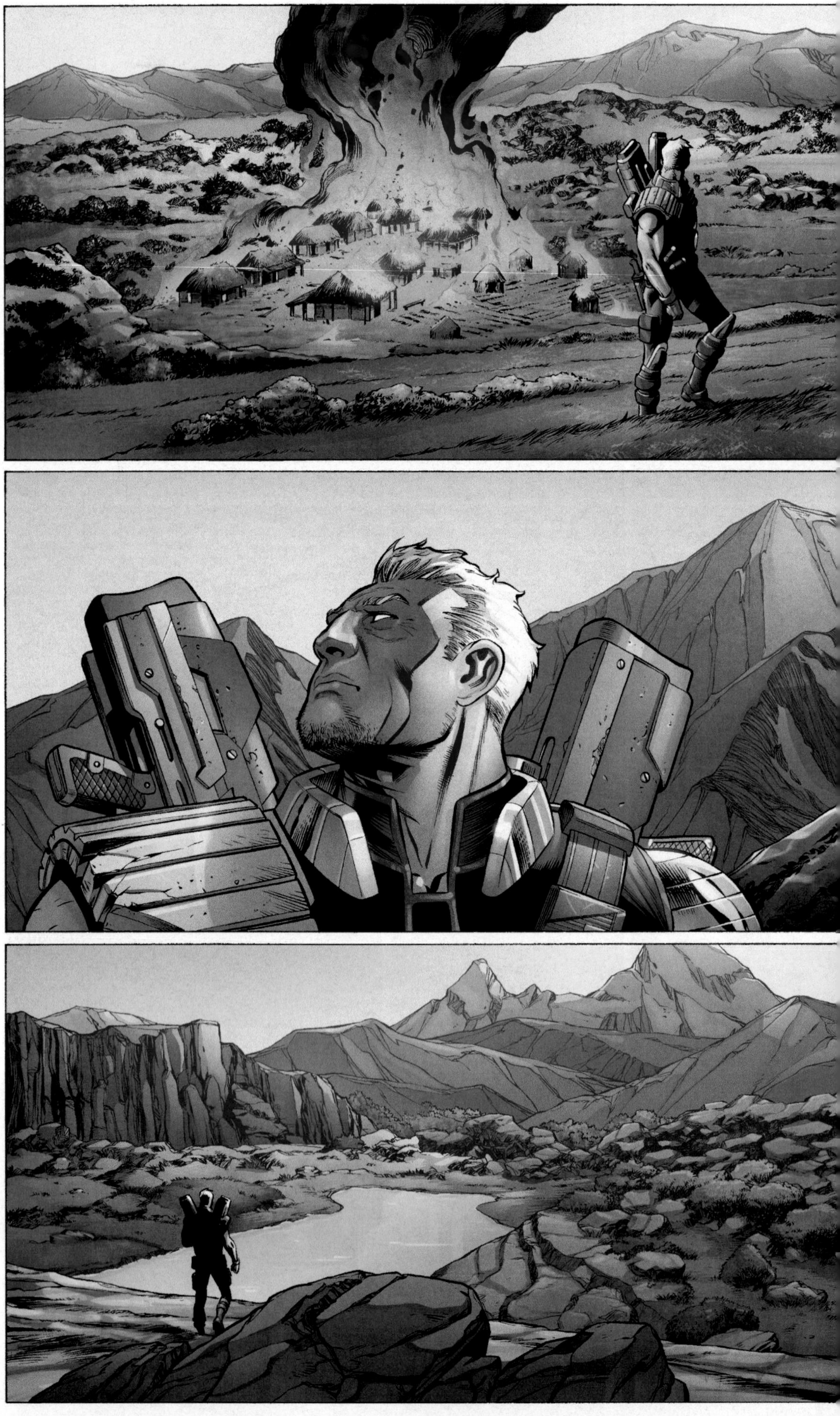

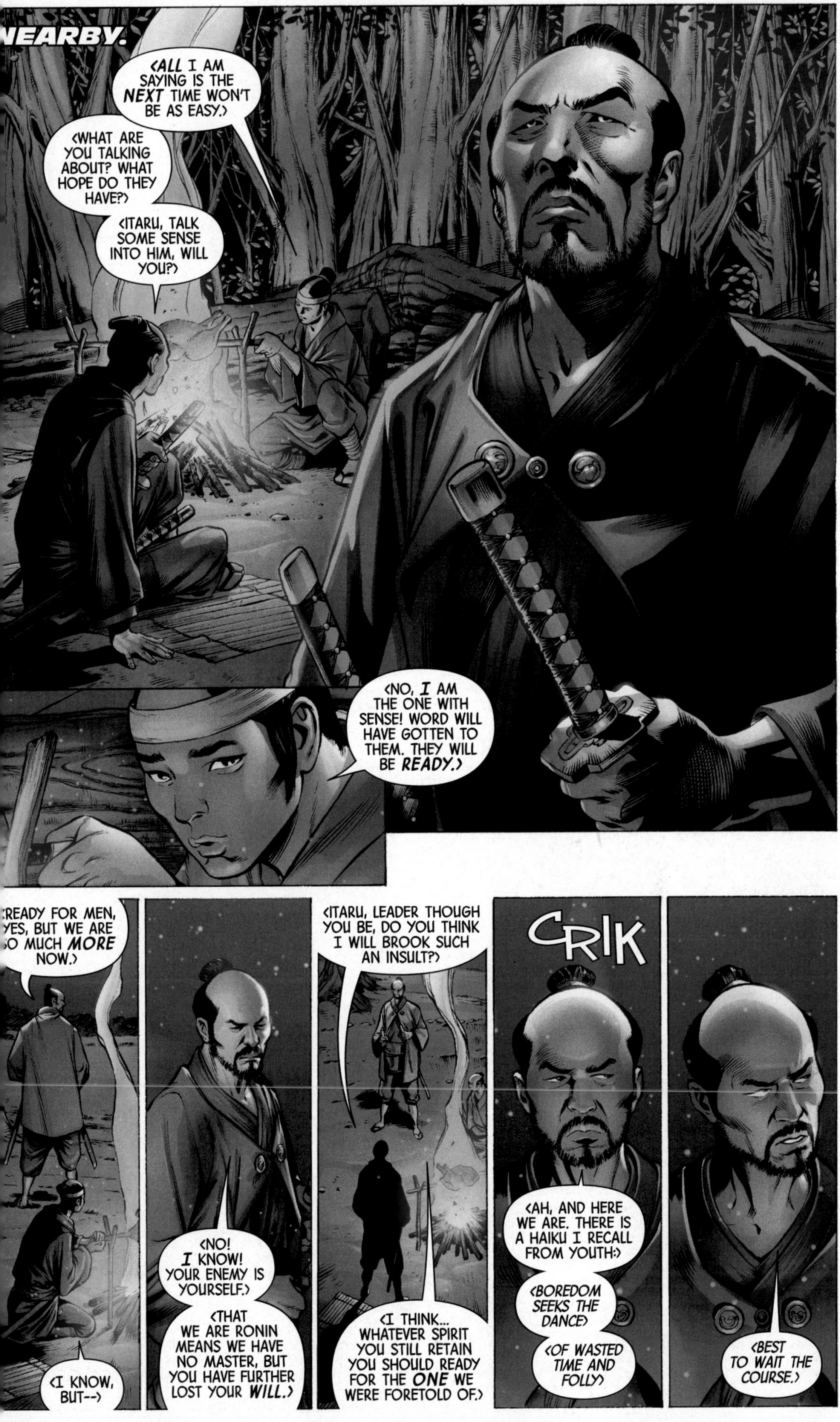
NEARBY.
<ALL I AM SAYING IS THE NEXT TIME WON'T BE AS EASY.>
<WHAT ARE YOU TALKING ABOUT? WHAT HOPE DO THEY HAVE?>
<ITARU, TALK SOME SENSE INTO HIM, WILL YOU?>
<NO, I AM THE ONE WITH SENSE! WORD WILL HAVE GOTTEN TO THEM. THEY WILL BE READY.>
<READY FOR MEN, YES, BUT WE ARE SO MUCH MORE NOW.>
<I KNOW, BUT-->
<NO! I KNOW! YOUR ENEMY IS YOURSELF.>
<THAT WE ARE RONIN MEANS WE HAVE NO MASTER, BUT YOU HAVE FURTHER LOST YOUR WILL.>
<ITARU, LEADER THOUGH YOU BE, DO YOU THINK I WILL BROOK SUCH AN INSULT?>
<I THINK... WHATEVER SPIRIT YOU STILL RETAIN YOU SHOULD READY FOR THE ONE WE WERE FORETOLD OF.>
CRIK
<AH, AND HERE WE ARE. THERE IS A HAIKU I RECALL FROM YOUTH:>
<BOREDOM SEEKS THE DANCE>
<OF WASTED TIME AND FOLLY>
<BEST TO WAIT THE COURSE.>

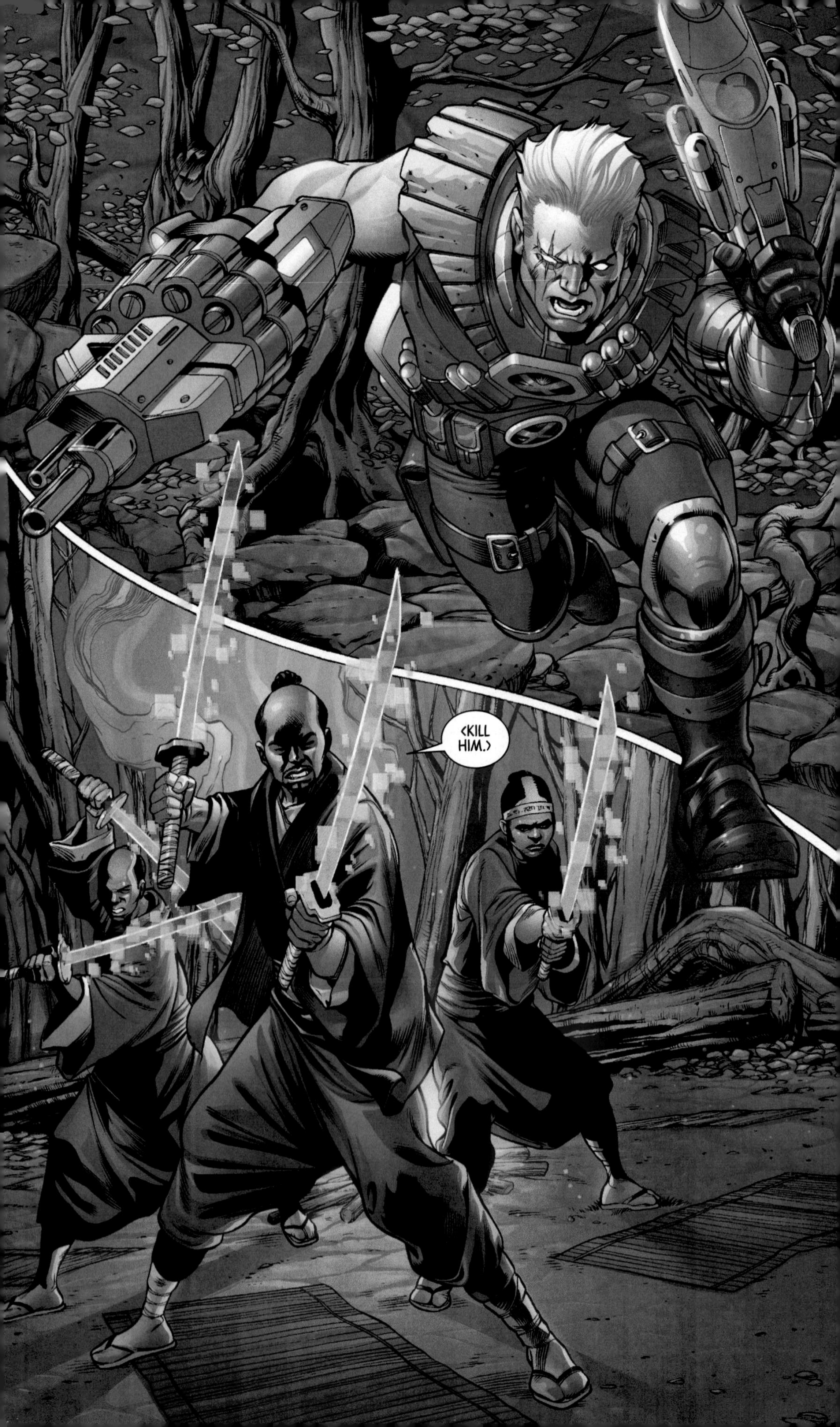
<KILL HIM.>

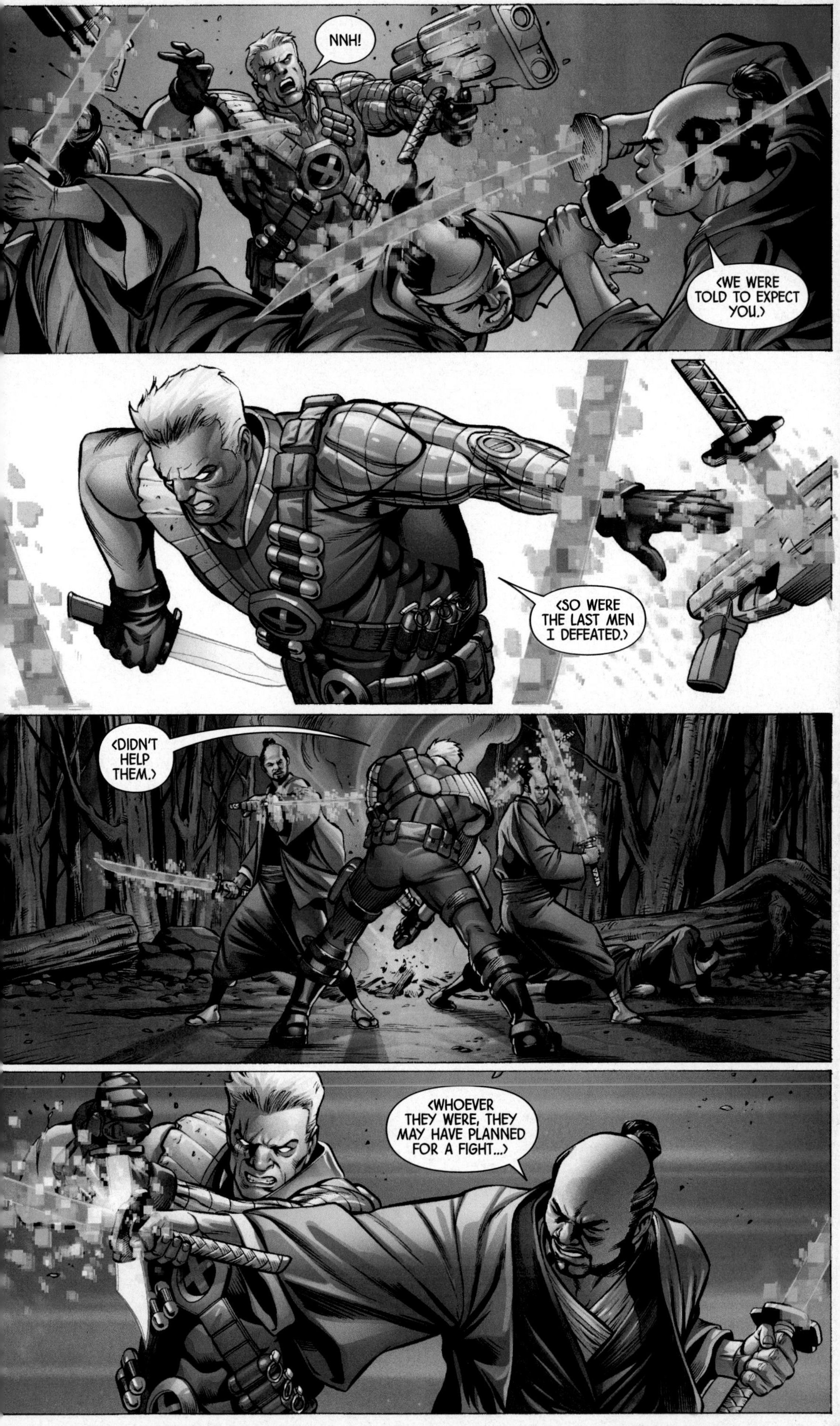
NNH!
<WE WERE TOLD TO EXPECT YOU.>
<SO WERE THE LAST MEN I DEFEATED.>
<DIDN'T HELP THEM.>
<WHOEVER THEY WERE, THEY MAY HAVE PLANNED FOR A FIGHT...>

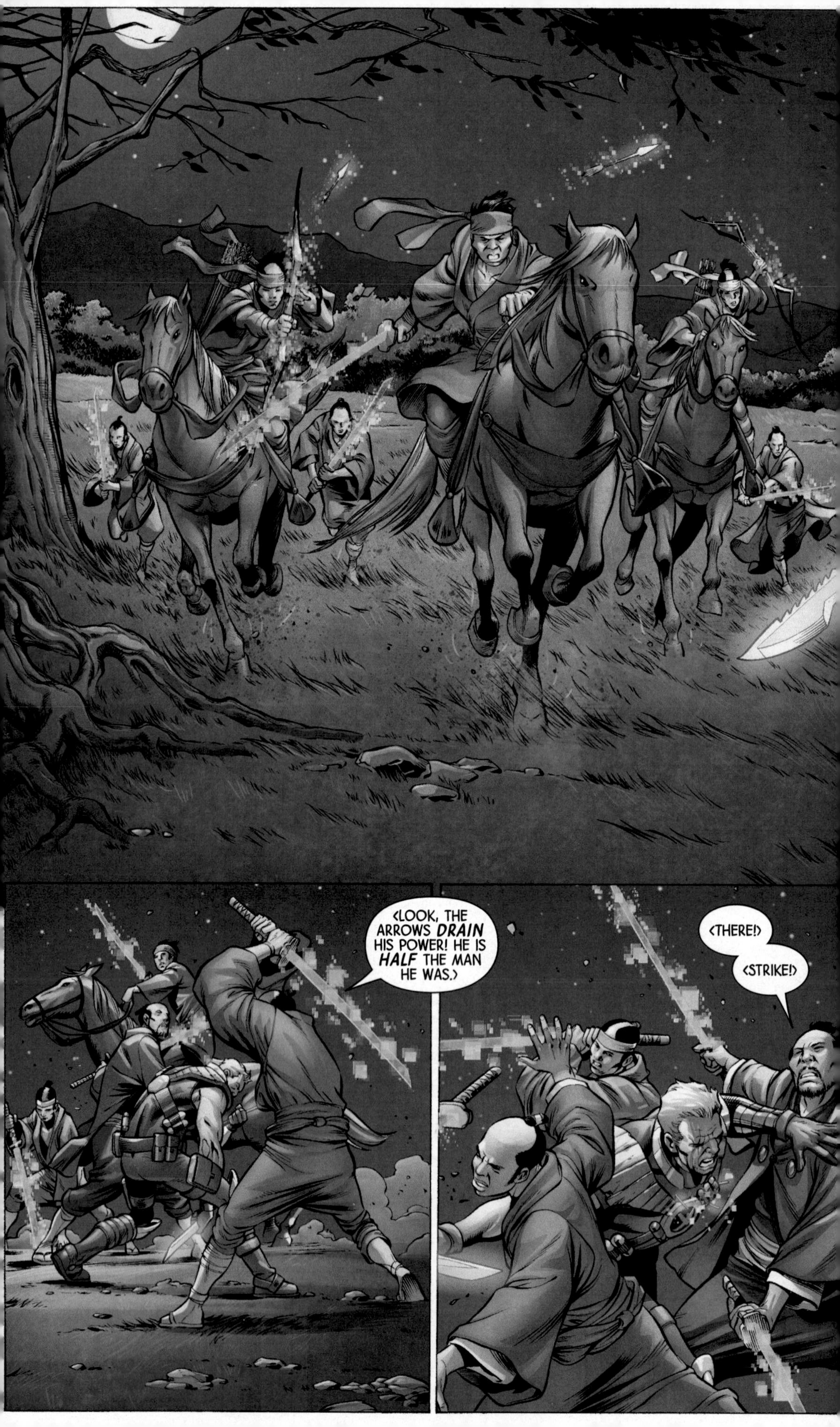

<LOOK, THE ARROWS DRAIN HIS POWER! HE IS HALF THE MAN HE WAS.>
<THERE!>
<STRIKE!>

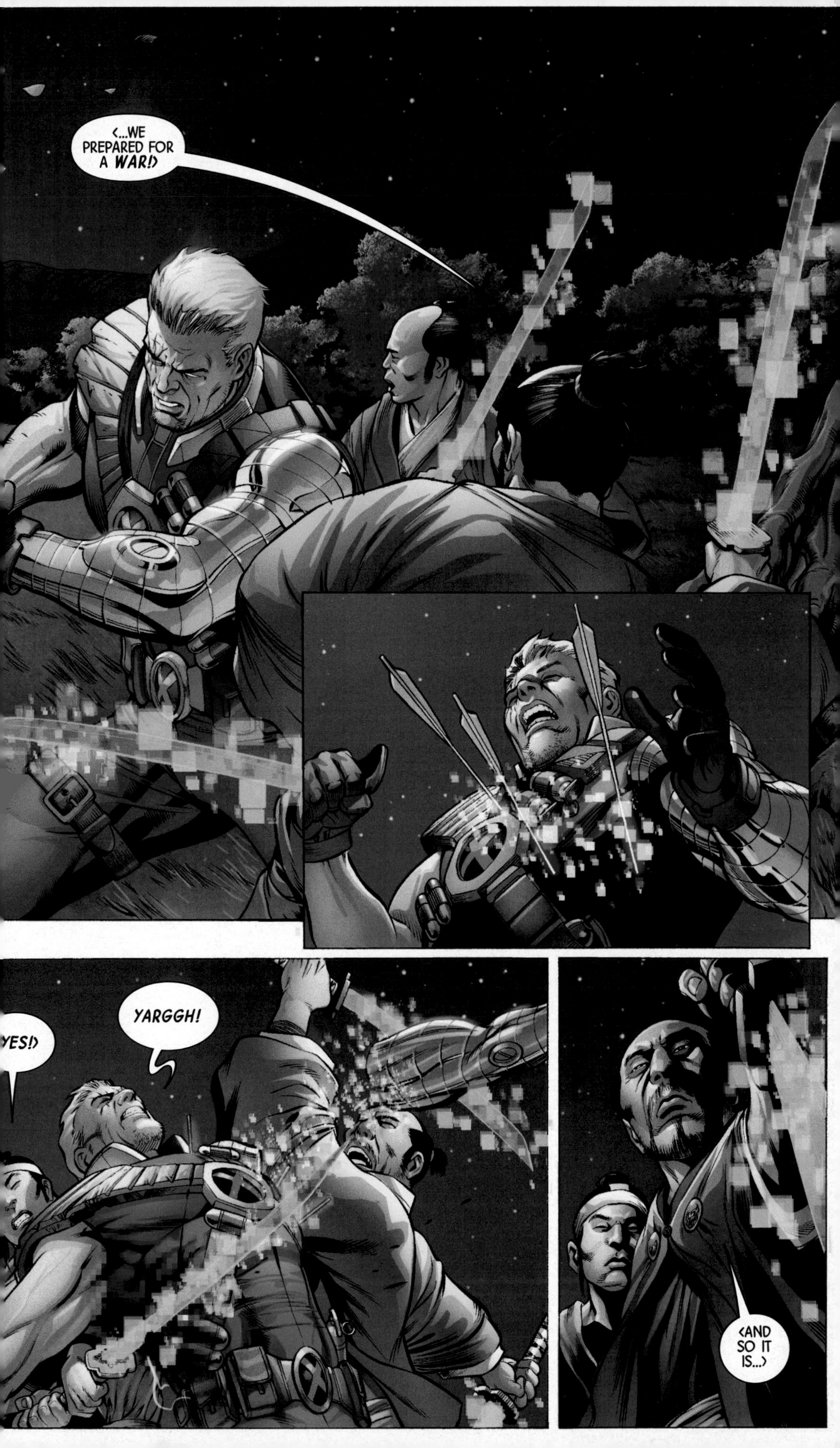
<...WE PREPARED FOR A WAR!>
YES!>
YARGGH!
<AND SO IT IS...>

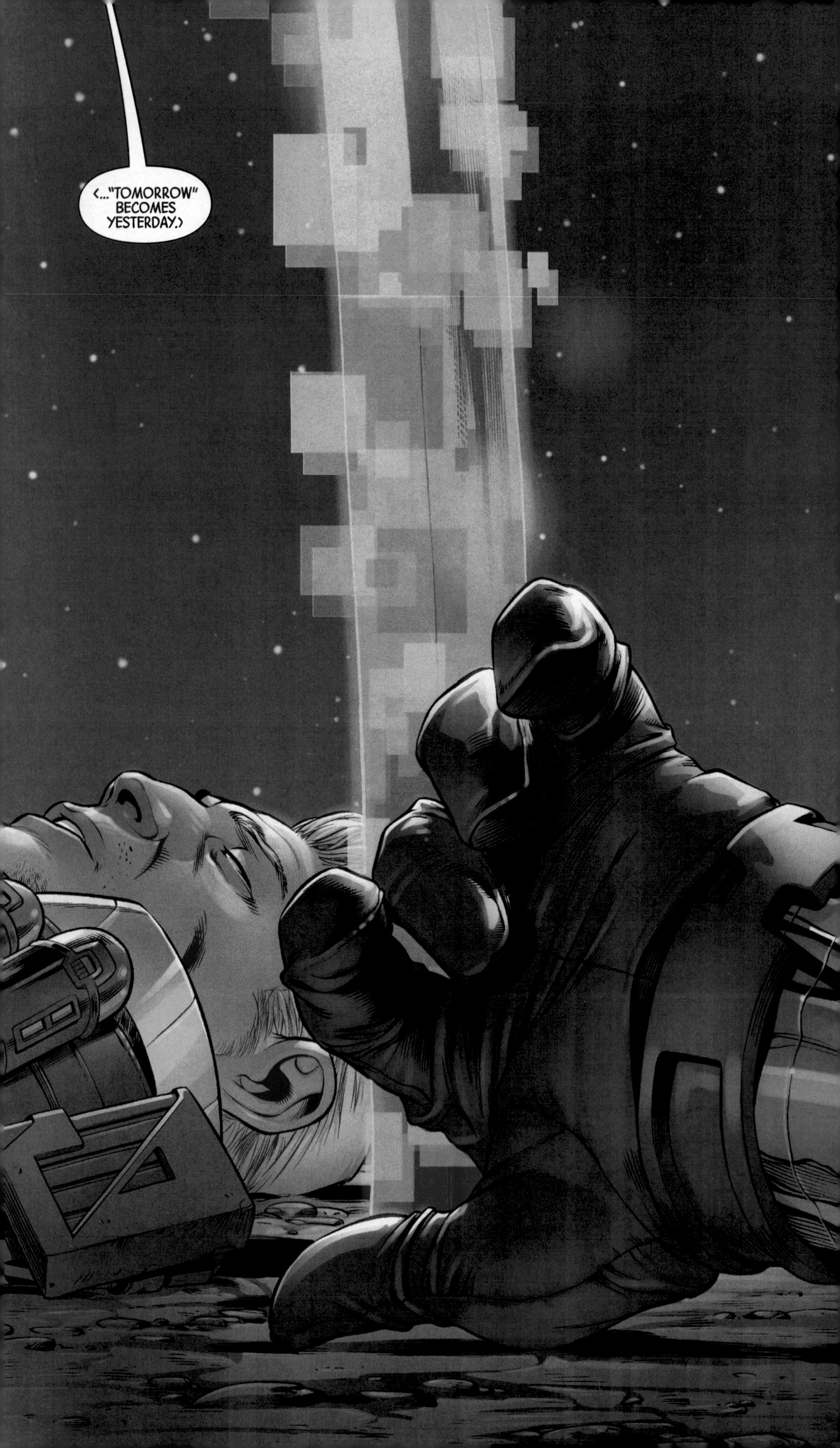
<..."TOMORROW" BECOMES YESTERDAY.>

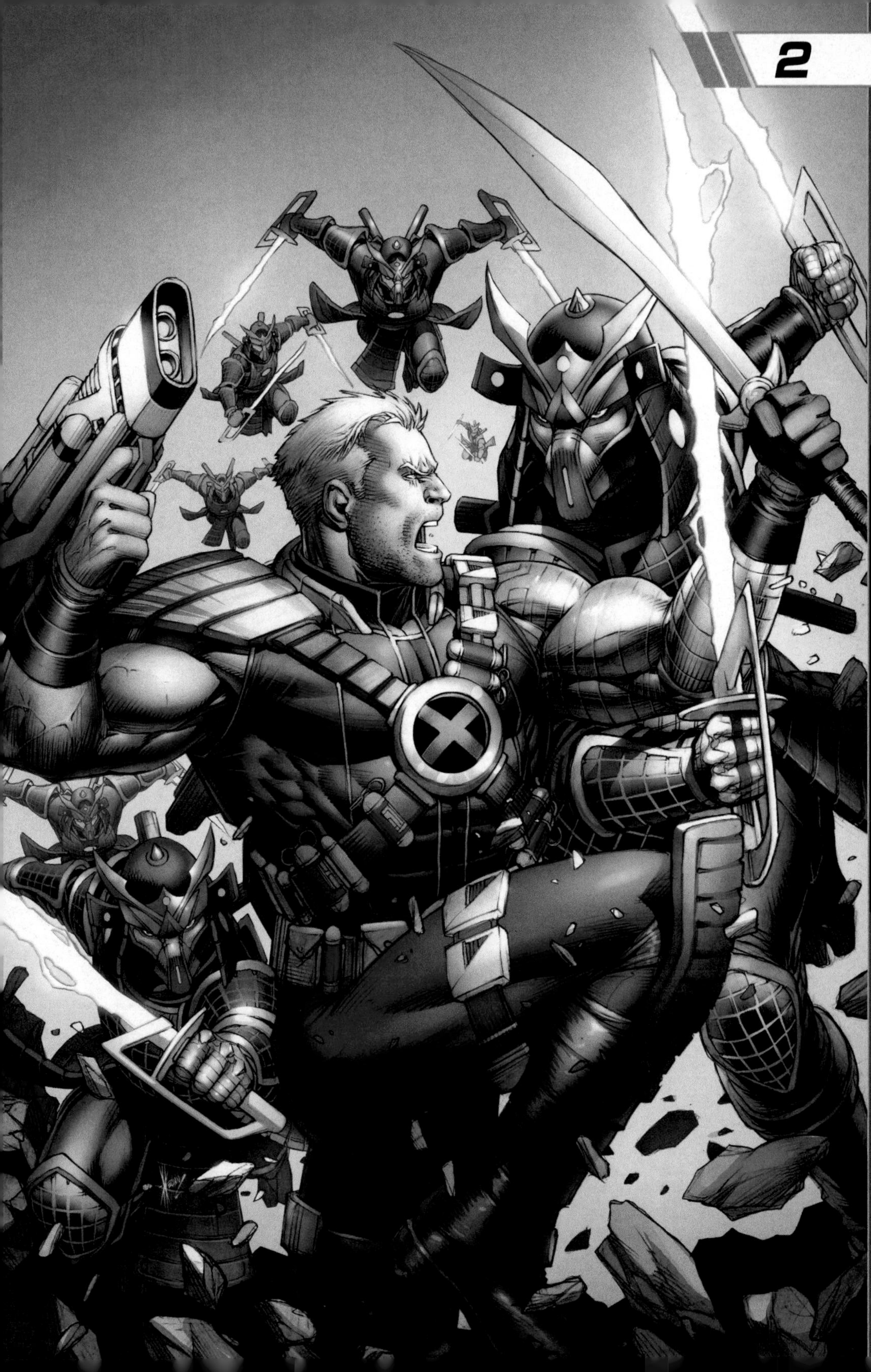
2

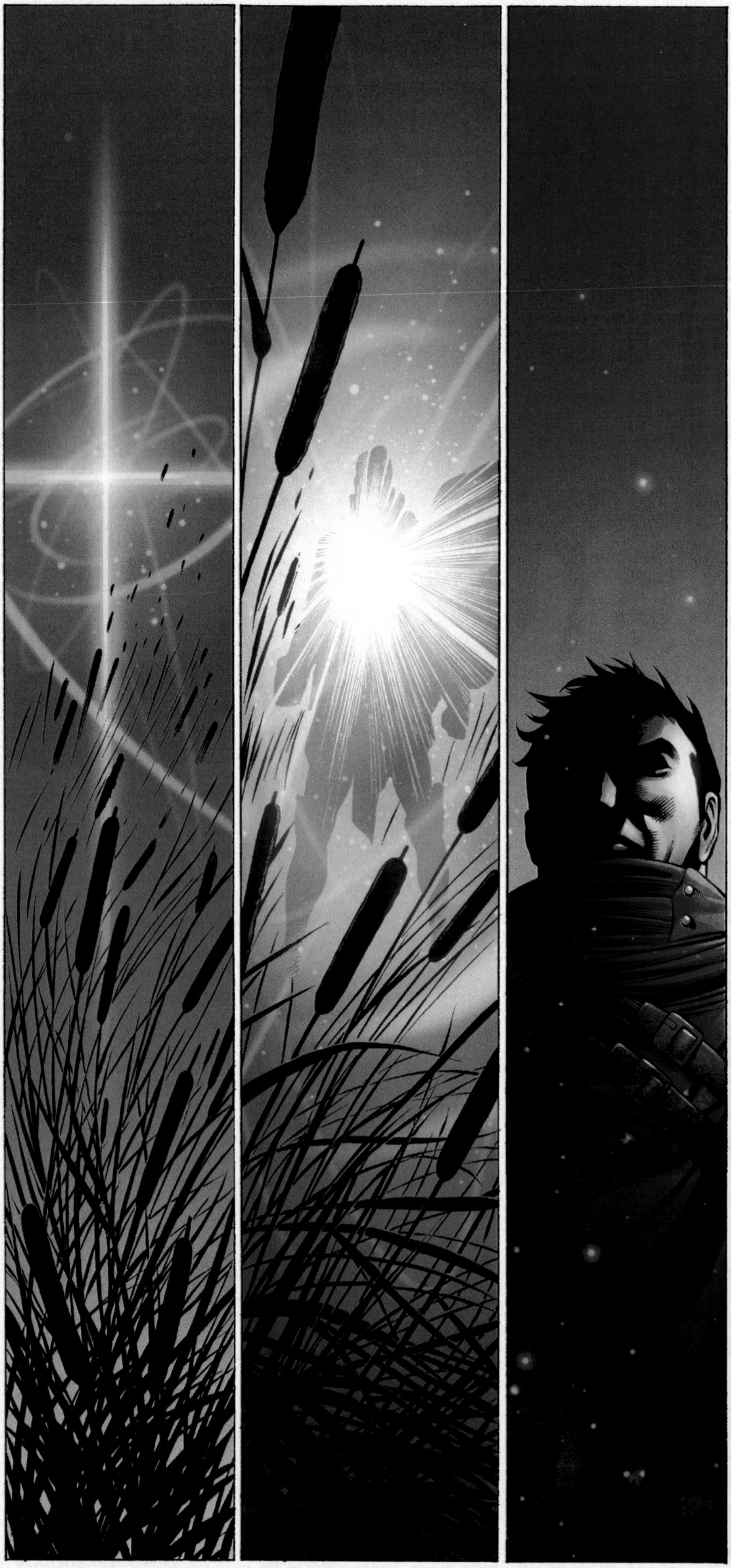

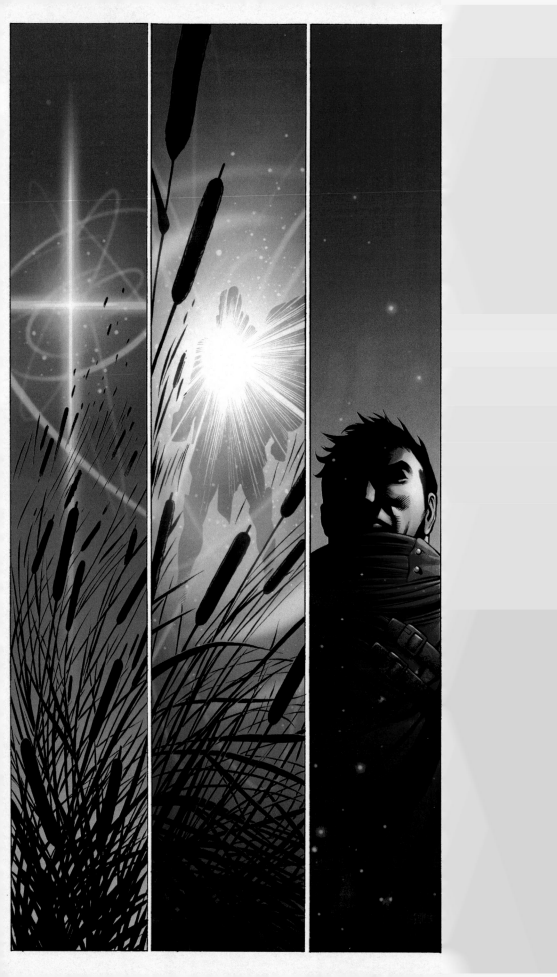

AMARU CASTLE.

UMMER PALACE OF THE
OST REVERED, ADMIRED
ND EXALTED DAIMYO (LORD)
MARU HIDEYOSHI.

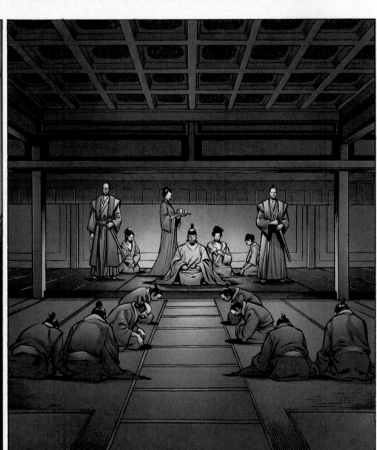

<YOU SHOCK
ME, MY DEAR...
AND *DELIGHT*
ME.>*

<I LOOK
FORWARD TO
RETIRING WITH
Y--->

*TRANSLATED
FROM JAPANESE.

FWWH

<WHO
IS THIS
DEVIL?!>

<NEVER MIND
WHO. HOW DID HE
GET IN HERE?>

<WELL,
DOG? SPEAK!>

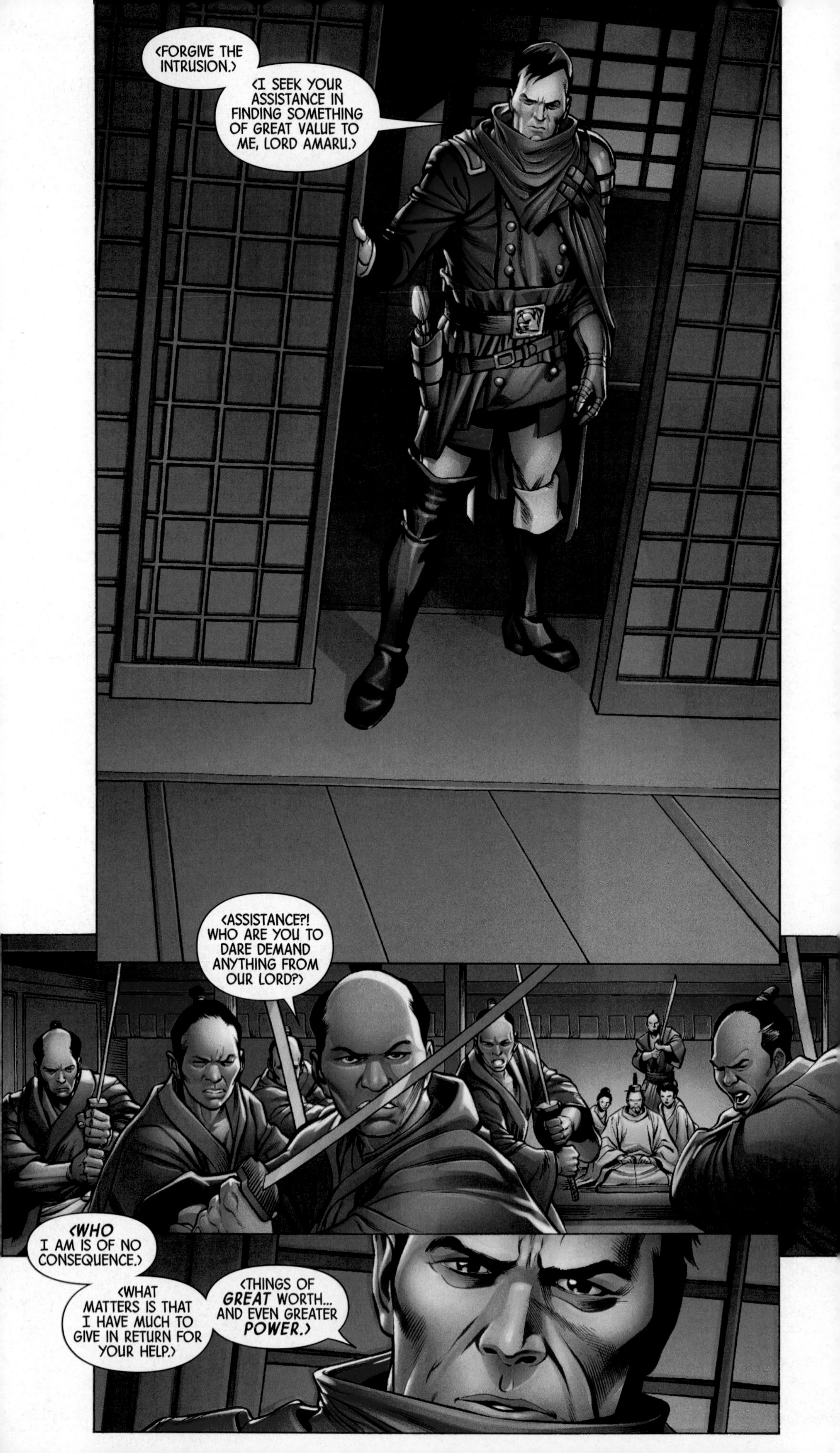

<FORGIVE THE INTRUSION.>
<I SEEK YOUR ASSISTANCE IN FINDING SOMETHING OF GREAT VALUE TO ME, LORD AMARU.>
<ASSISTANCE?! WHO ARE YOU TO DARE DEMAND ANYTHING FROM OUR LORD?>
<*WHO* I AM IS OF NO CONSEQUENCE.>
<WHAT MATTERS IS THAT I HAVE MUCH TO GIVE IN RETURN FOR YOUR HELP.>
<THINGS OF ***GREAT*** WORTH... AND EVEN GREATER ***POWER.***>

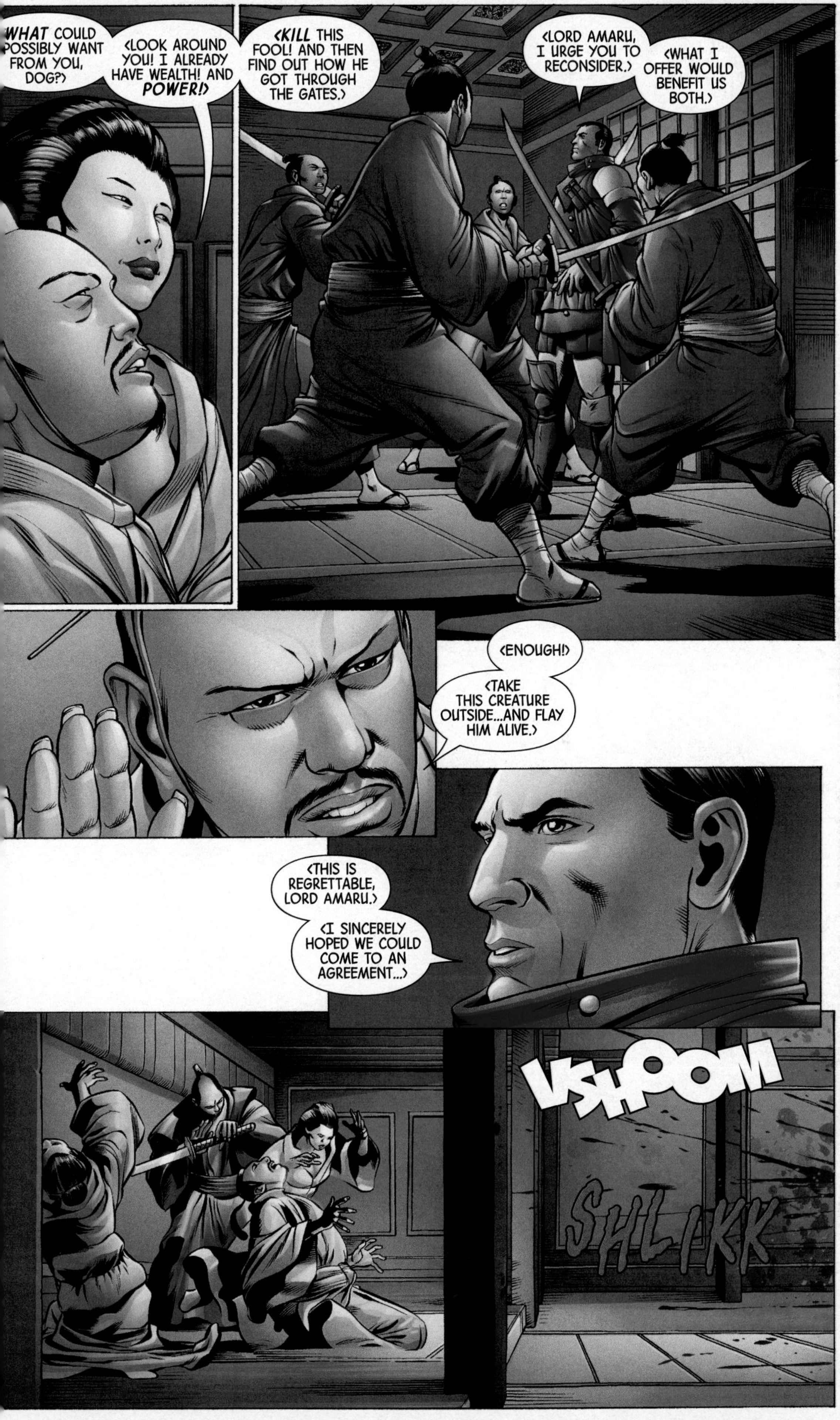
‹WHAT COULD POSSIBLY WANT FROM YOU, DOG?›
‹LOOK AROUND YOU! I ALREADY HAVE WEALTH! AND POWER!›
‹KILL THIS FOOL! AND THEN FIND OUT HOW HE GOT THROUGH THE GATES.›
‹LORD AMARU, I URGE YOU TO RECONSIDER.›
‹WHAT I OFFER WOULD BENEFIT US BOTH.›
‹ENOUGH!›
‹TAKE THIS CREATURE OUTSIDE...AND FLAY HIM ALIVE.›
‹THIS IS REGRETTABLE, LORD AMARU.›
‹I SINCERELY HOPED WE COULD COME TO AN AGREEMENT...›
VSHOOM
SHLIKK

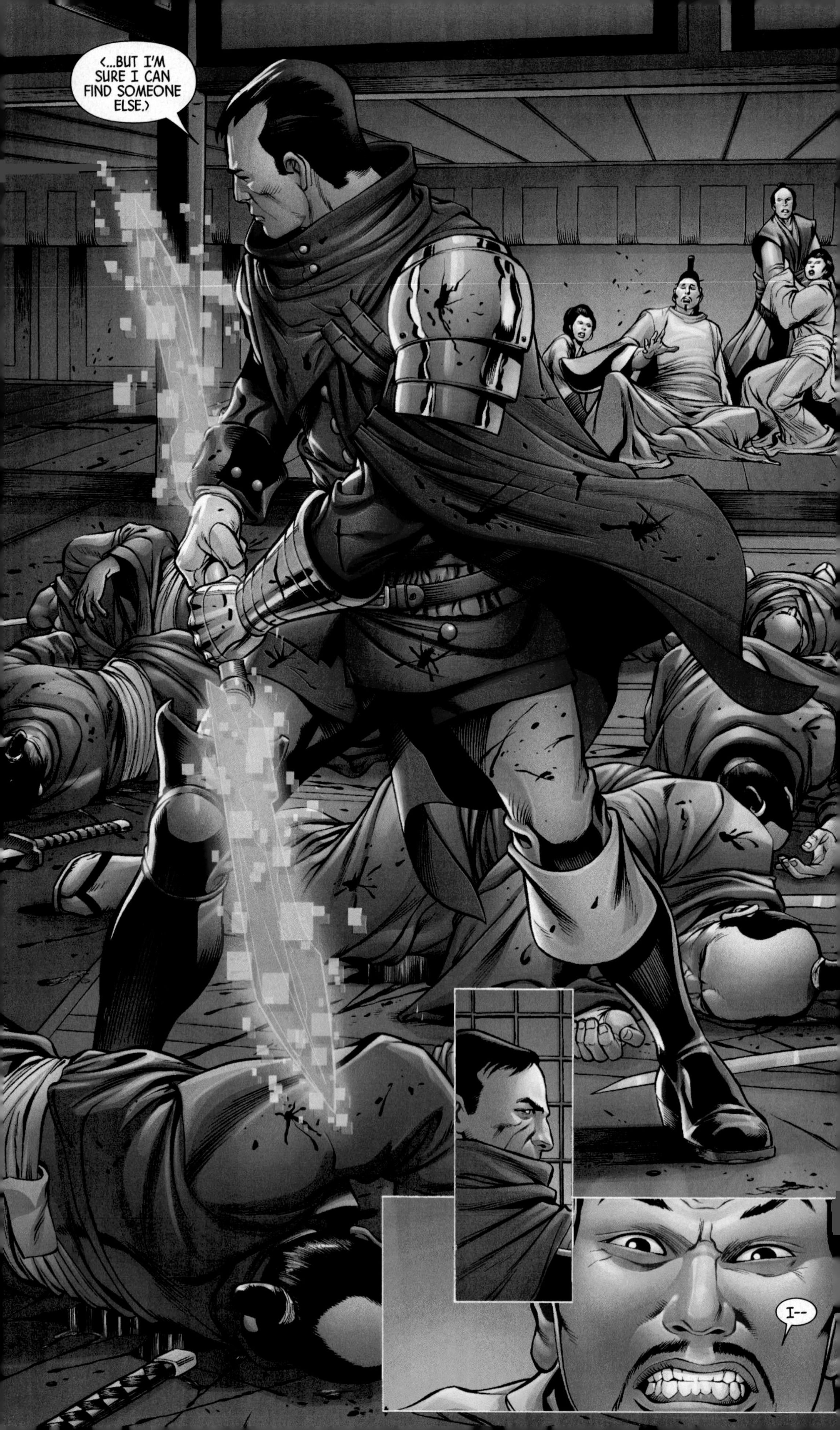

<...BUT I'M SURE I CAN FIND SOMEONE ELSE.>
I--

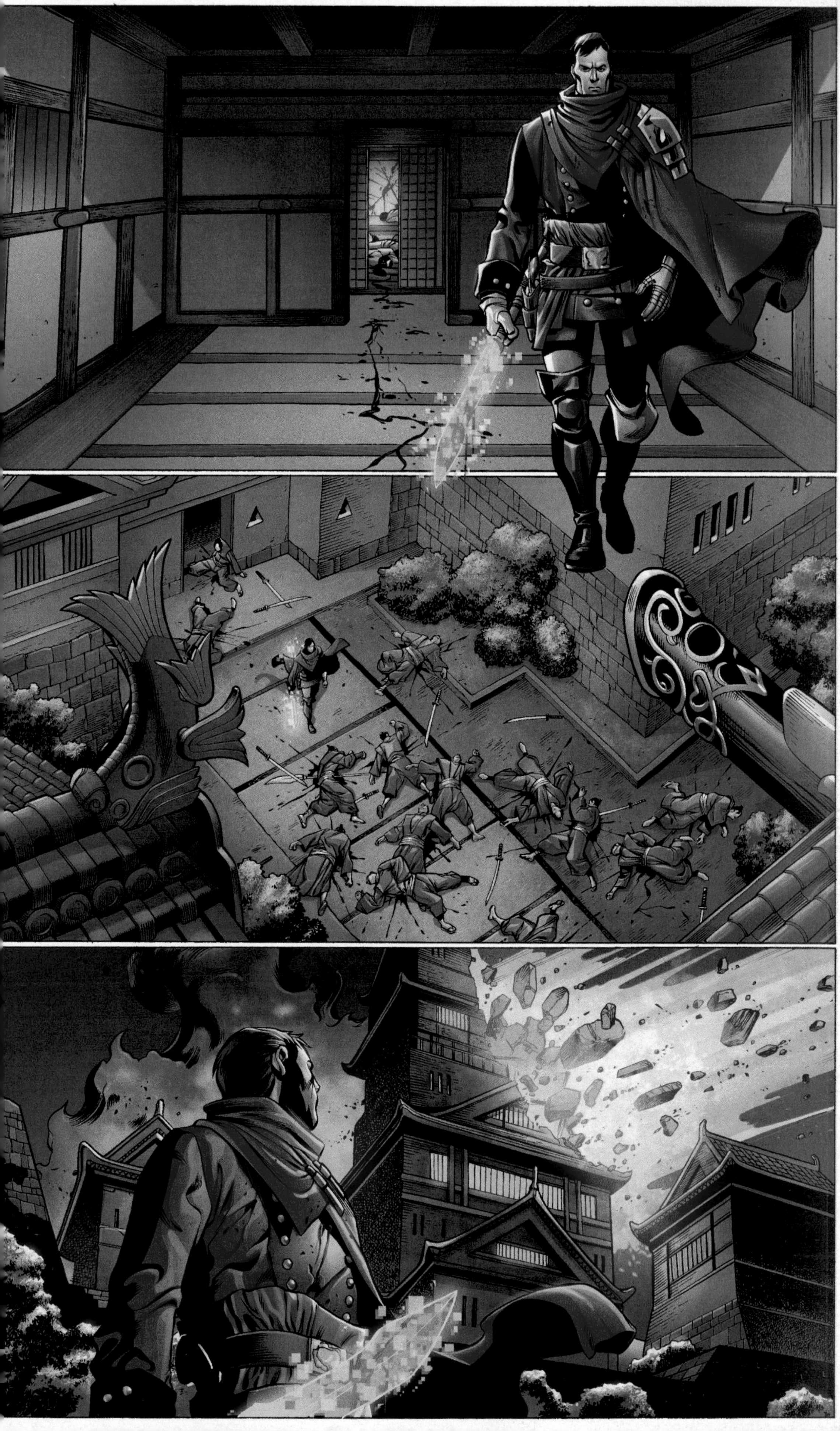

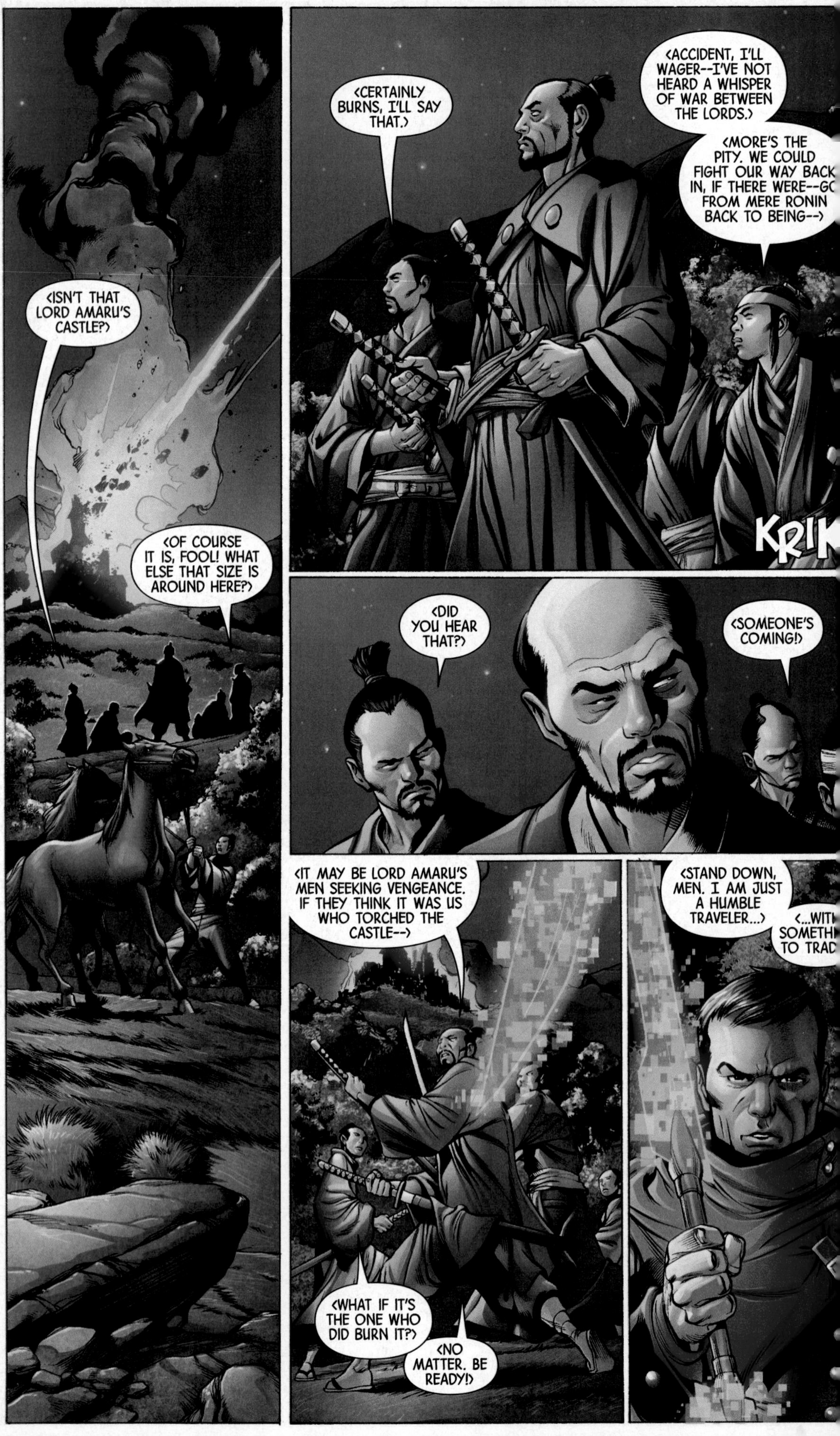
<ISN'T THAT LORD AMARU'S CASTLE?>
<OF COURSE IT IS, FOOL! WHAT ELSE THAT SIZE IS AROUND HERE?>
<CERTAINLY BURNS, I'LL SAY THAT.>
<ACCIDENT, I'LL WAGER--I'VE NOT HEARD A WHISPER OF WAR BETWEEN THE LORDS.>
<MORE'S THE PITY. WE COULD FIGHT OUR WAY BACK IN, IF THERE WERE--GO FROM MERE RONIN BACK TO BEING-->
KRIK
<DID YOU HEAR THAT?>
<SOMEONE'S COMING!>
<IT MAY BE LORD AMARU'S MEN SEEKING VENGEANCE. IF THEY THINK IT WAS US WHO TORCHED THE CASTLE-->
<WHAT IF IT'S THE ONE WHO DID BURN IT?>
<NO MATTER. BE READY!>
<STAND DOWN, MEN. I AM JUST A HUMBLE TRAVELER...>

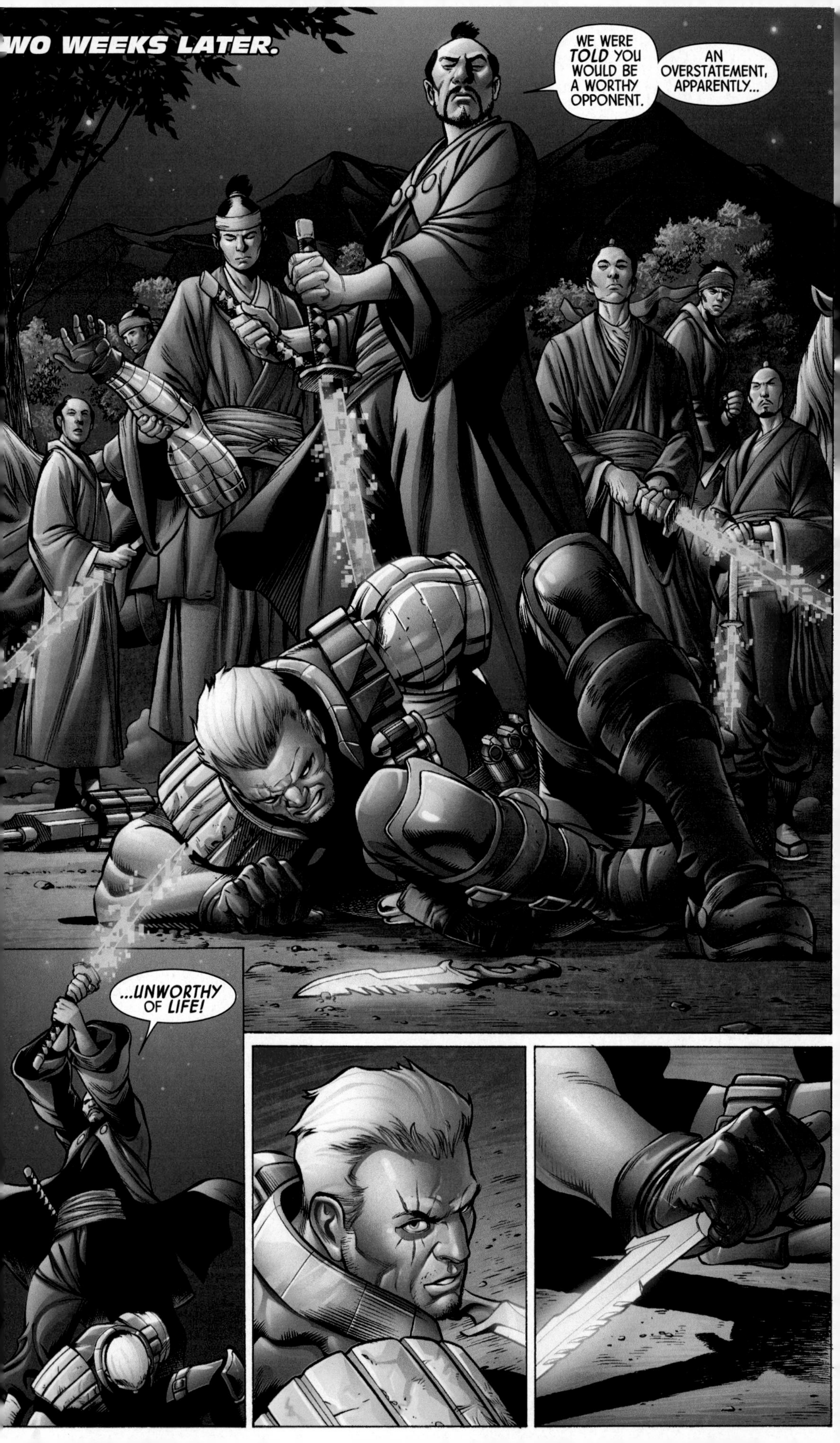
WO WEEKS LATER.
WE WERE TOLD YOU WOULD BE A WORTHY OPPONENT.
AN OVERSTATEMENT, APPARENTLY...
...UNWORTHY OF LIFE!

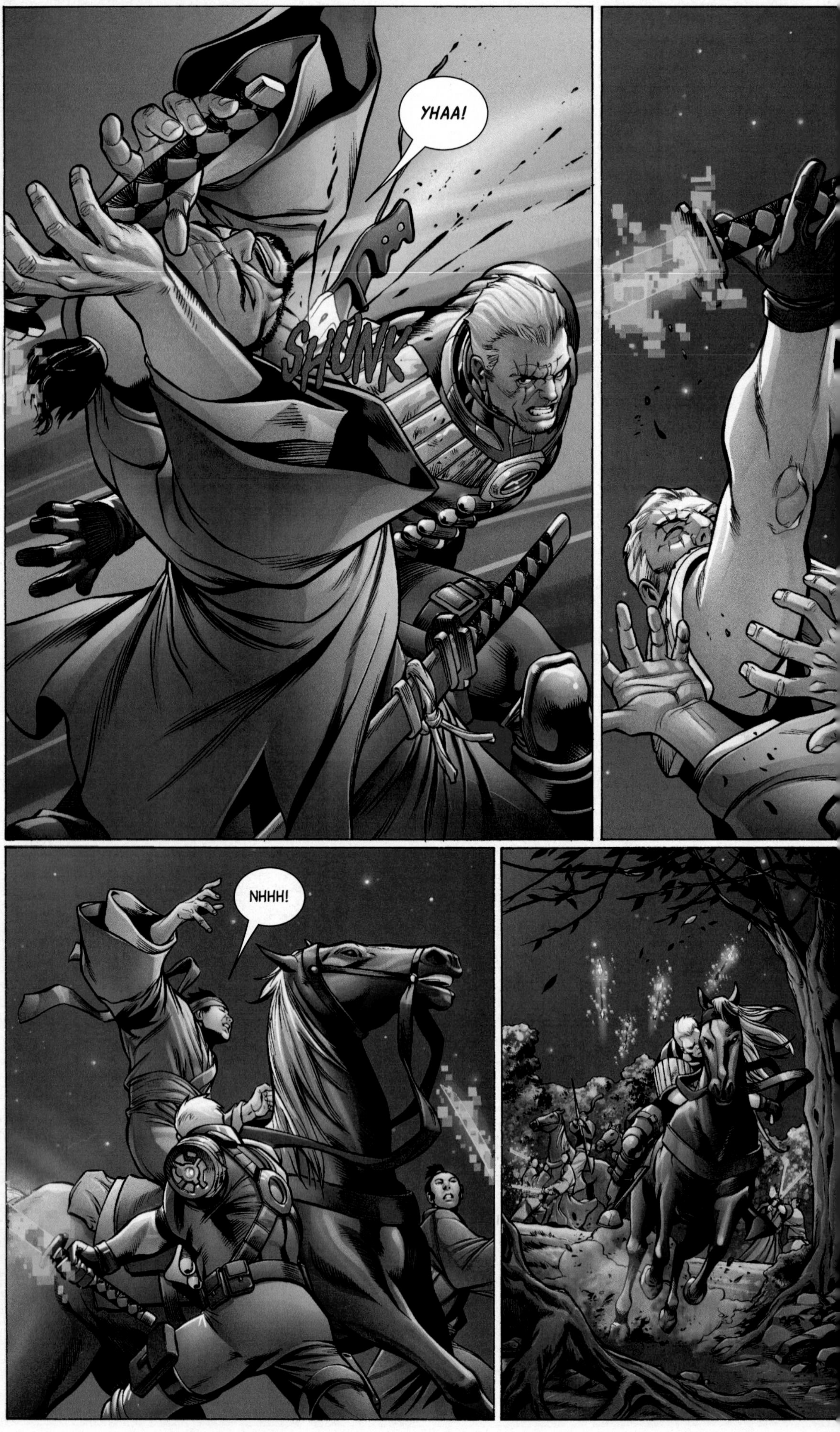
YHAA!
SHUNK
NHHH!

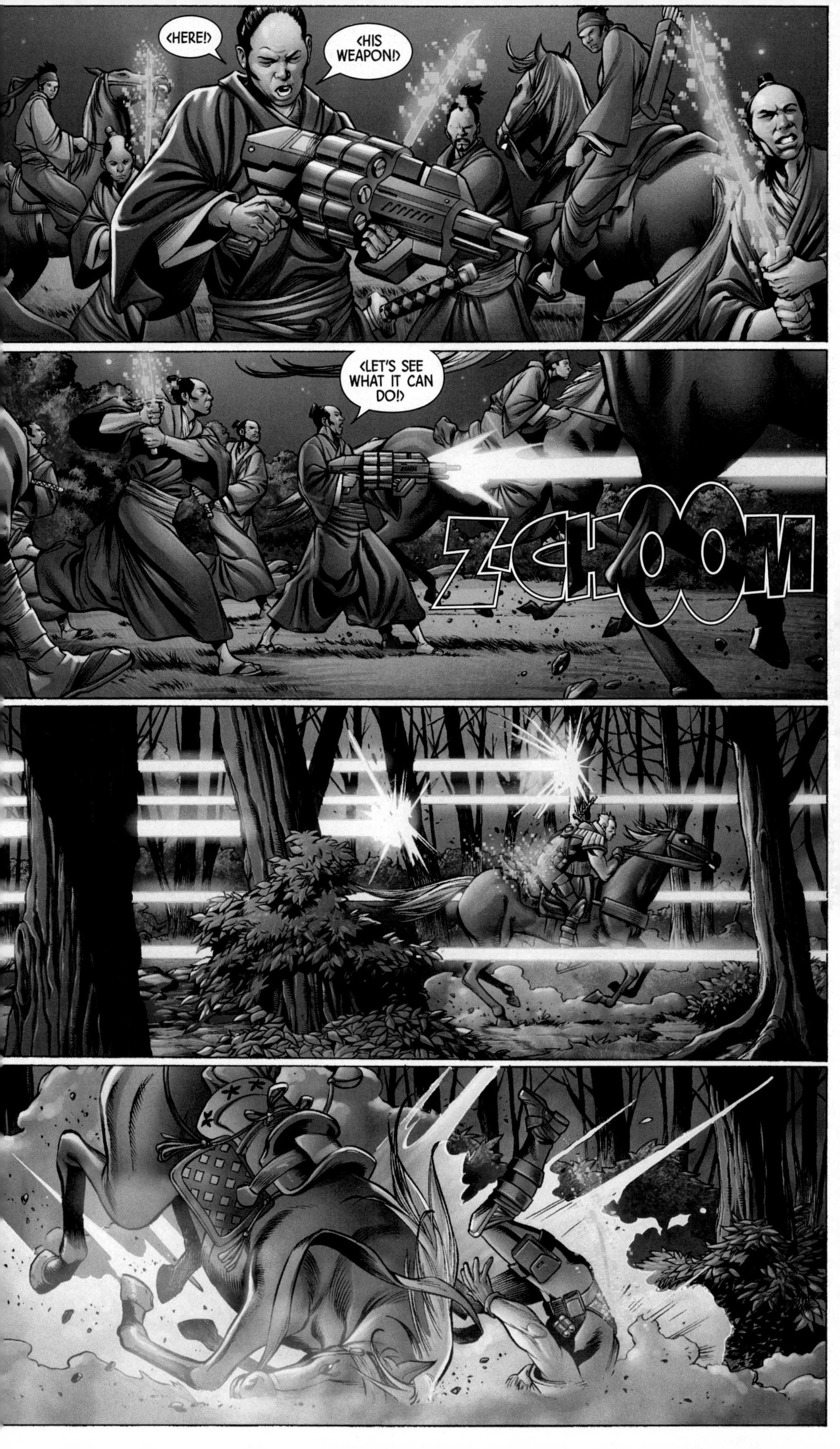

‹HERE!›
‹HIS WEAPON!›
‹LET'S SEE WHAT IT CAN DO!›
Z-CHOOM

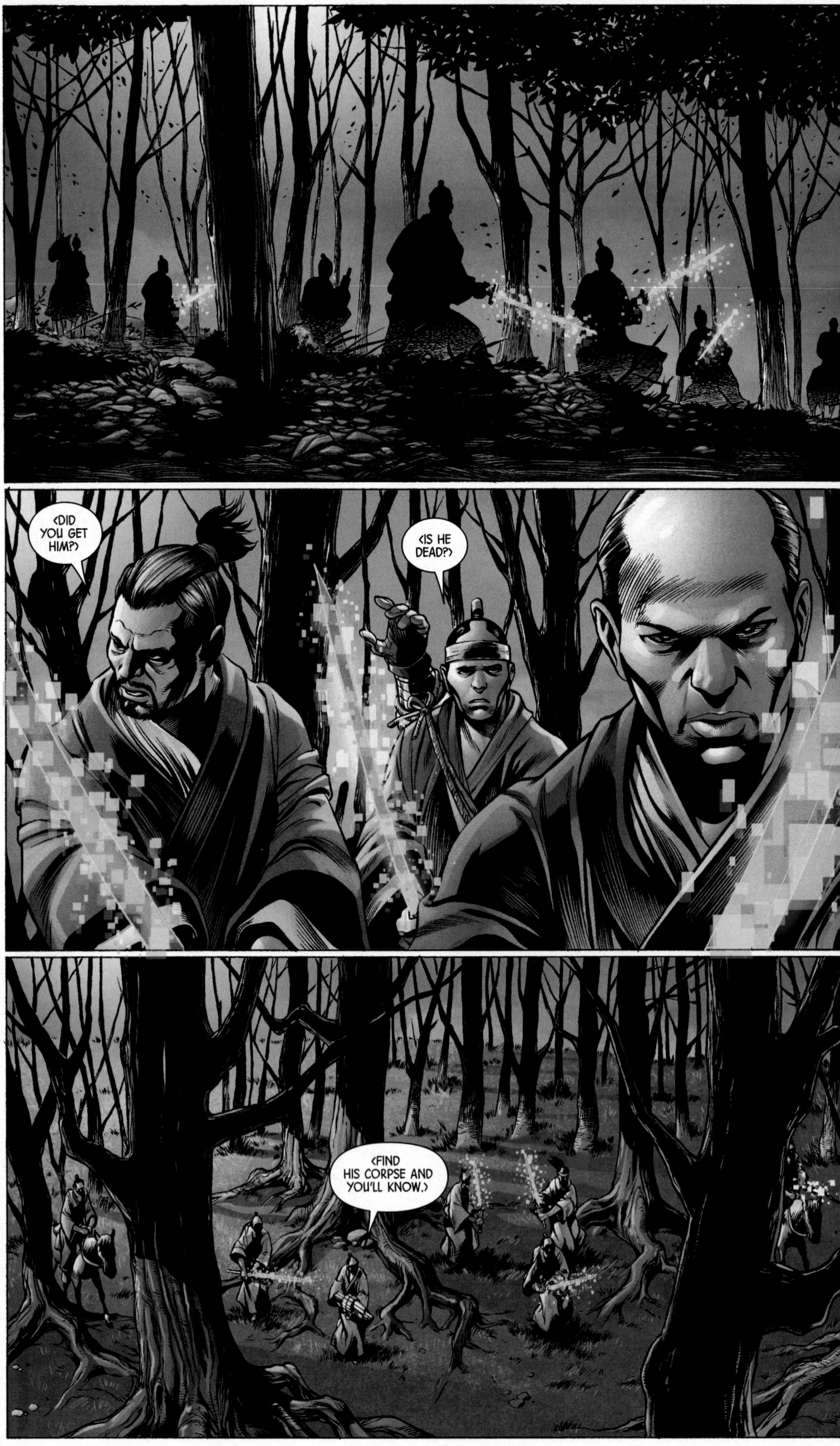
<DID YOU GET HIM?>
<IS HE DEAD?>
<FIND HIS CORPSE AND YOU'LL KNOW.>

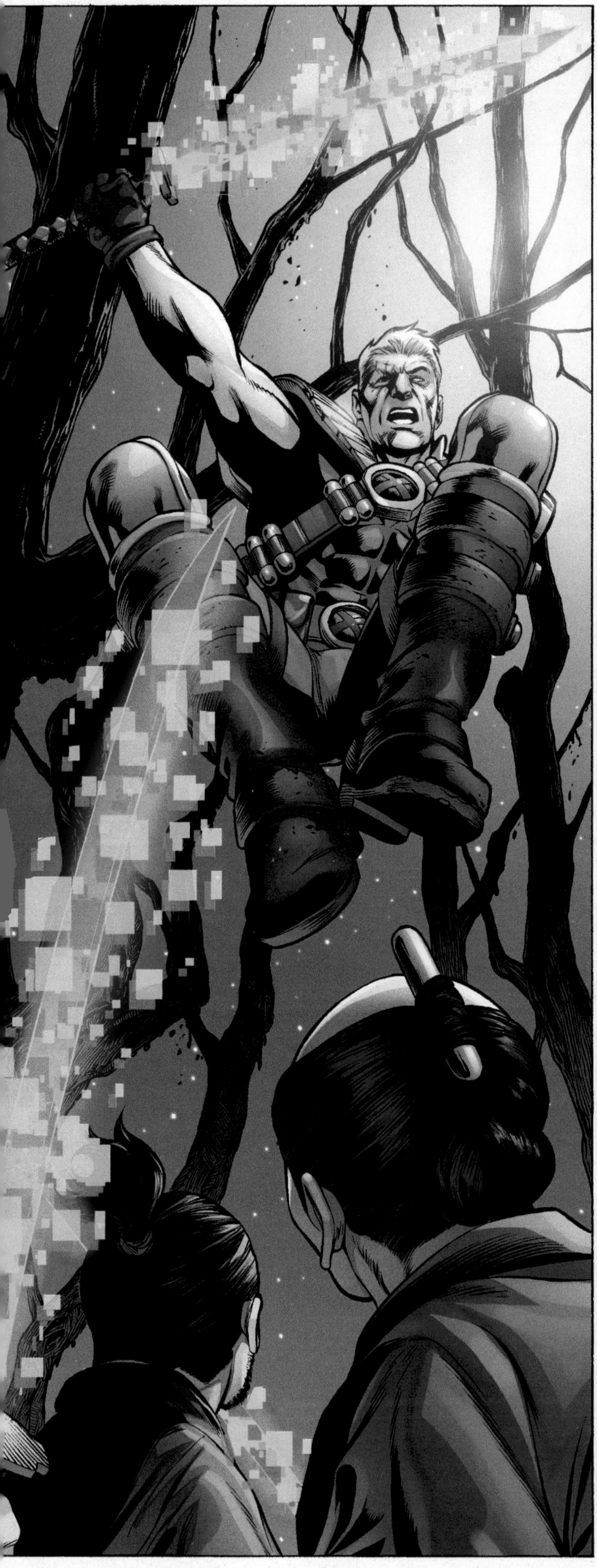

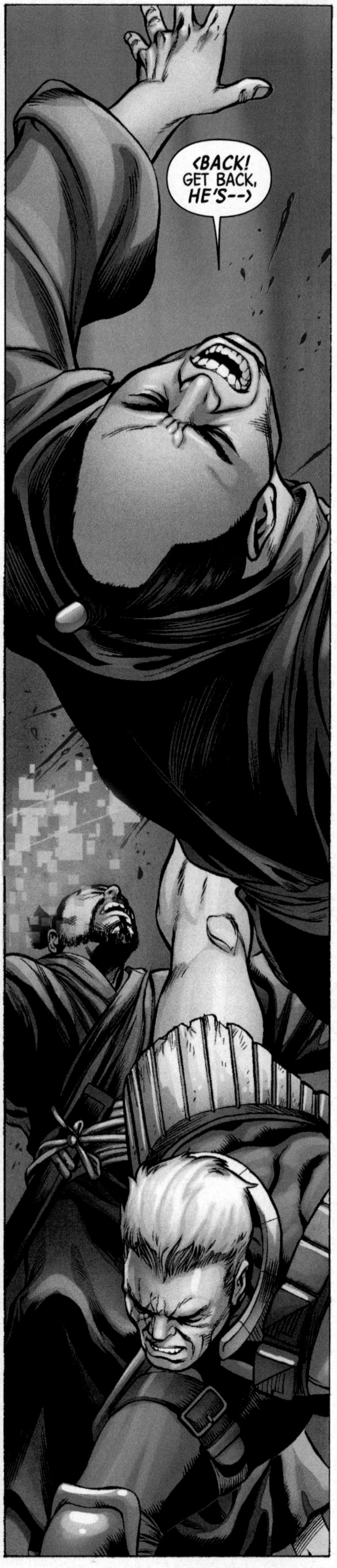

‹BACK! GET BACK, HE'S--›

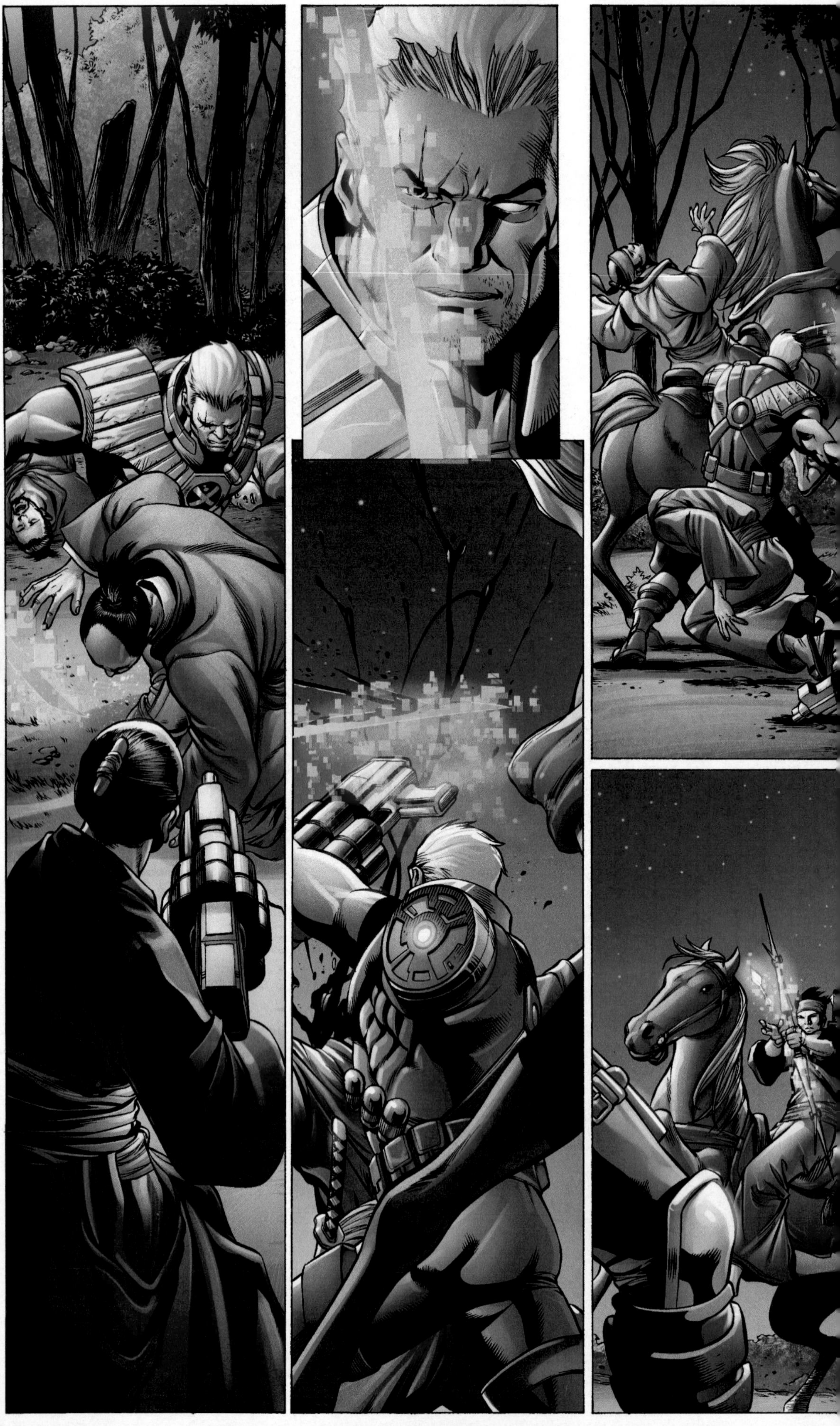

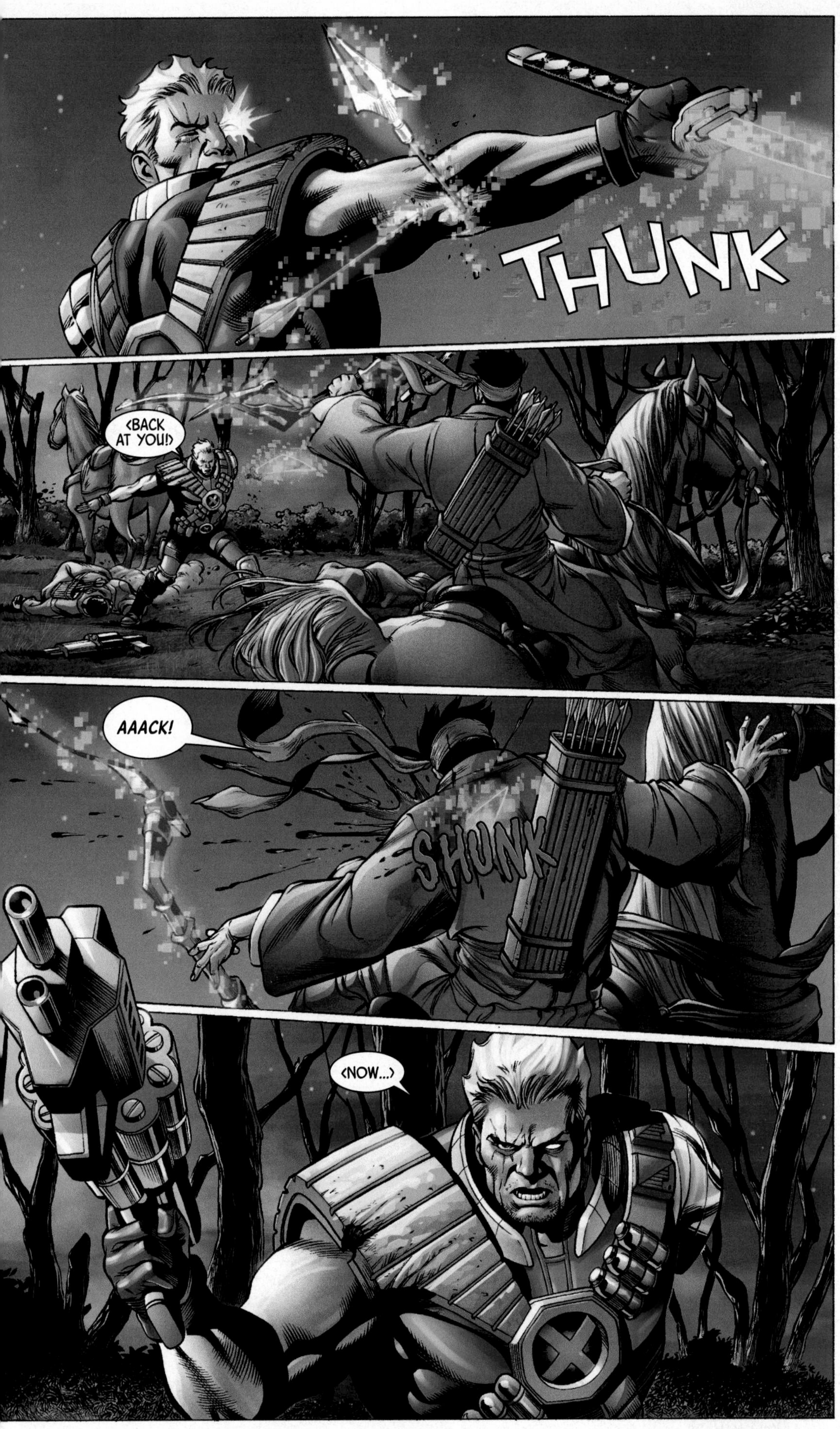
THUNK
‹BACK AT YOU!›
AAACK!
SHUNK
‹NOW...›

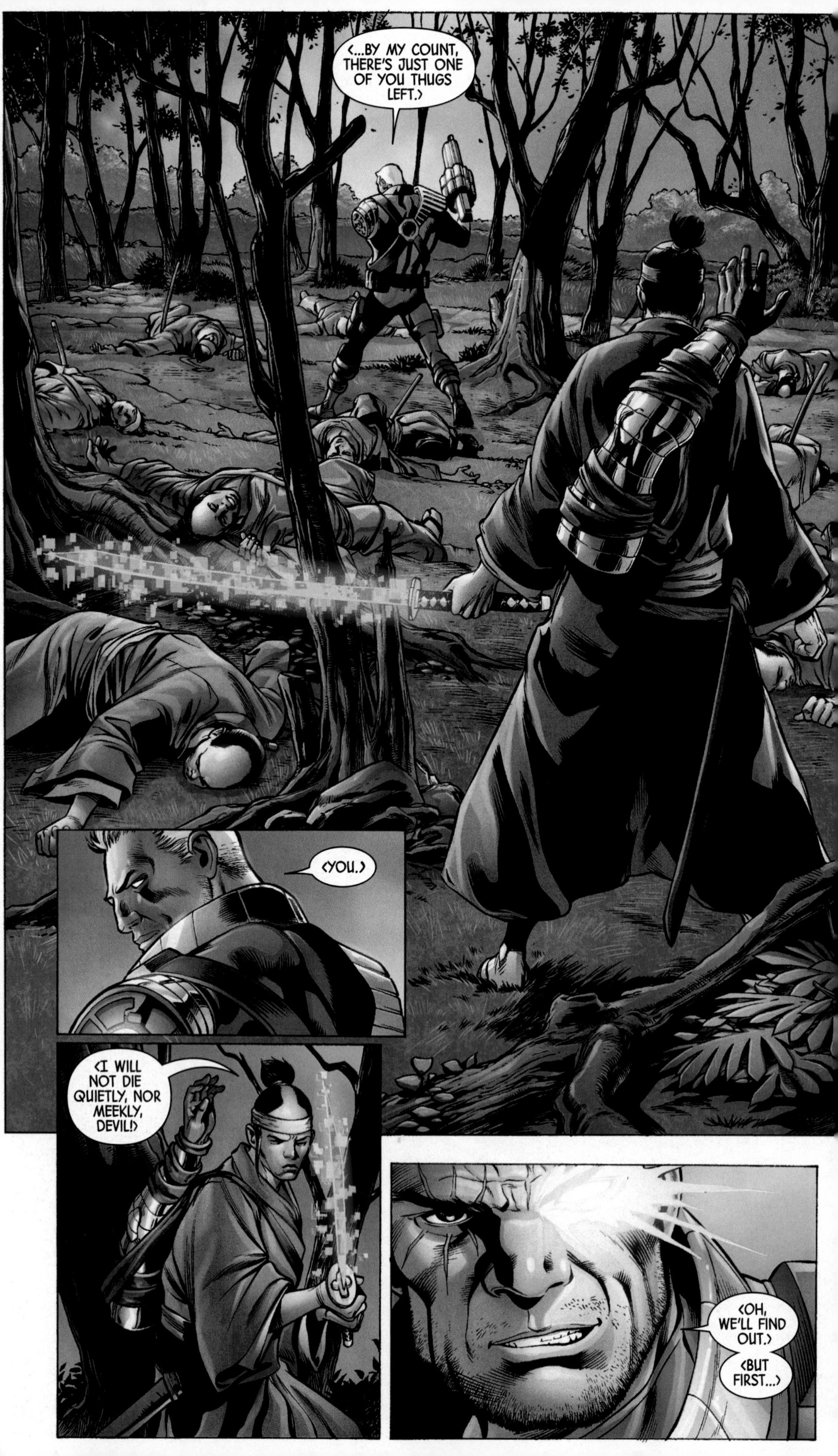
<...BY MY COUNT, THERE'S JUST ONE OF YOU THUGS LEFT.>
<YOU.>
<I WILL NOT DIE QUIETLY, NOR MEEKLY, DEVIL!>
<OH, WE'LL FIND OUT.>
<BUT FIRST...>

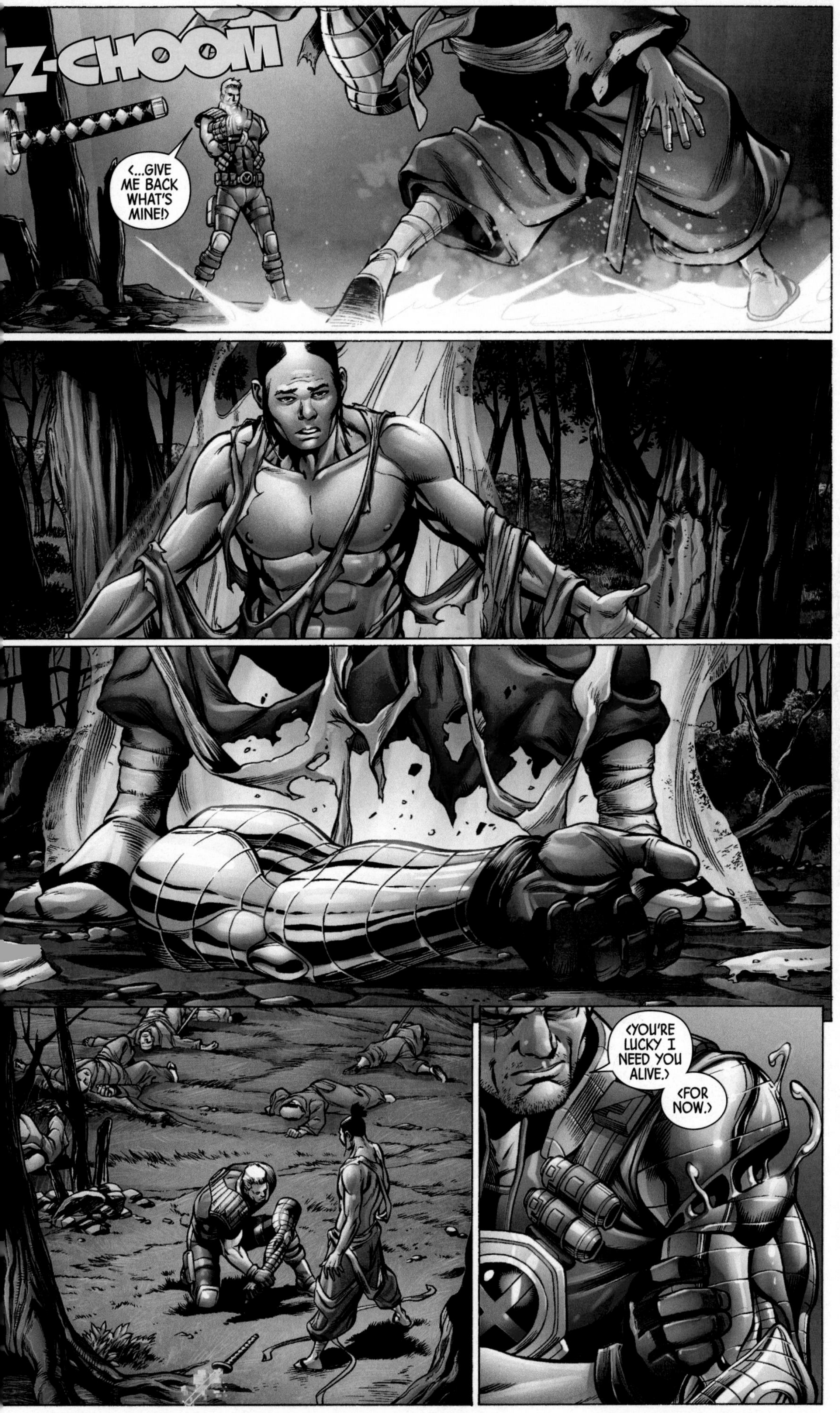
Z-CHOOM
<...GIVE ME BACK WHAT'S MINE!>
<YOU'RE LUCKY I NEED YOU ALIVE.>
<FOR NOW.>

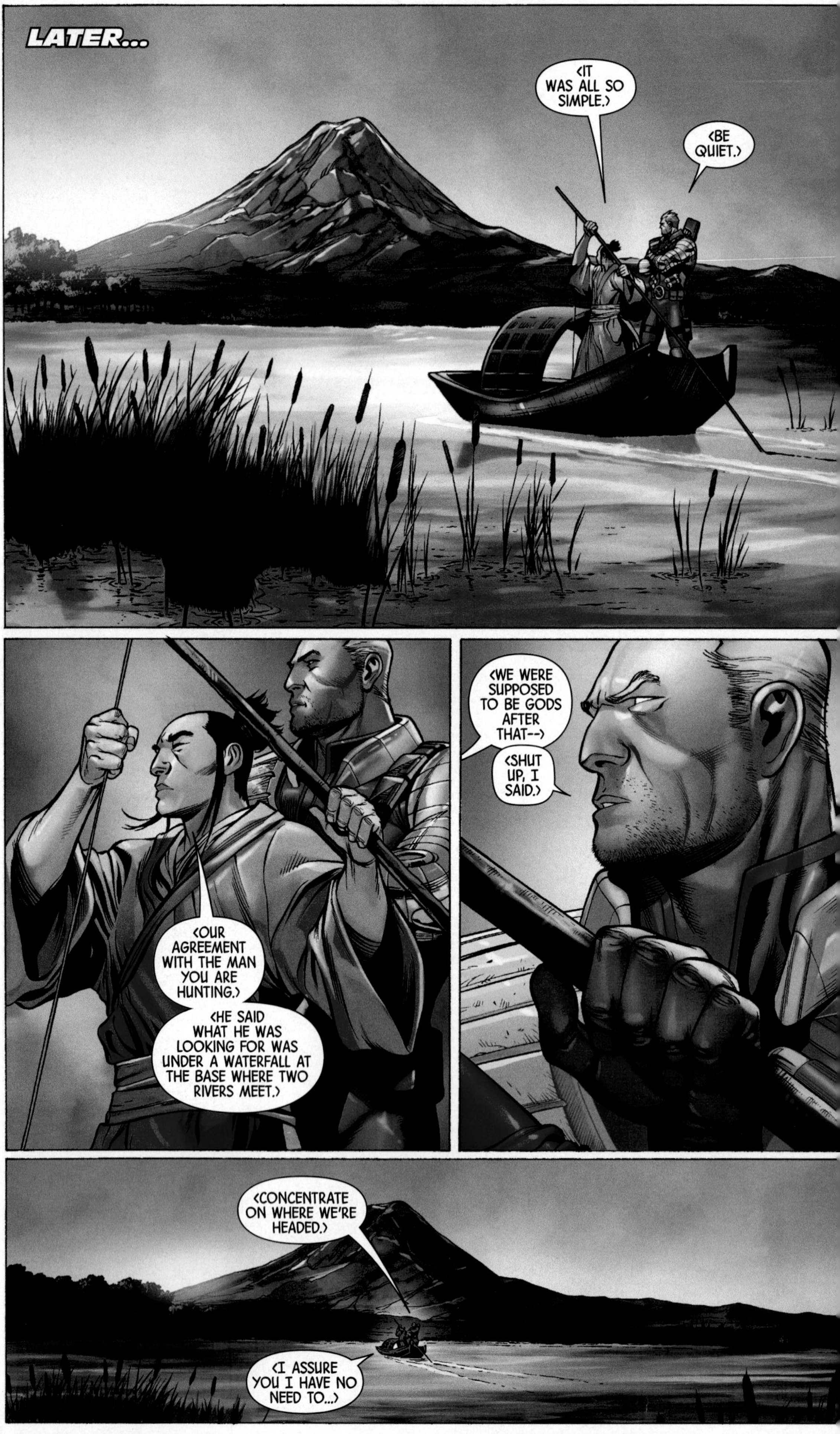
LATER...
<IT WAS ALL SO SIMPLE.>
<BE QUIET.>
<OUR AGREEMENT WITH THE MAN YOU ARE HUNTING.>
<HE SAID WHAT HE WAS LOOKING FOR WAS UNDER A WATERFALL AT THE BASE WHERE TWO RIVERS MEET.>
<WE WERE SUPPOSED TO BE GODS AFTER THAT-->
<SHUT UP, I SAID.>
<CONCENTRATE ON WHERE WE'RE HEADED.>
<I ASSURE YOU I HAVE NO NEED TO...>

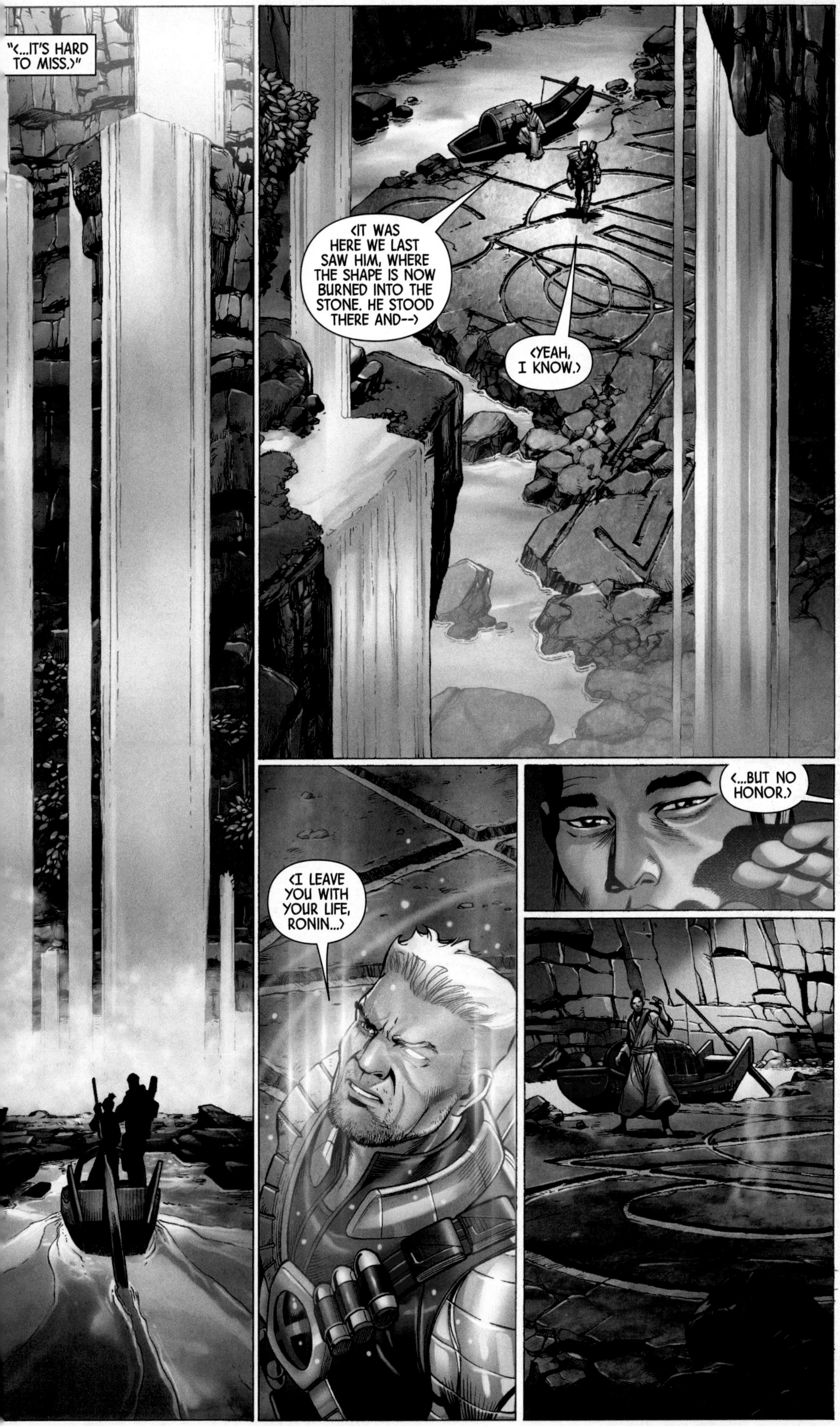
"<...IT'S HARD TO MISS.>"
<IT WAS HERE WE LAST SAW HIM, WHERE THE SHAPE IS NOW BURNED INTO THE STONE. HE STOOD THERE AND-->
<YEAH, I KNOW.>
<I LEAVE YOU WITH YOUR LIFE, RONIN...>
<...BUT NO HONOR.>

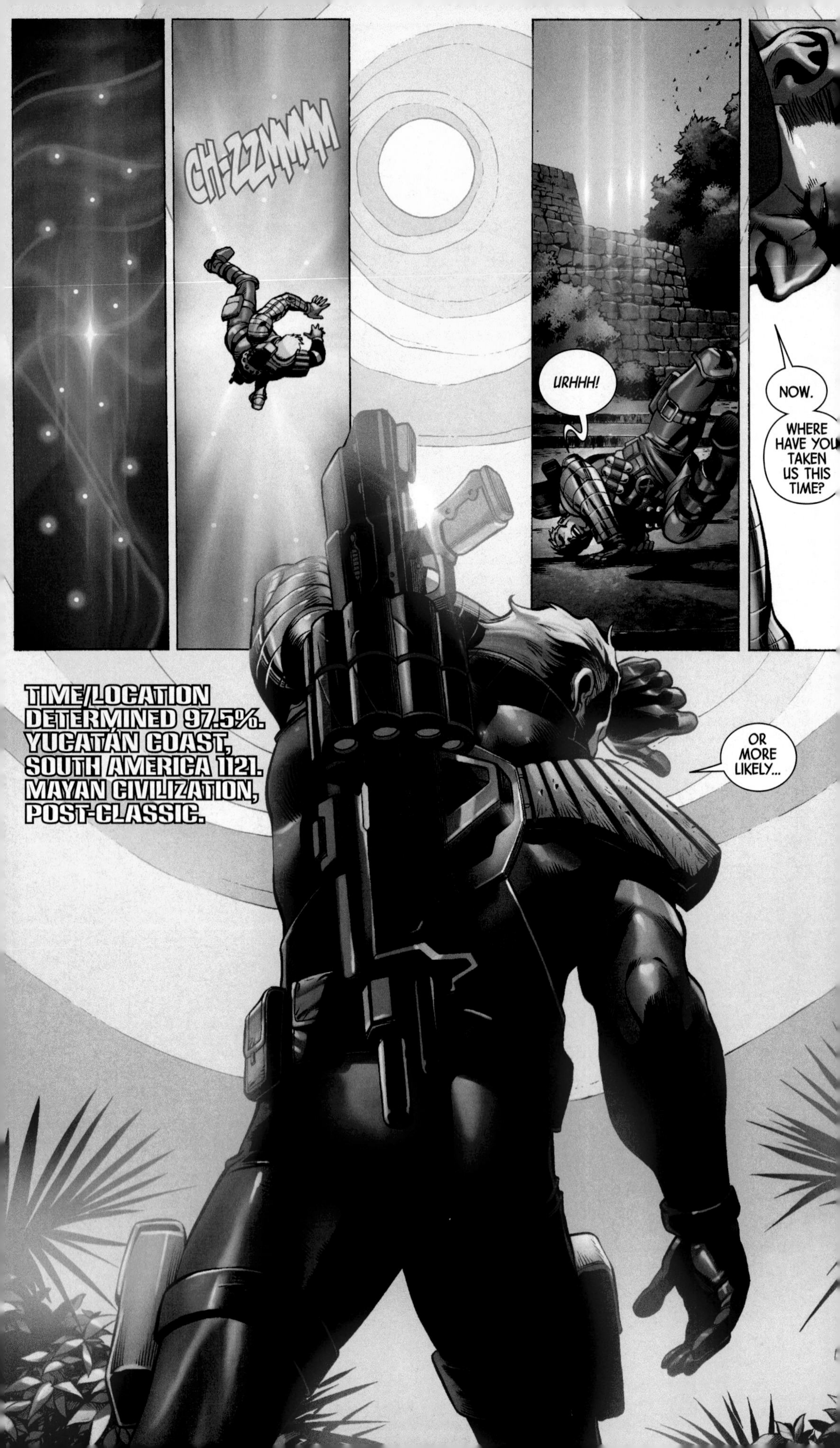
CH-ZZMMM
URHHH!
NOW.
WHERE HAVE YOU TAKEN US THIS TIME?
TIME/LOCATION DETERMINED 97.5%. YUCATÁN COAST, SOUTH AMERICA 1121. MAYAN CIVILIZATION, POST-CLASSIC.
OR MORE LIKELY...

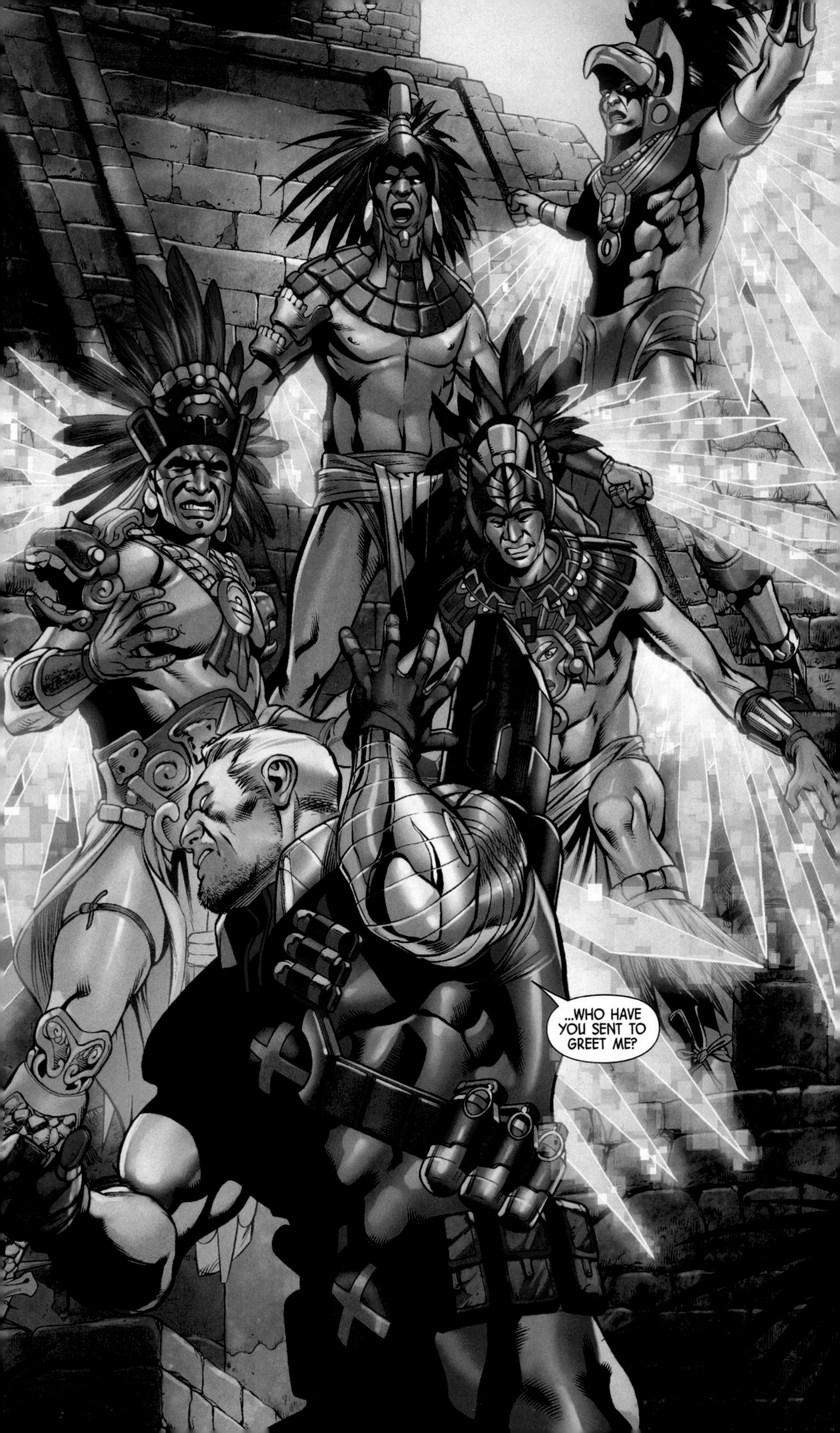
...WHO HAVE YOU SENT TO GREET ME?

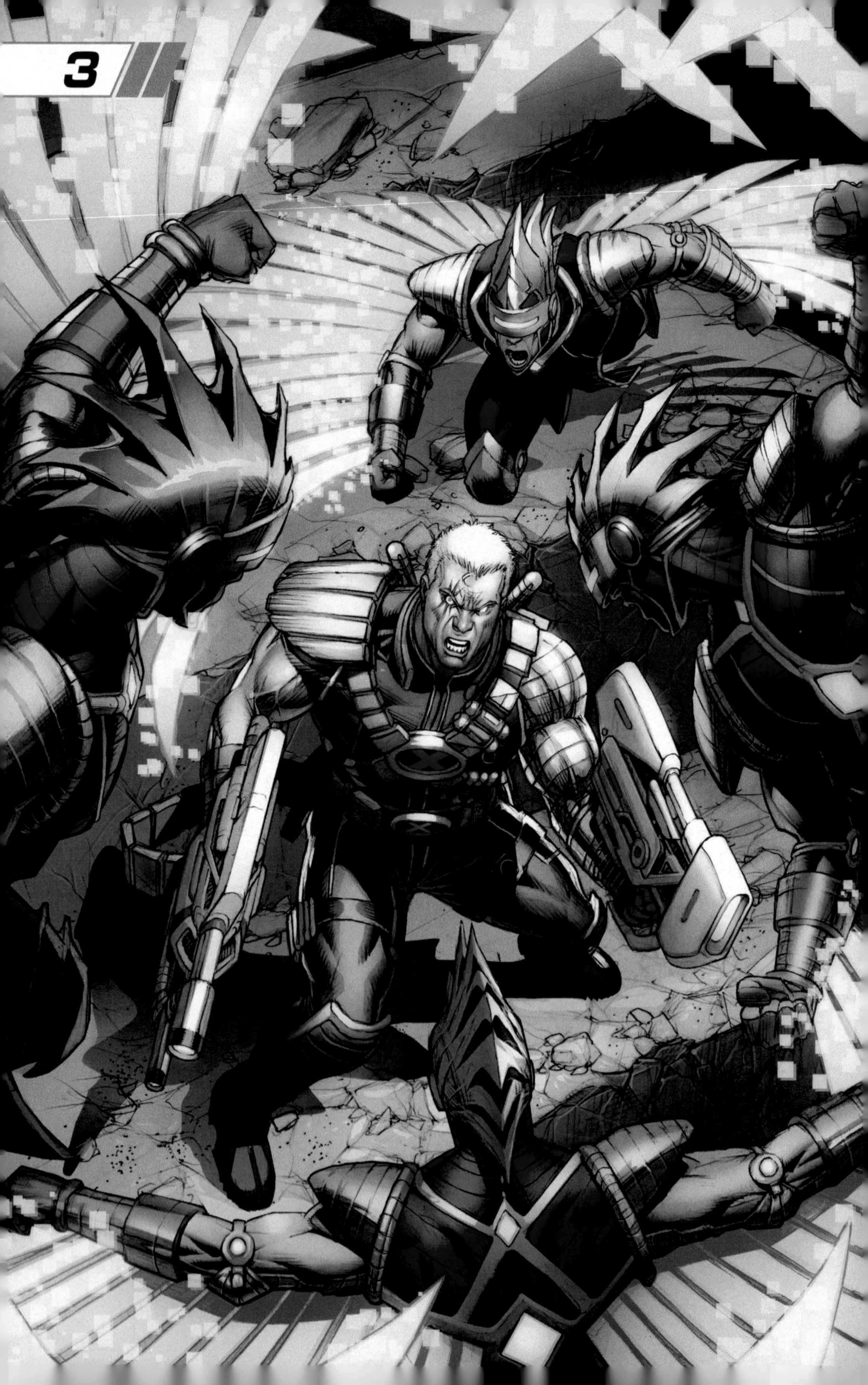
3

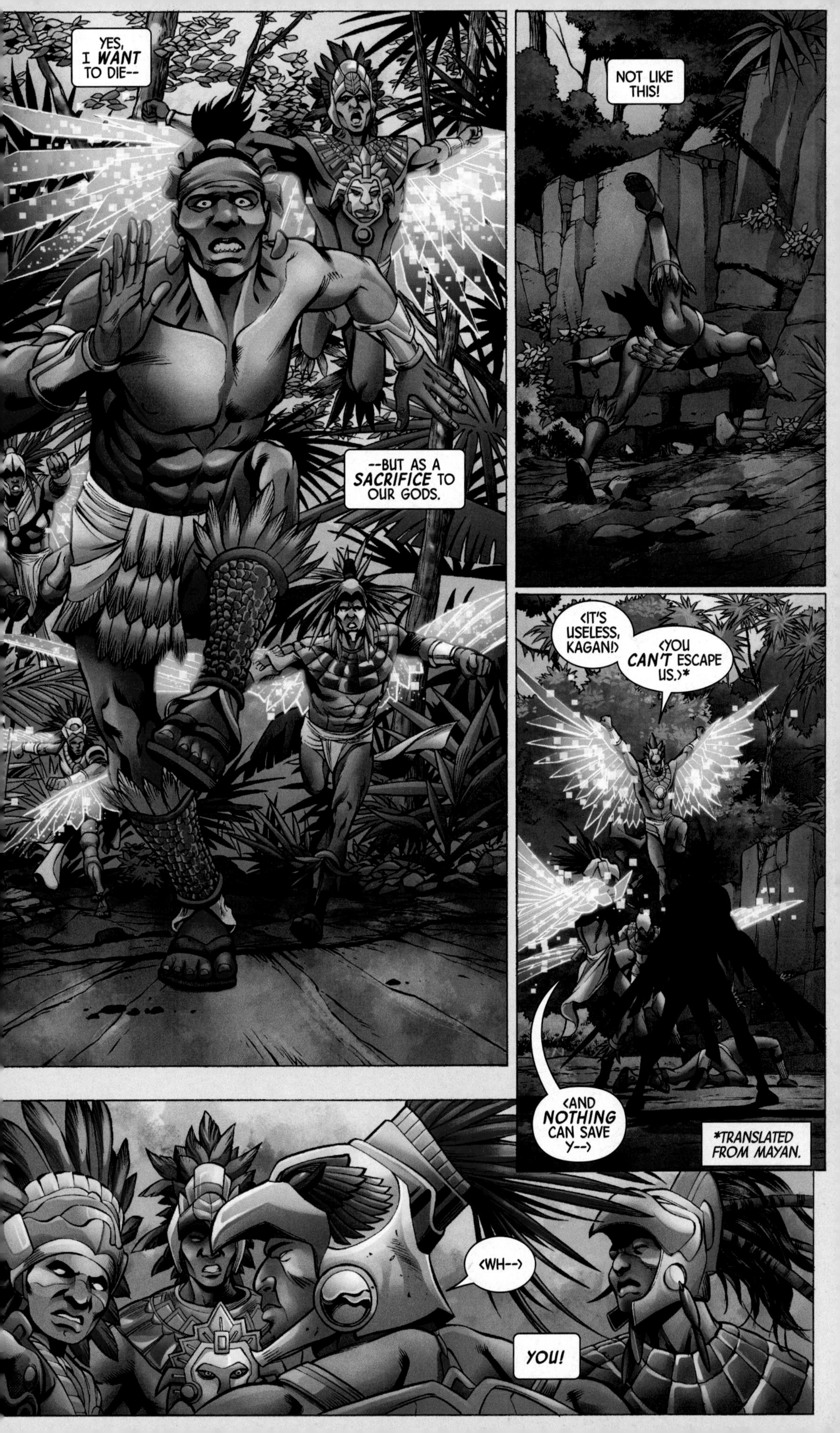
YES, I WANT TO DIE--
--BUT AS A SACRIFICE TO OUR GODS.
NOT LIKE THIS!
<IT'S USELESS, KAGAN!>
<YOU CAN'T ESCAPE US.>*
<AND NOTHING CAN SAVE Y-->
*TRANSLATED FROM MAYAN.
<WH-->
YOU!

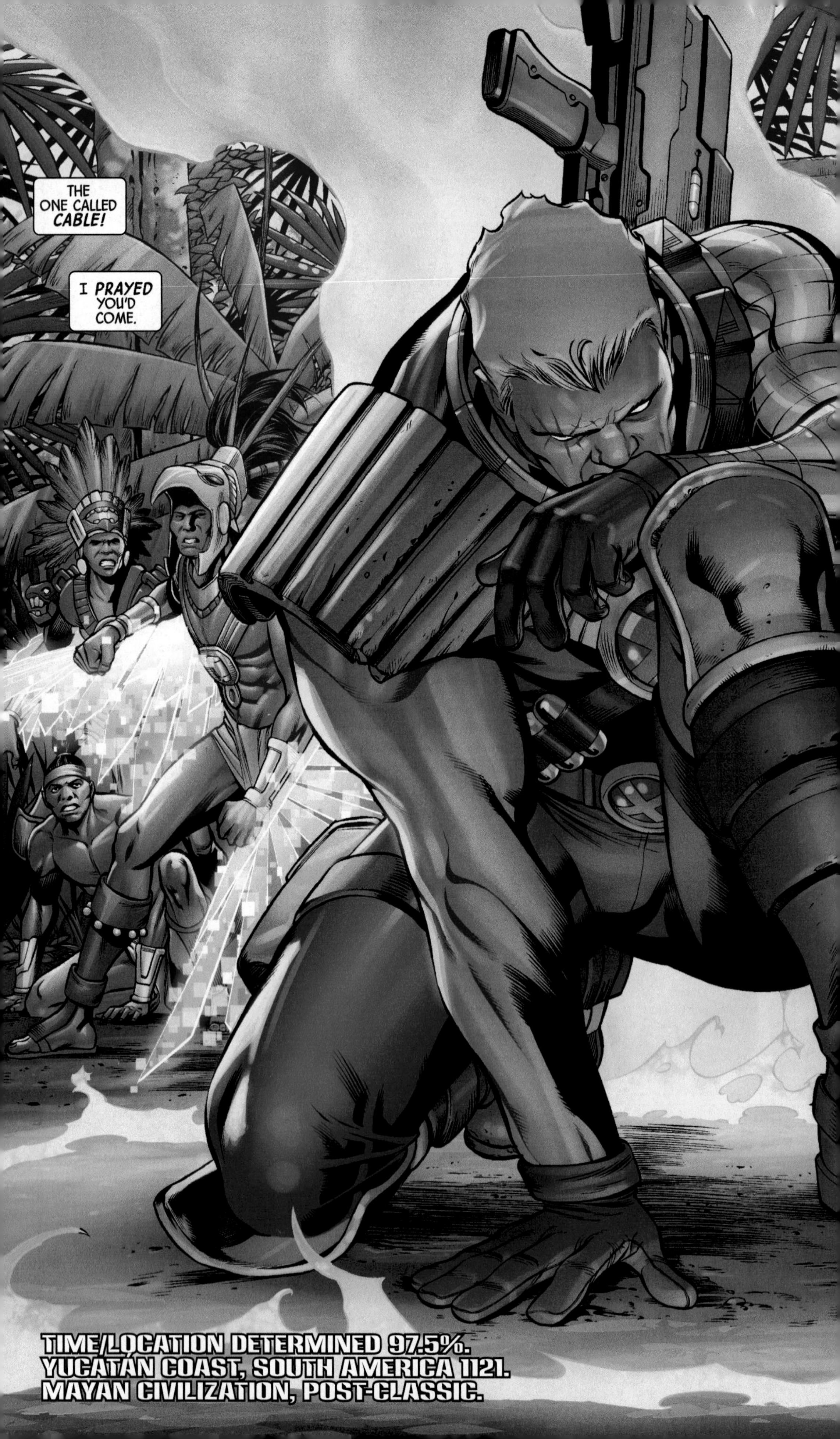

THE ONE CALLED CABLE!
I PRAYED YOU'D COME.
TIME/LOCATION DETERMINED 97.5%.
YUCATÁN COAST, SOUTH AMERICA 1121.
MAYAN CIVILIZATION, POST-CLASSIC.

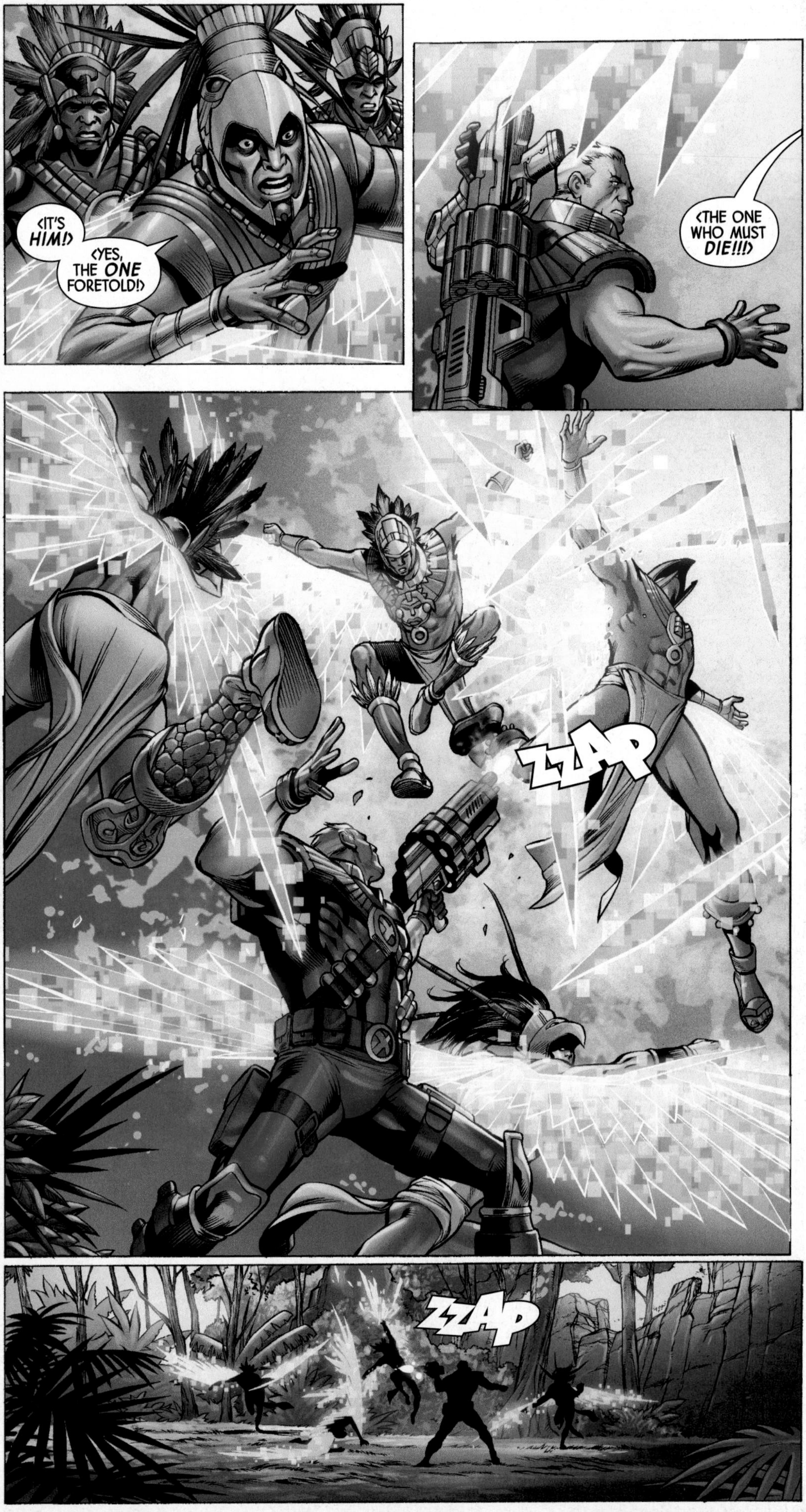

‹IT'S HIM!›
‹YES, THE ONE FORETOLD!›
‹THE ONE WHO MUST DIE!!!›
ZZAP
ZZAP

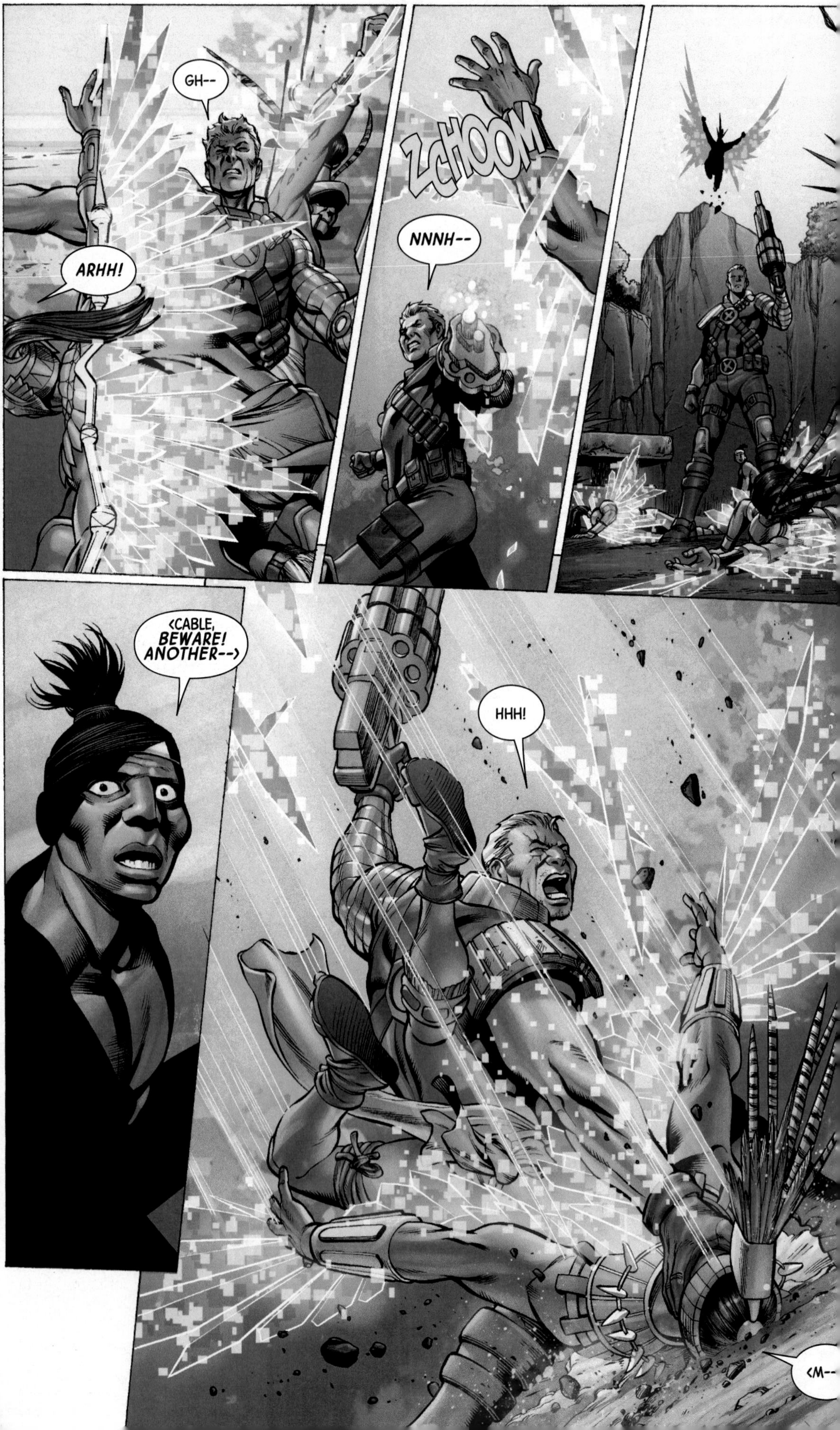
GH--
ARHH!
ZCHOOM
NNNH--
<CABLE,
BEWARE!
ANOTHER-->
HHH!
<M--

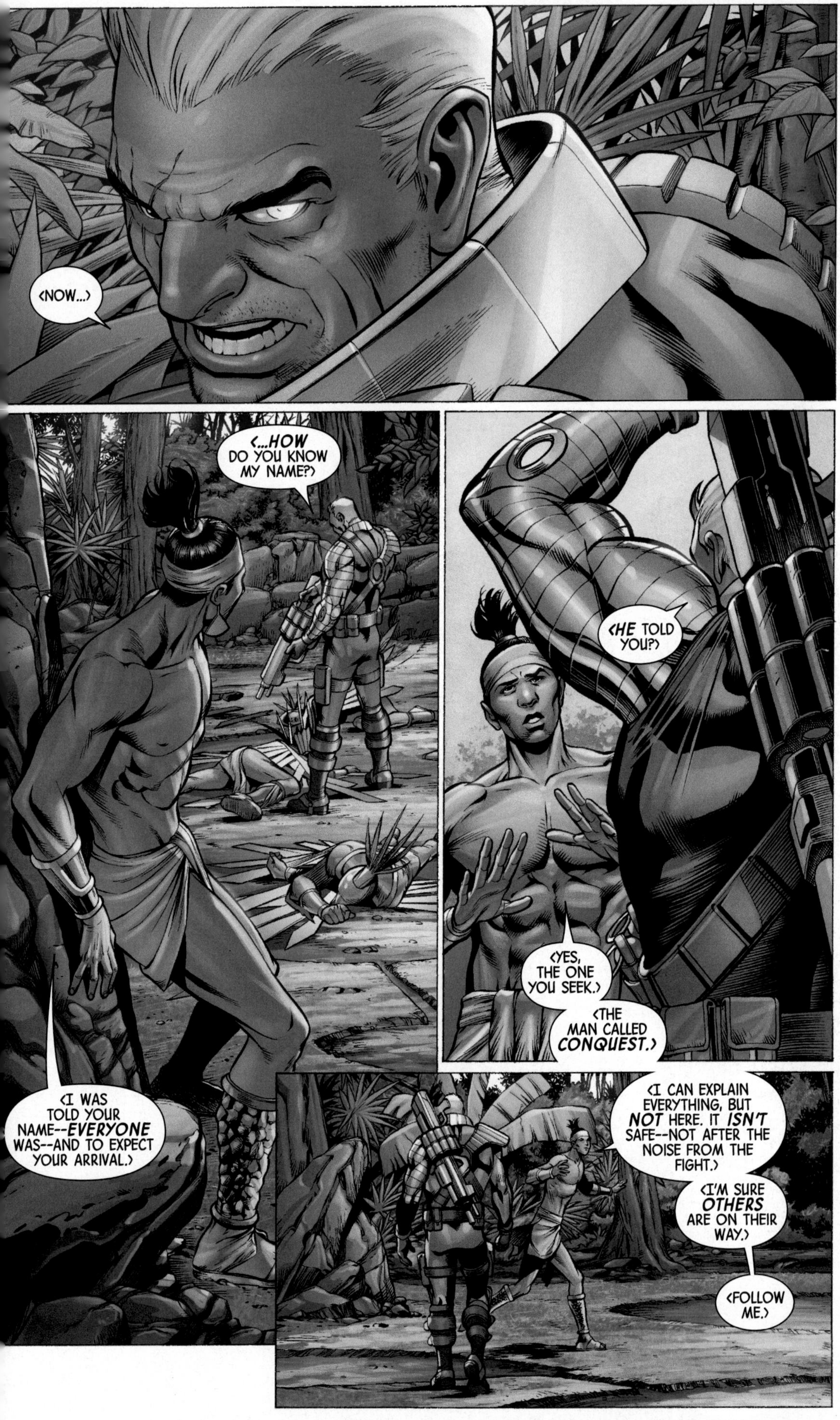

‹NOW...›
‹...HOW DO YOU KNOW MY NAME?›
‹I WAS TOLD YOUR NAME--EVERYONE WAS--AND TO EXPECT YOUR ARRIVAL.›
‹HE TOLD YOU?›
‹YES, THE ONE YOU SEEK.›
‹THE MAN CALLED CONQUEST.›
‹I CAN EXPLAIN EVERYTHING, BUT NOT HERE. IT ISN'T SAFE--NOT AFTER THE NOISE FROM THE FIGHT.›
‹I'M SURE OTHERS ARE ON THEIR WAY.›
‹FOLLOW ME.›

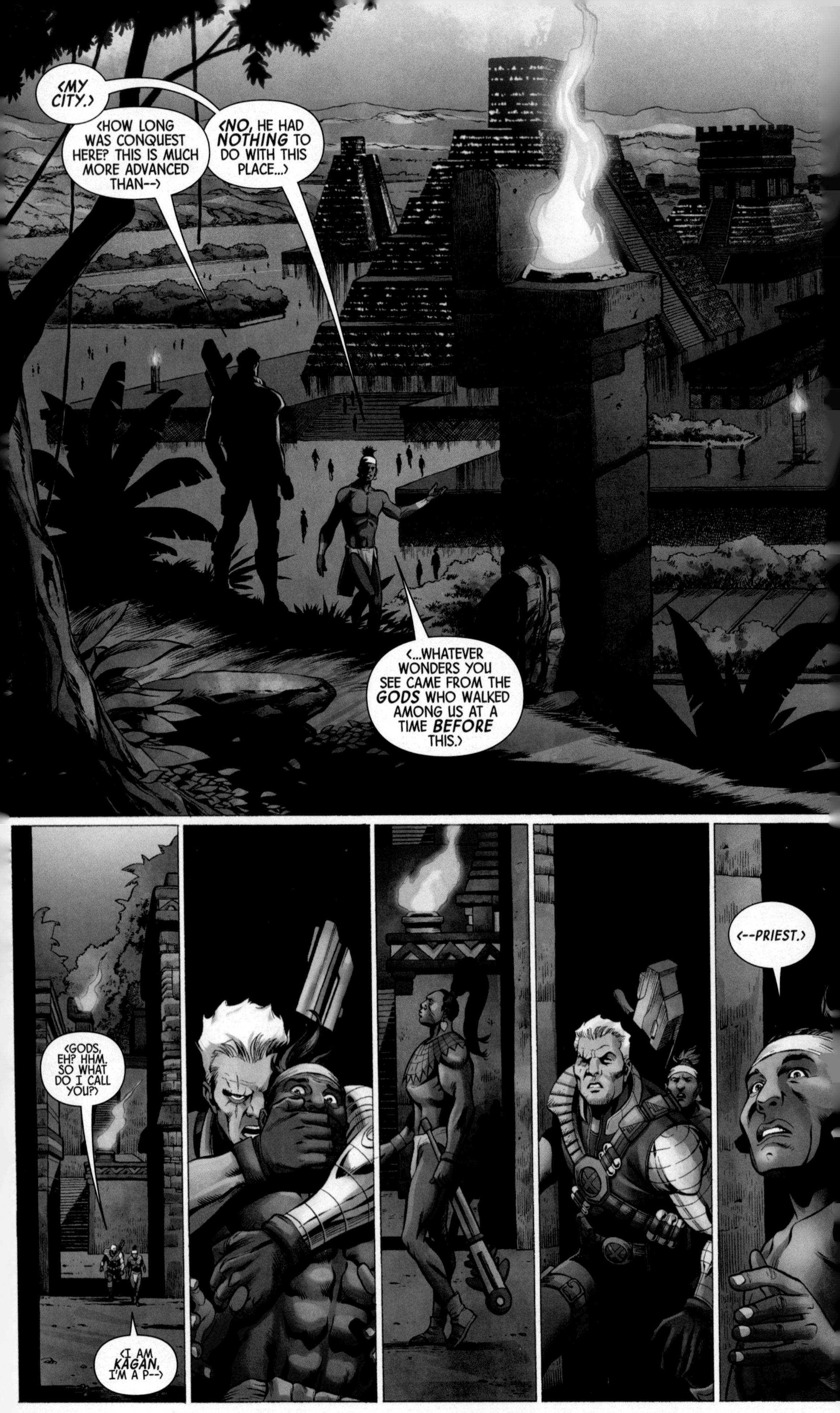
<MY CITY.>
<HOW LONG WAS CONQUEST HERE? THIS IS MUCH MORE ADVANCED THAN-->
<NO, HE HAD NOTHING TO DO WITH THIS PLACE...>
<...WHATEVER WONDERS YOU SEE CAME FROM THE GODS WHO WALKED AMONG US AT A TIME BEFORE THIS.>
<GODS, EH? HHM. SO WHAT DO I CALL YOU?>
<I AM KAGAN, I'M A P-->
<--PRIEST.>

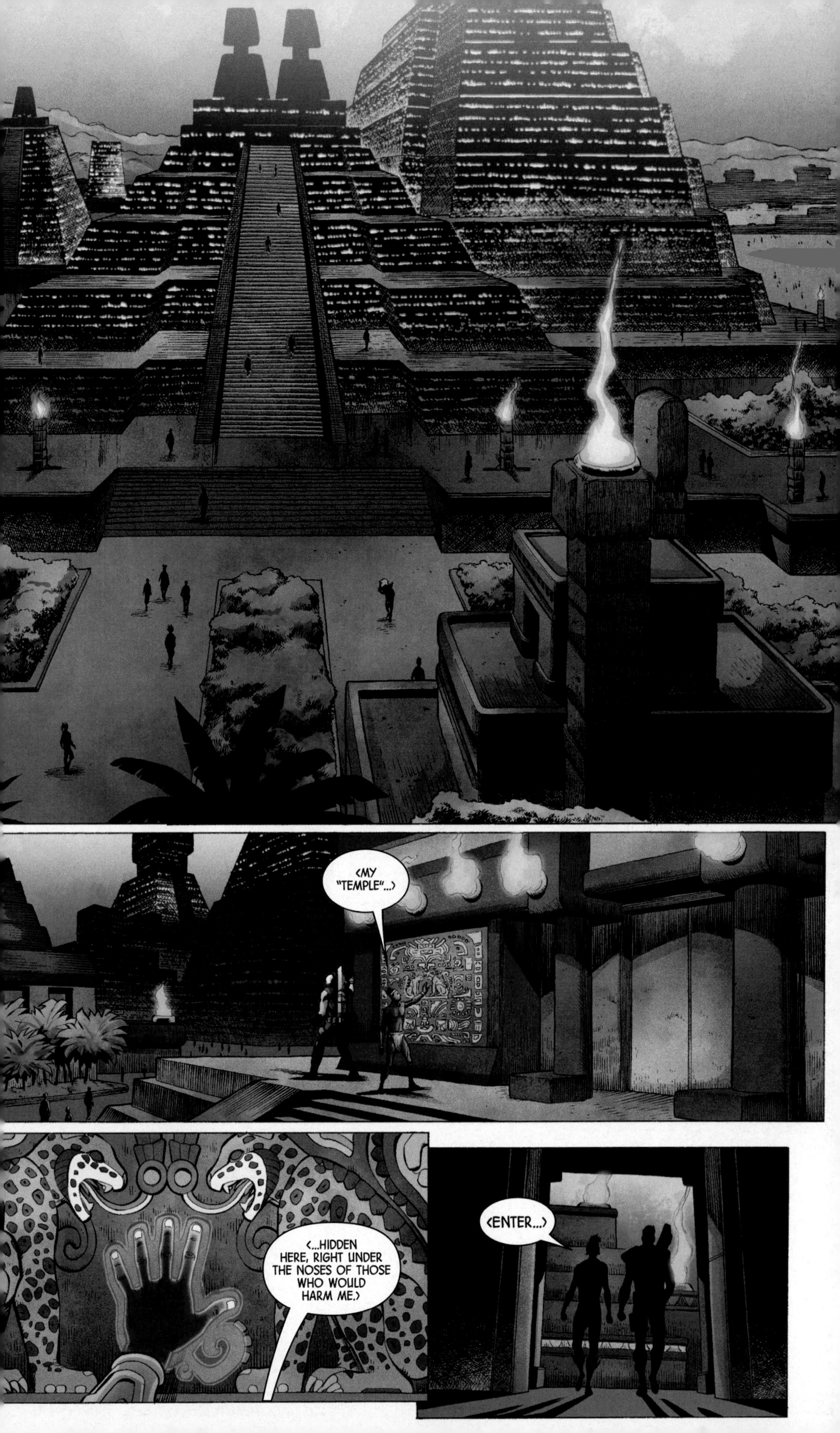
‹MY "TEMPLE"...›
‹...HIDDEN HERE, RIGHT UNDER THE NOSES OF THOSE WHO WOULD HARM ME.›
‹ENTER...›

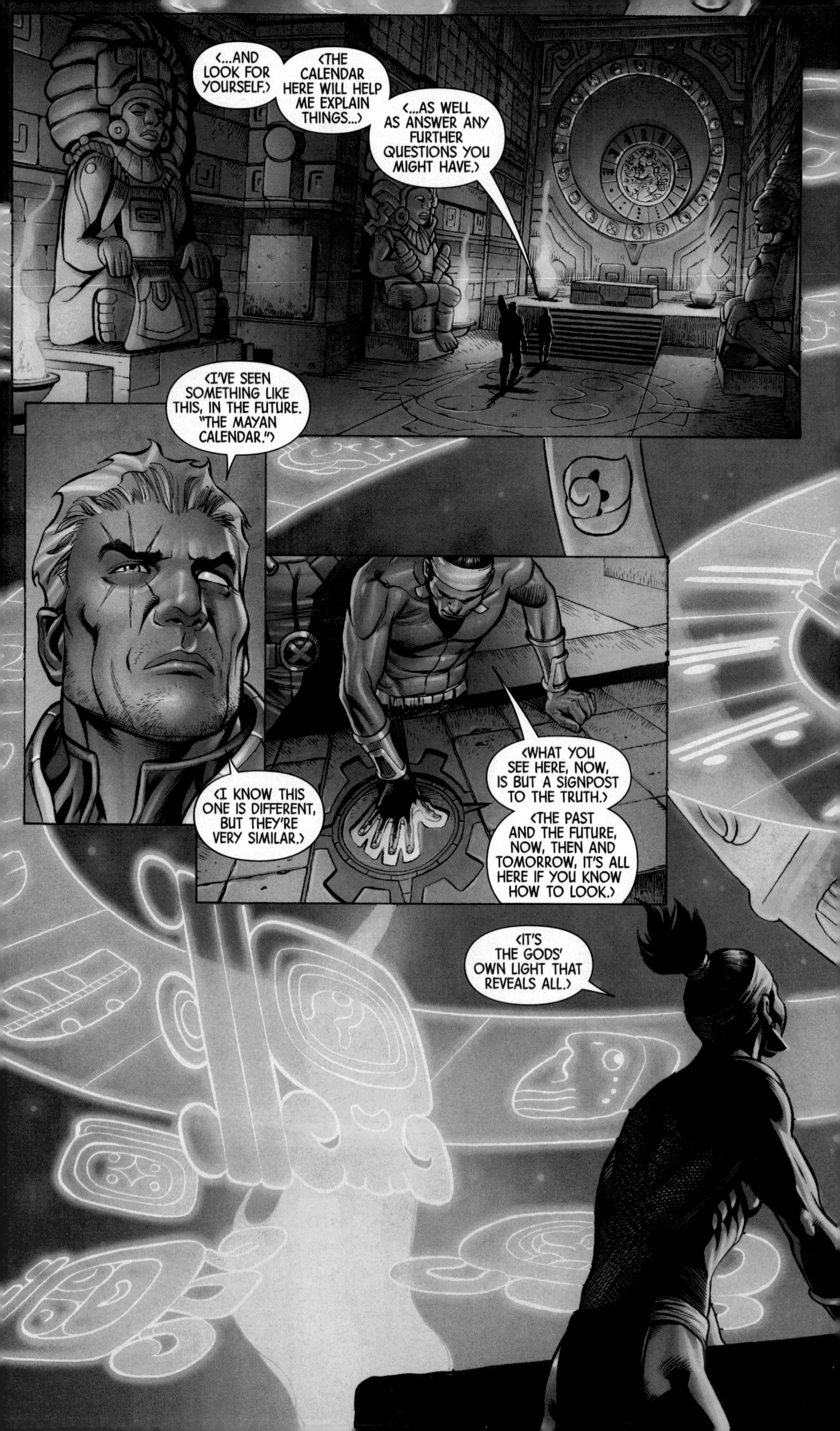
<...AND LOOK FOR YOURSELF.>
<THE CALENDAR HERE WILL HELP ME EXPLAIN THINGS...>
<...AS WELL AS ANSWER ANY FURTHER QUESTIONS YOU MIGHT HAVE.>
<I'VE SEEN SOMETHING LIKE THIS, IN THE FUTURE. "THE MAYAN CALENDAR.">
<I KNOW THIS ONE IS DIFFERENT, BUT THEY'RE VERY SIMILAR.>
<WHAT YOU SEE HERE, NOW, IS BUT A SIGNPOST TO THE TRUTH.>
<THE PAST AND THE FUTURE, NOW, THEN AND TOMORROW, IT'S ALL HERE IF YOU KNOW HOW TO LOOK.>
<IT'S THE GODS' OWN LIGHT THAT REVEALS ALL.>

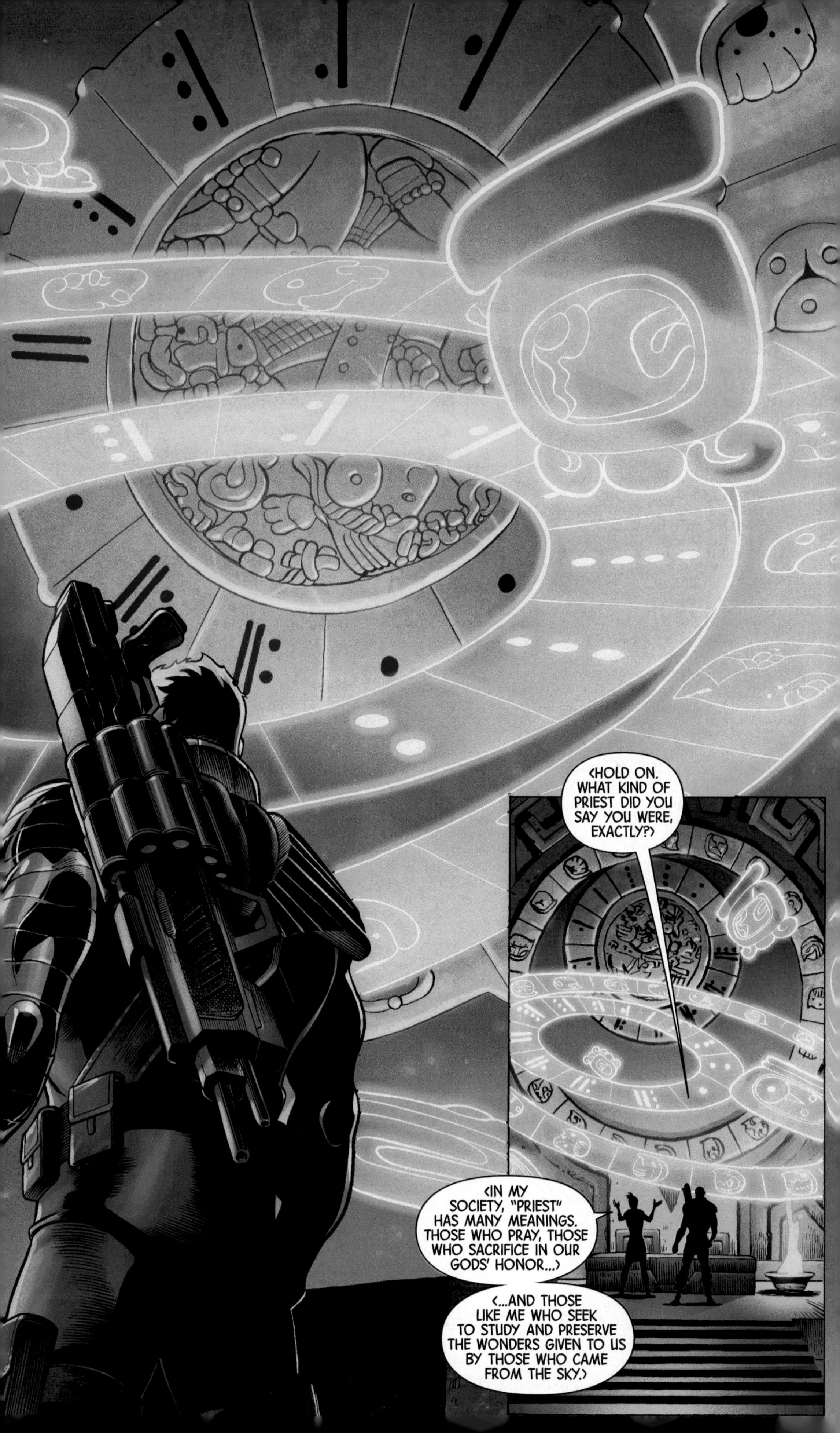

<HOLD ON. WHAT KIND OF PRIEST DID YOU SAY YOU WERE, EXACTLY?>
<IN MY SOCIETY, "PRIEST" HAS MANY MEANINGS. THOSE WHO PRAY, THOSE WHO SACRIFICE IN OUR GODS' HONOR...>
<...AND THOSE LIKE ME WHO SEEK TO STUDY AND PRESERVE THE WONDERS GIVEN TO US BY THOSE WHO CAME FROM THE SKY.>

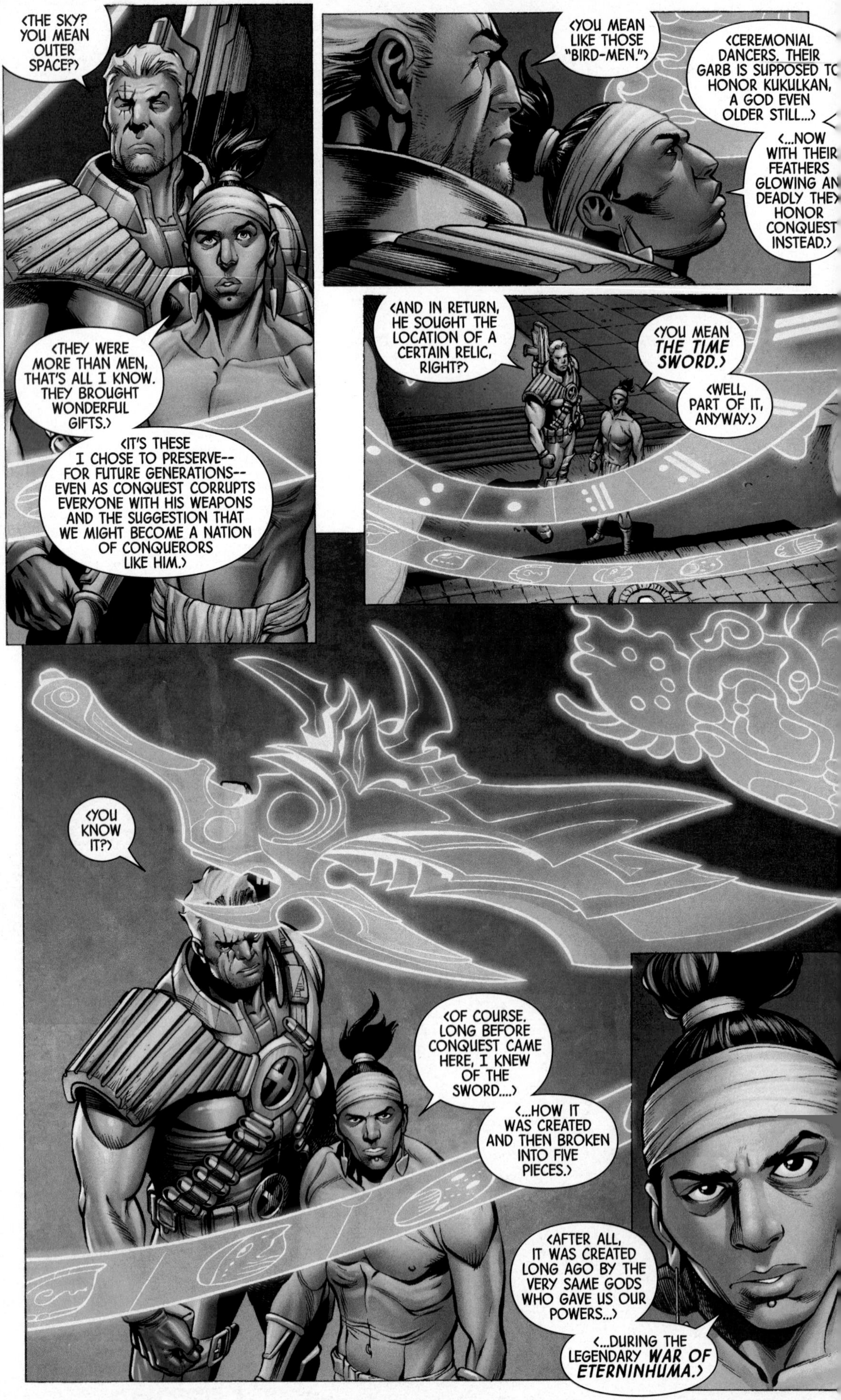

<THE SKY? YOU MEAN OUTER SPACE?>
<THEY WERE MORE THAN MEN, THAT'S ALL I KNOW. THEY BROUGHT WONDERFUL GIFTS.>
<IT'S THESE I CHOSE TO PRESERVE-- FOR FUTURE GENERATIONS-- EVEN AS CONQUEST CORRUPTS EVERYONE WITH HIS WEAPONS AND THE SUGGESTION THAT WE MIGHT BECOME A NATION OF CONQUERORS LIKE HIM.>
<YOU MEAN LIKE THOSE "BIRD-MEN.">
<CEREMONIAL DANCERS. THEIR GARB IS SUPPOSED TO HONOR KUKULKAN, A GOD EVEN OLDER STILL...>
<...NOW WITH THEIR FEATHERS GLOWING AN DEADLY THEY HONOR CONQUEST INSTEAD.>
<AND IN RETURN, HE SOUGHT THE LOCATION OF A CERTAIN RELIC, RIGHT?>
<YOU MEAN *THE TIME SWORD.*>
<WELL, PART OF IT, ANYWAY.>
<YOU KNOW IT?>
<OF COURSE. LONG BEFORE CONQUEST CAME HERE, I KNEW OF THE SWORD....>
<...HOW IT WAS CREATED AND THEN BROKEN INTO FIVE PIECES.>
<AFTER ALL, IT WAS CREATED LONG AGO BY THE VERY SAME GODS WHO GAVE US OUR POWERS...>
<...DURING THE LEGENDARY *WAR OF ETERNINHUMA.*>

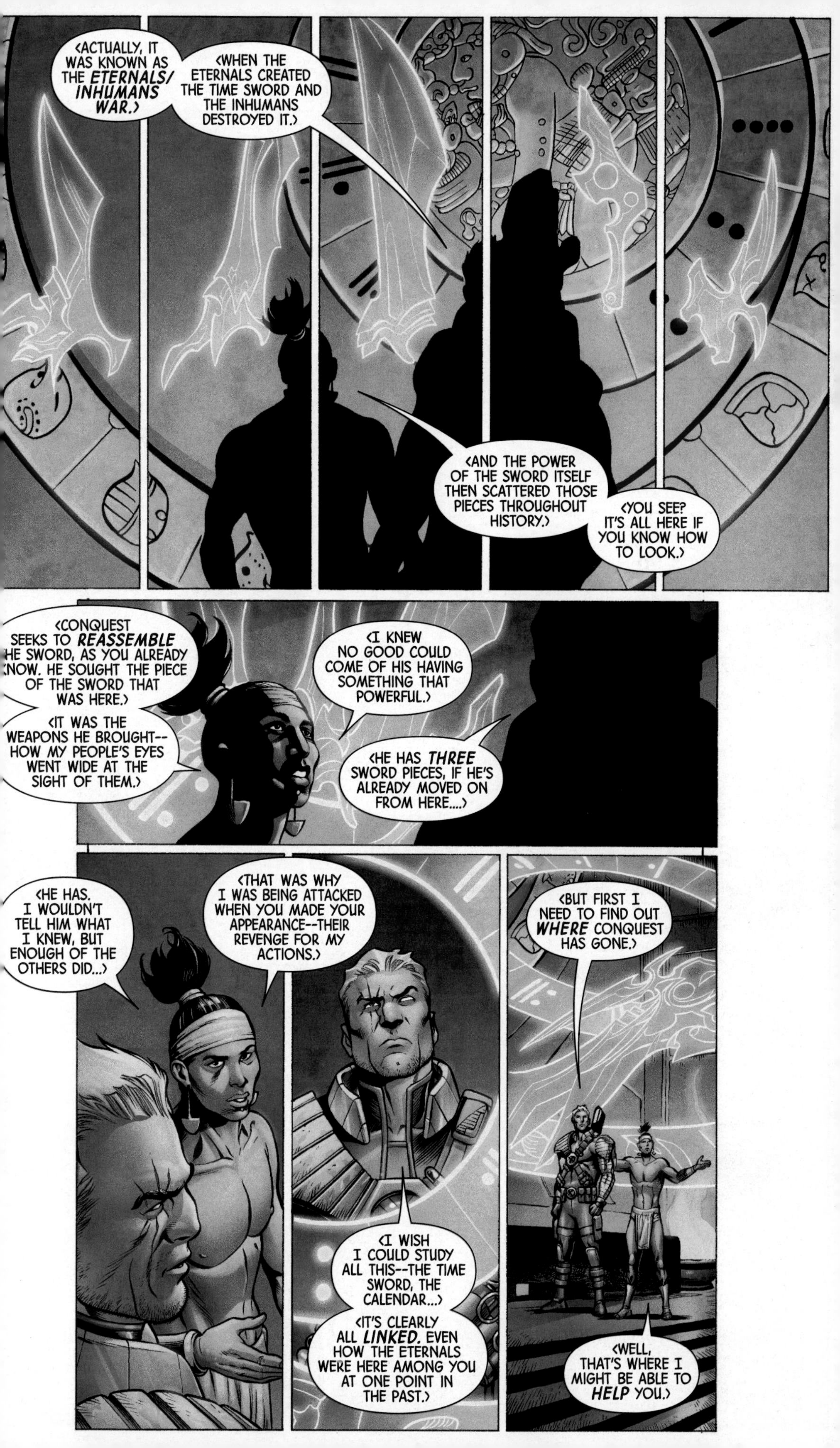

<ACTUALLY, IT WAS KNOWN AS THE ETERNALS/ INHUMANS WAR.>
<WHEN THE ETERNALS CREATED THE TIME SWORD AND THE INHUMANS DESTROYED IT.>
<AND THE POWER OF THE SWORD ITSELF THEN SCATTERED THOSE PIECES THROUGHOUT HISTORY.>
<YOU SEE? IT'S ALL HERE IF YOU KNOW HOW TO LOOK.>
<CONQUEST SEEKS TO REASSEMBLE HE SWORD, AS YOU ALREADY NOW. HE SOUGHT THE PIECE OF THE SWORD THAT WAS HERE.>
<IT WAS THE WEAPONS HE BROUGHT-- HOW MY PEOPLE'S EYES WENT WIDE AT THE SIGHT OF THEM.>
<I KNEW NO GOOD COULD COME OF HIS HAVING SOMETHING THAT POWERFUL.>
<HE HAS THREE SWORD PIECES, IF HE'S ALREADY MOVED ON FROM HERE....>
<HE HAS. I WOULDN'T TELL HIM WHAT I KNEW, BUT ENOUGH OF THE OTHERS DID...>
<THAT WAS WHY I WAS BEING ATTACKED WHEN YOU MADE YOUR APPEARANCE--THEIR REVENGE FOR MY ACTIONS.>
<I WISH I COULD STUDY ALL THIS--THE TIME SWORD, THE CALENDAR...>
<IT'S CLEARLY ALL LINKED. EVEN HOW THE ETERNALS WERE HERE AMONG YOU AT ONE POINT IN THE PAST.>
<BUT FIRST I NEED TO FIND OUT WHERE CONQUEST HAS GONE.>
<WELL, THAT'S WHERE I MIGHT BE ABLE TO HELP YOU.>

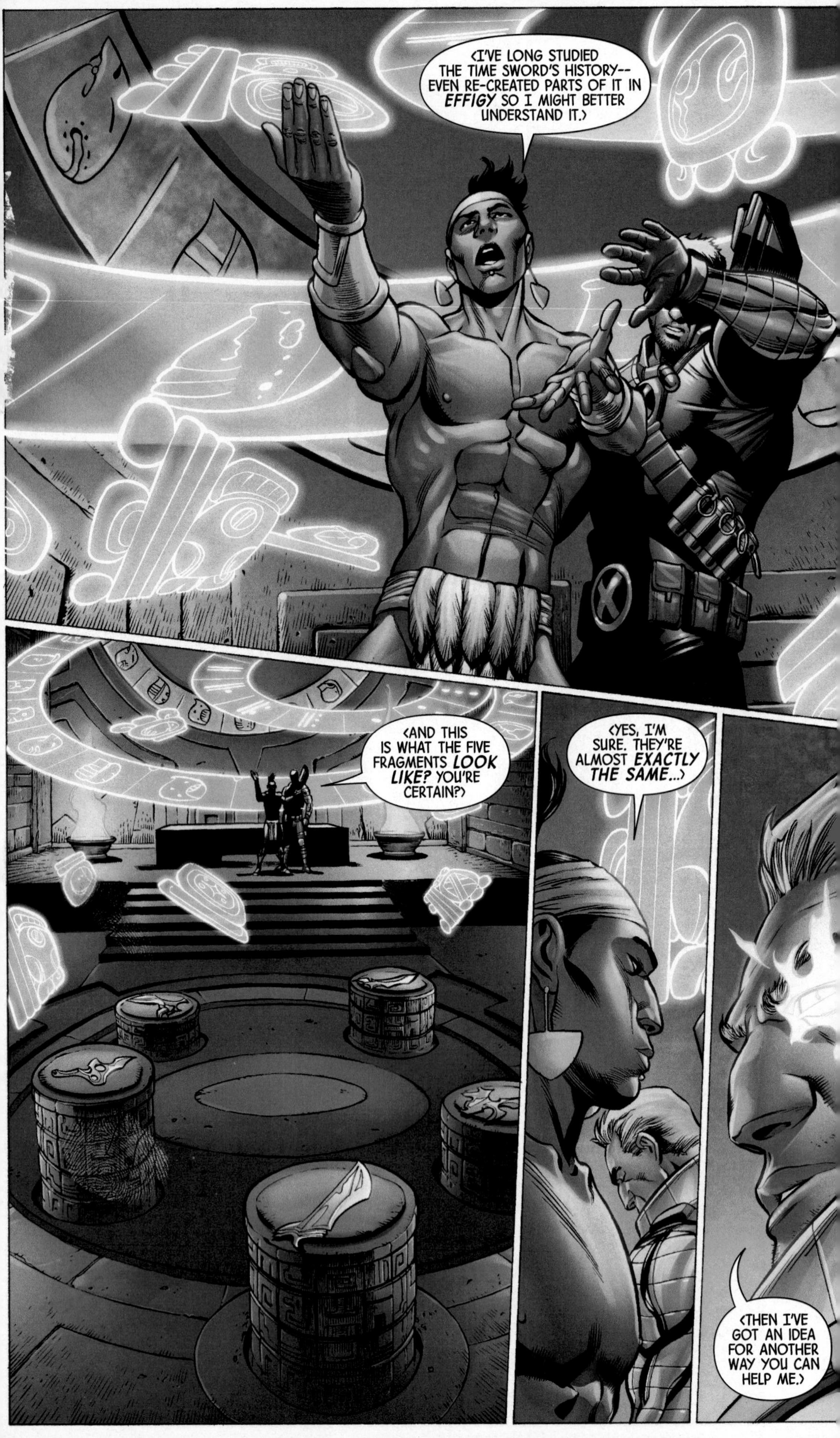
‹I'VE LONG STUDIED THE TIME SWORD'S HISTORY-- EVEN RE-CREATED PARTS OF IT IN EFFIGY SO I MIGHT BETTER UNDERSTAND IT.›
‹AND THIS IS WHAT THE FIVE FRAGMENTS LOOK LIKE? YOU'RE CERTAIN?›
‹YES, I'M SURE. THEY'RE ALMOST EXACTLY THE SAME...›
‹THEN I'VE GOT AN IDEA FOR ANOTHER WAY YOU CAN HELP ME.›

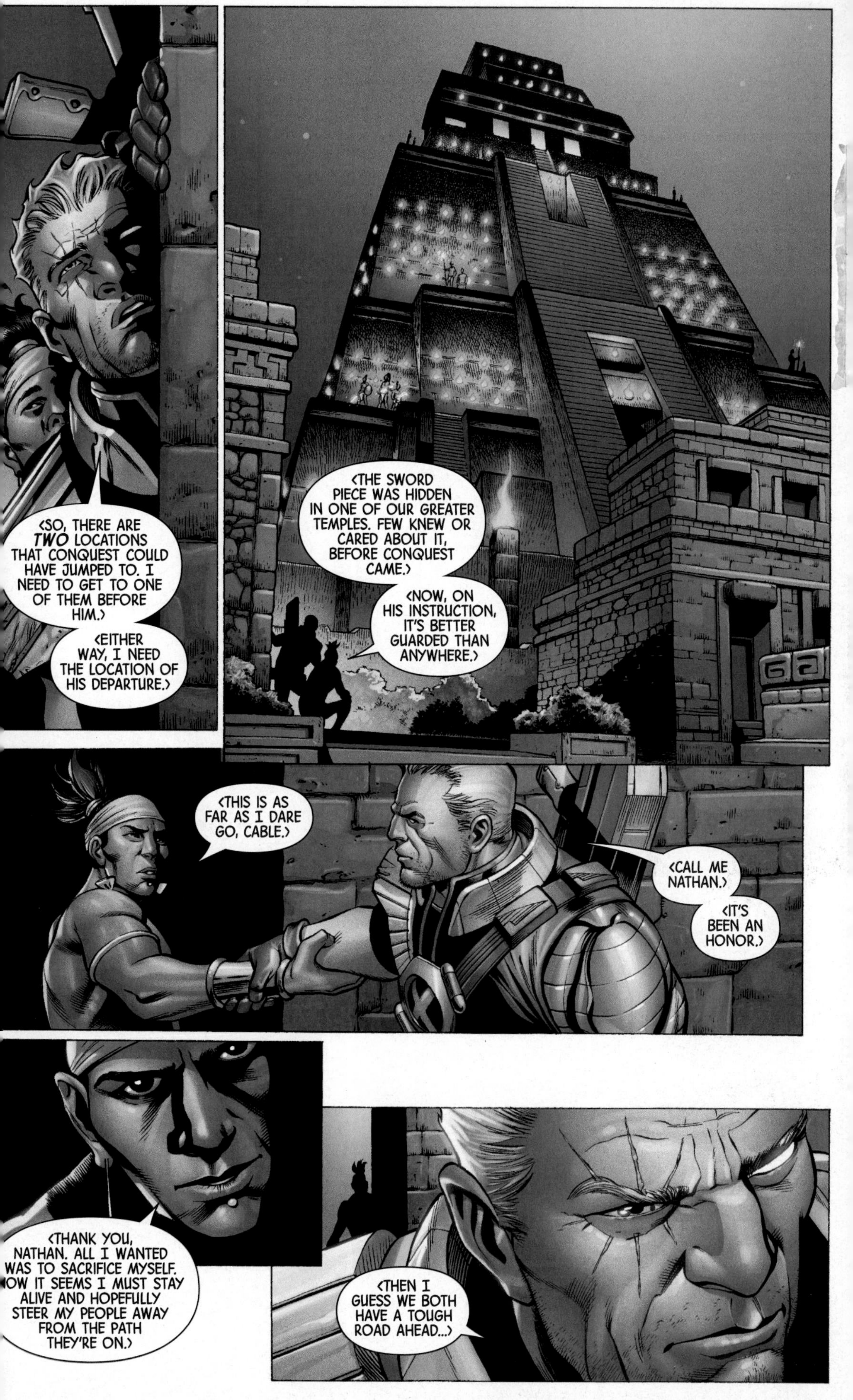

<SO, THERE ARE *TWO* LOCATIONS THAT CONQUEST COULD HAVE JUMPED TO. I NEED TO GET TO ONE OF THEM BEFORE HIM.>
<EITHER WAY, I NEED THE LOCATION OF HIS DEPARTURE.>
<THE SWORD PIECE WAS HIDDEN IN ONE OF OUR GREATER TEMPLES. FEW KNEW OR CARED ABOUT IT, BEFORE CONQUEST CAME.>
<NOW, ON HIS INSTRUCTION, IT'S BETTER GUARDED THAN ANYWHERE.>
<THIS IS AS FAR AS I DARE GO, CABLE.>
<CALL ME NATHAN.>
<IT'S BEEN AN HONOR.>
<THANK YOU, NATHAN. ALL I WANTED WAS TO SACRIFICE MYSELF. OW IT SEEMS I MUST STAY ALIVE AND HOPEFULLY STEER MY PEOPLE AWAY FROM THE PATH THEY'RE ON.>
<THEN I GUESS WE BOTH HAVE A TOUGH ROAD AHEAD...>

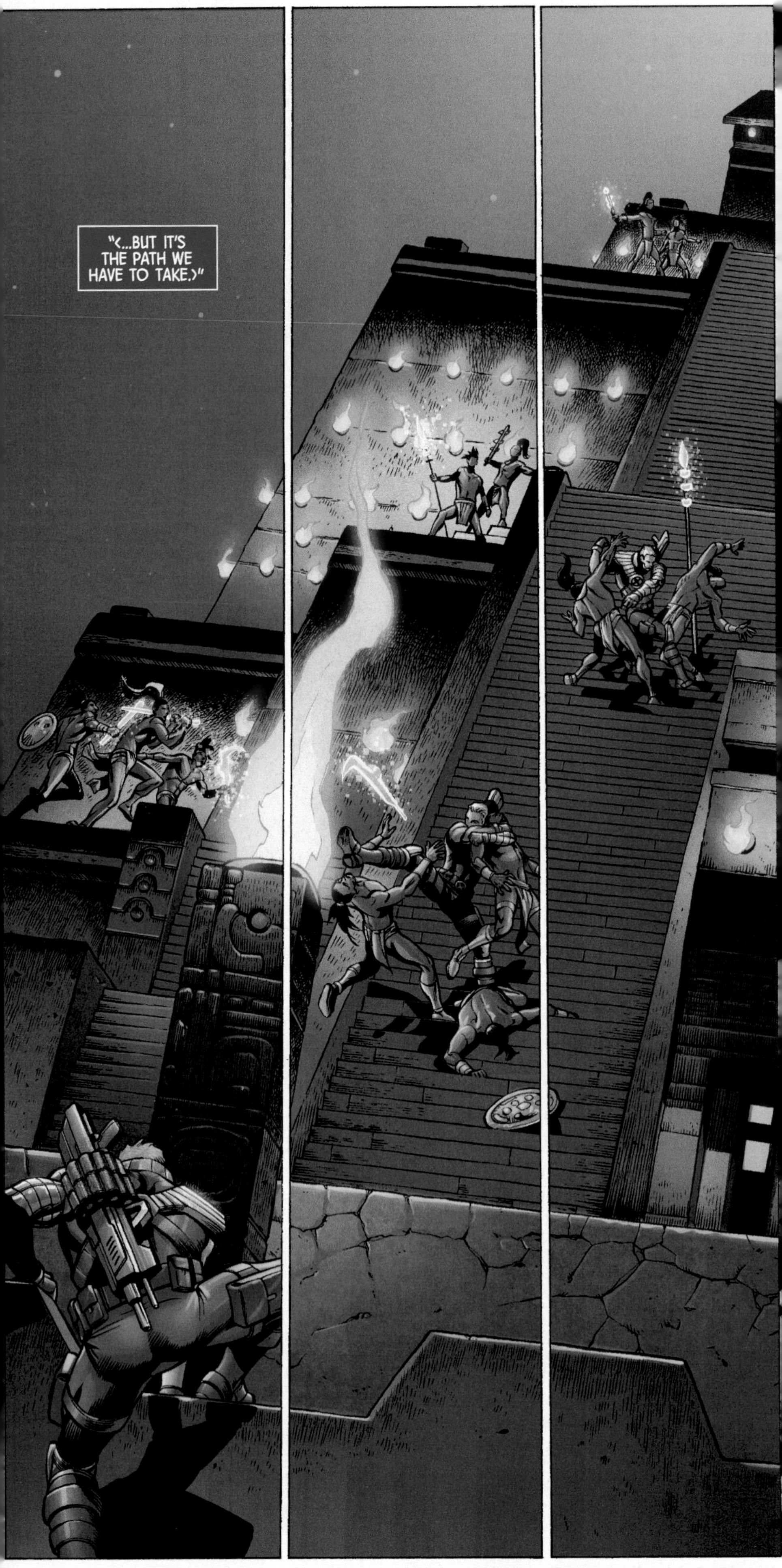
"<...BUT IT'S THE PATH WE HAVE TO TAKE.>"

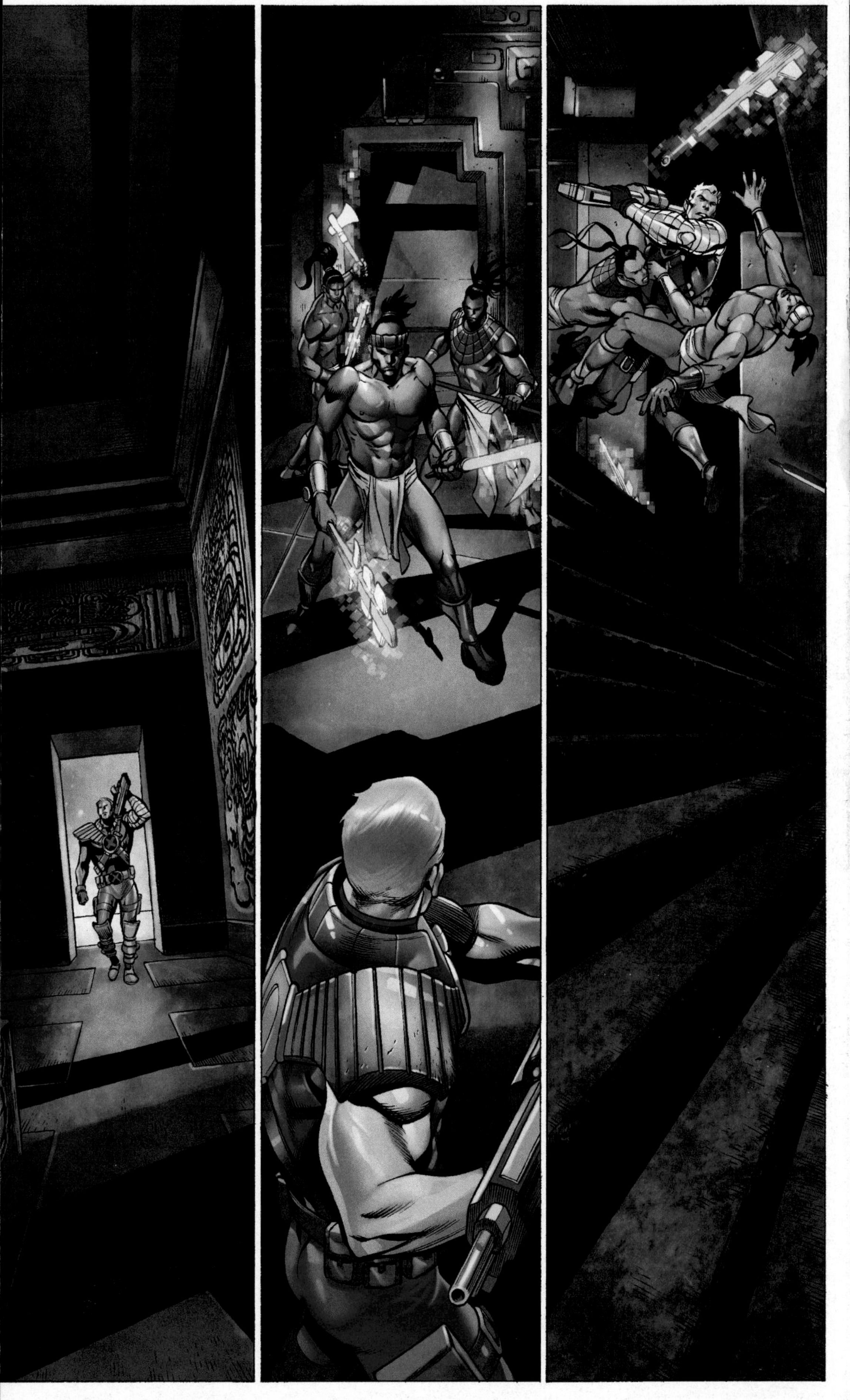

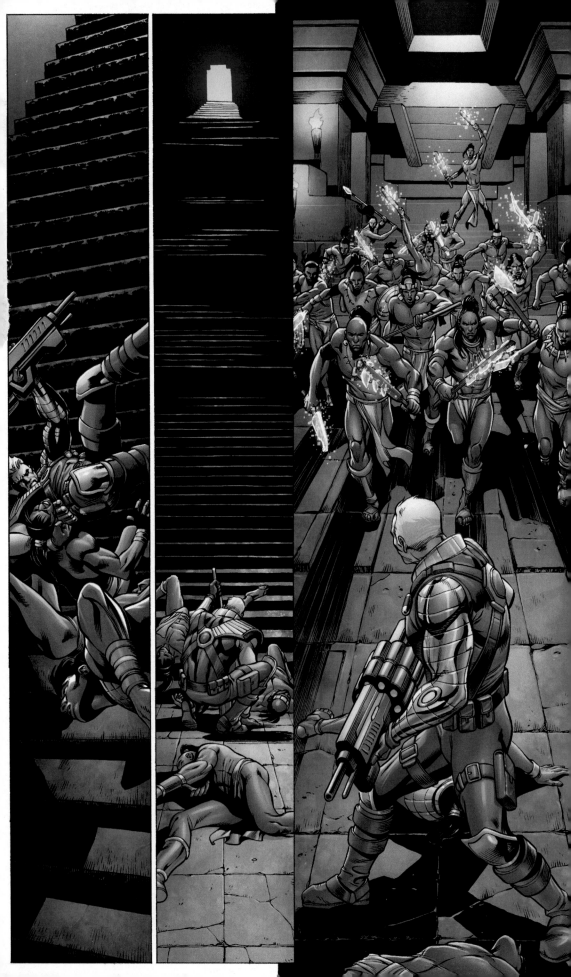

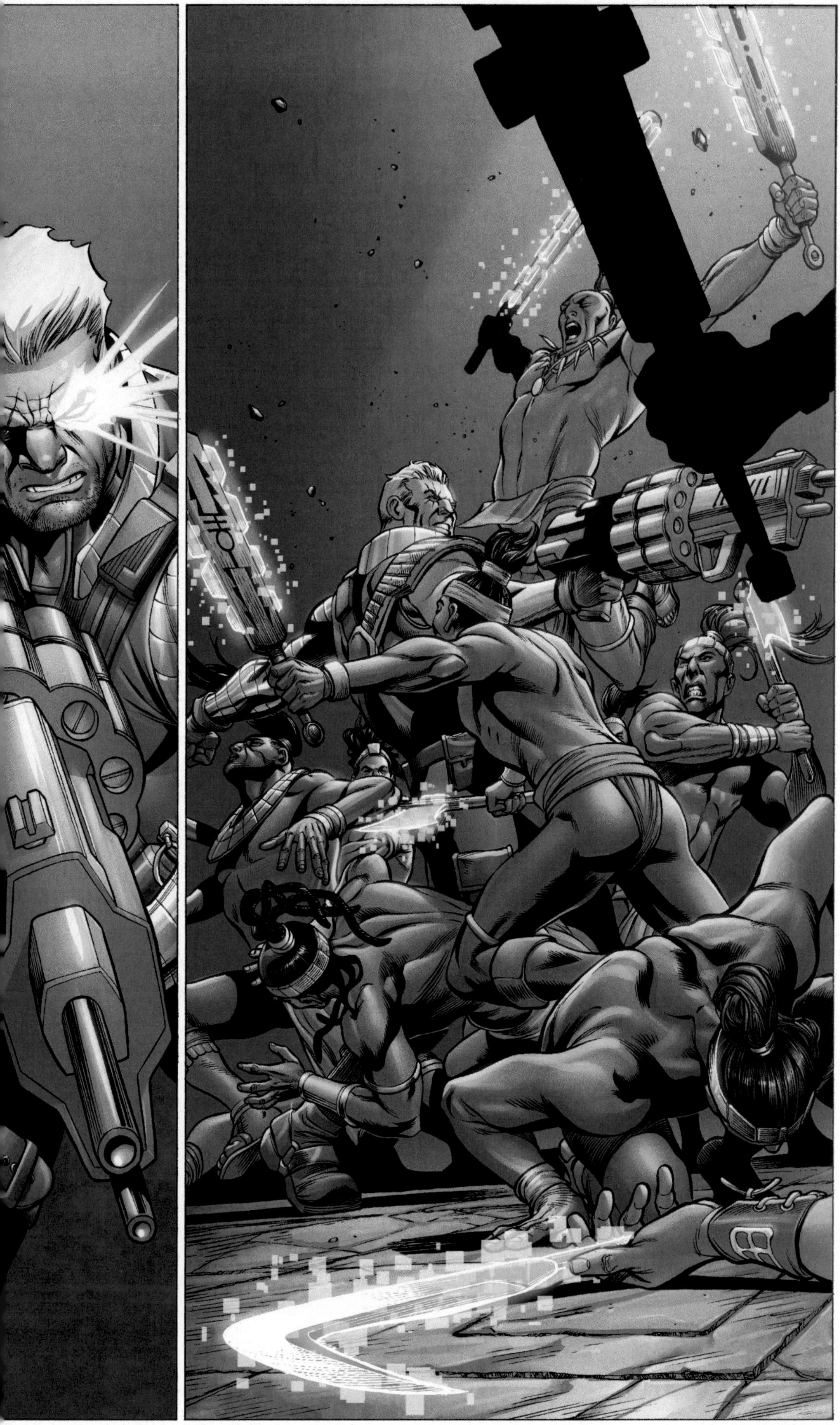

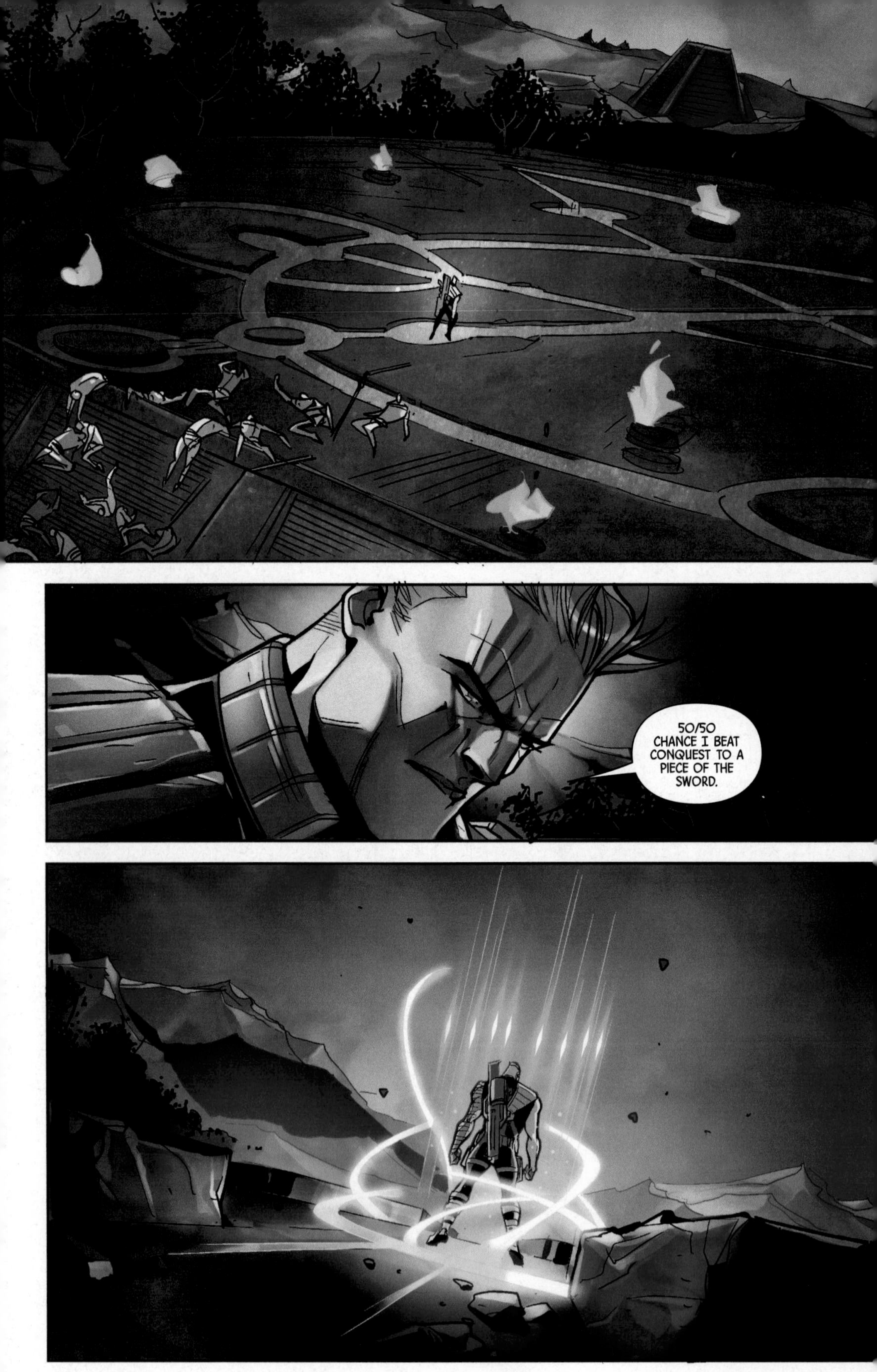
50/50 CHANCE I BEAT CONQUEST TO A PIECE OF THE SWORD.

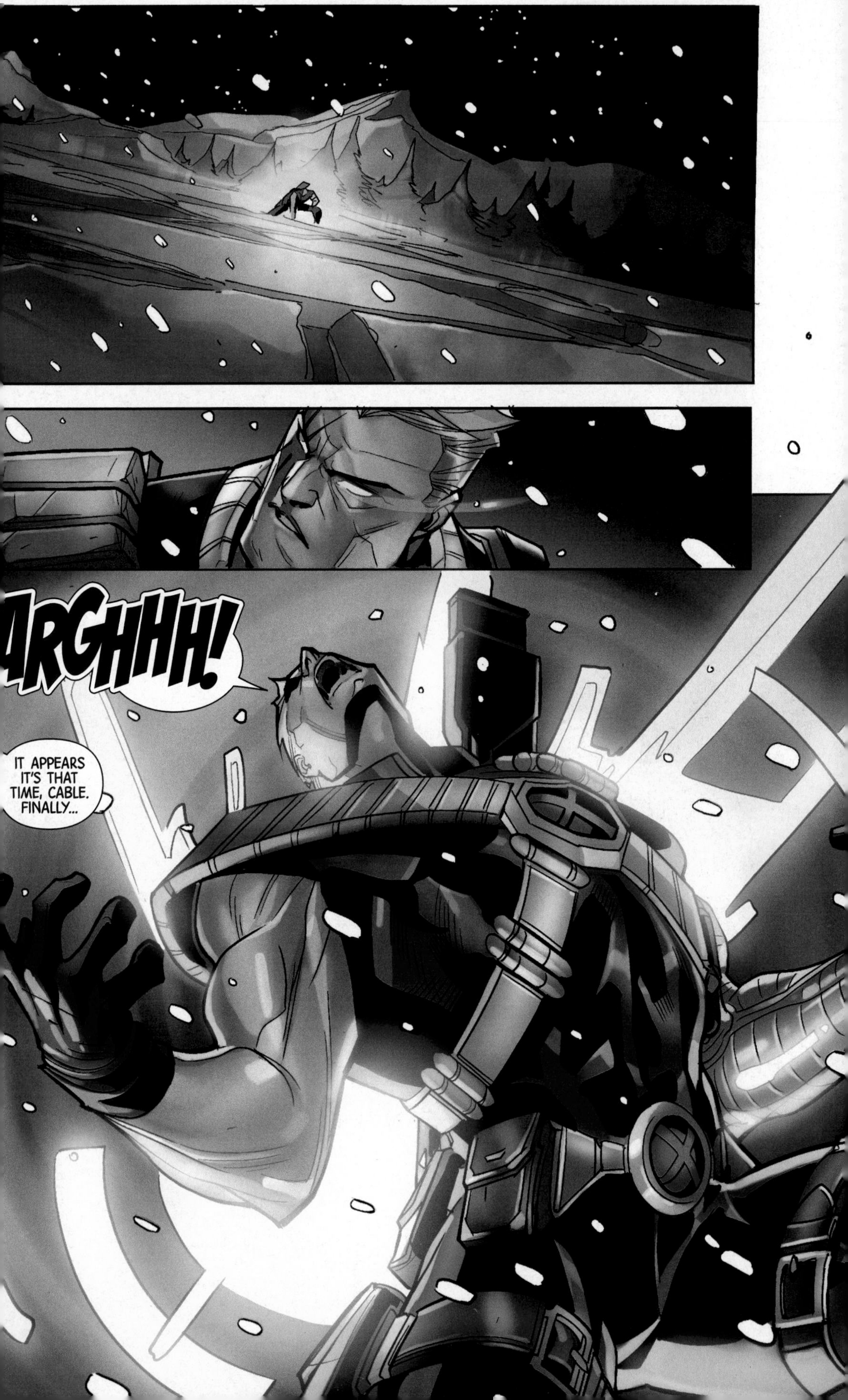

RGHHH!
IT APPEARS IT'S THAT TIME, CABLE. FINALLY...

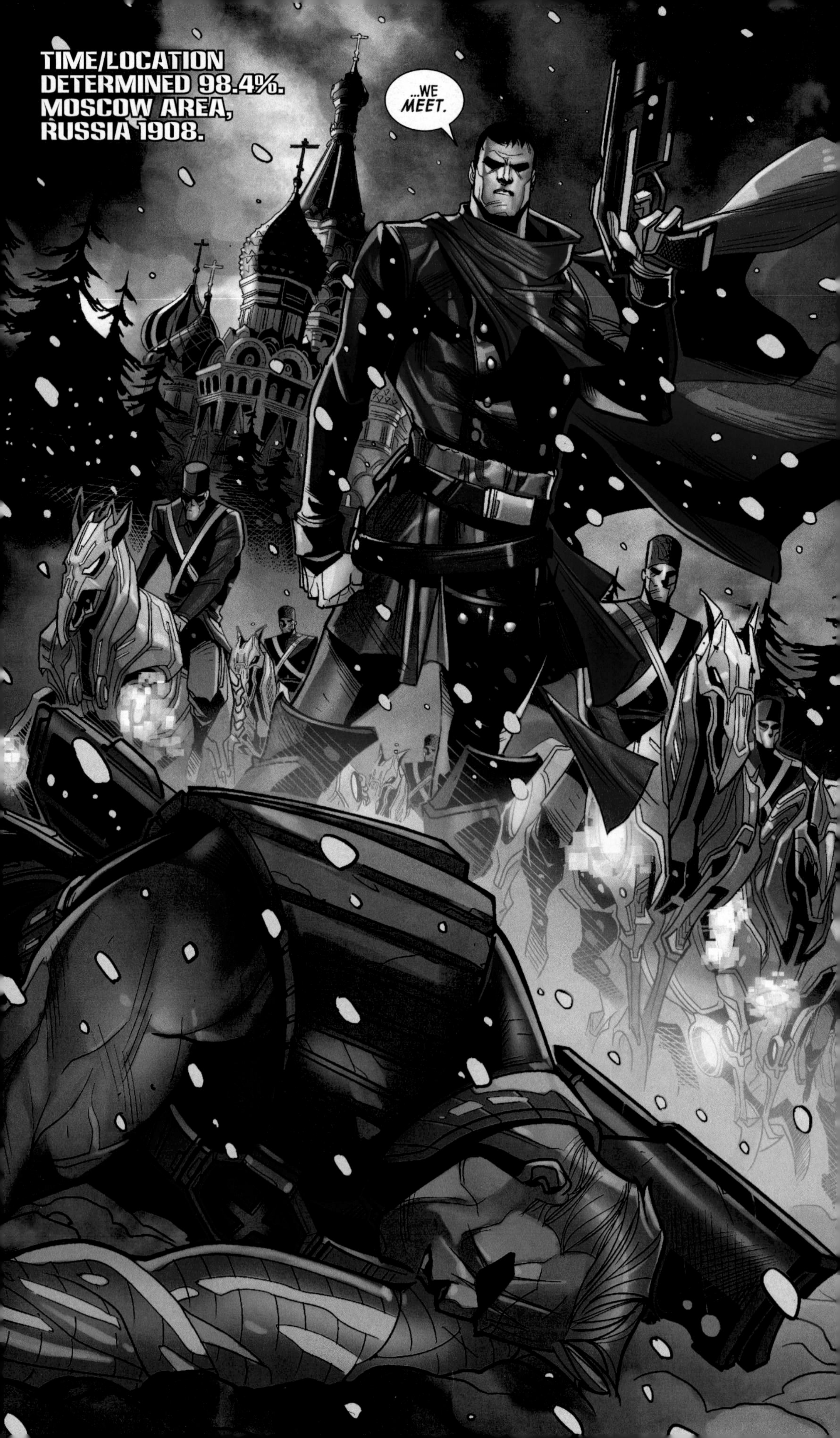
TIME/LOCATION DETERMINED 98.4%. MOSCOW AREA, RUSSIA 1908.
...WE MEET.

#1 VARIANT BY **ADAM KUBERT** & **FRANK MARTIN**

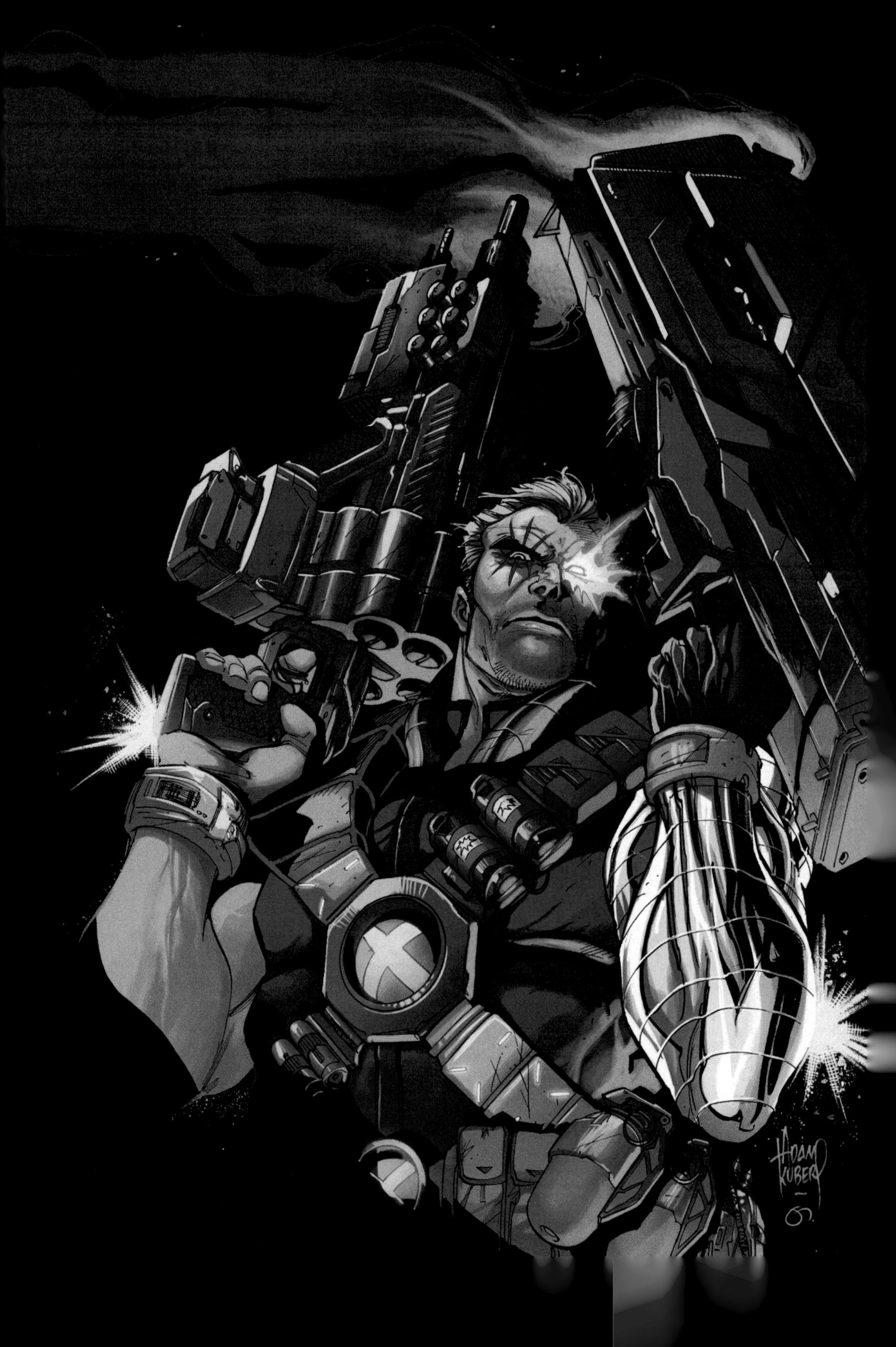

ADAM KUBERT

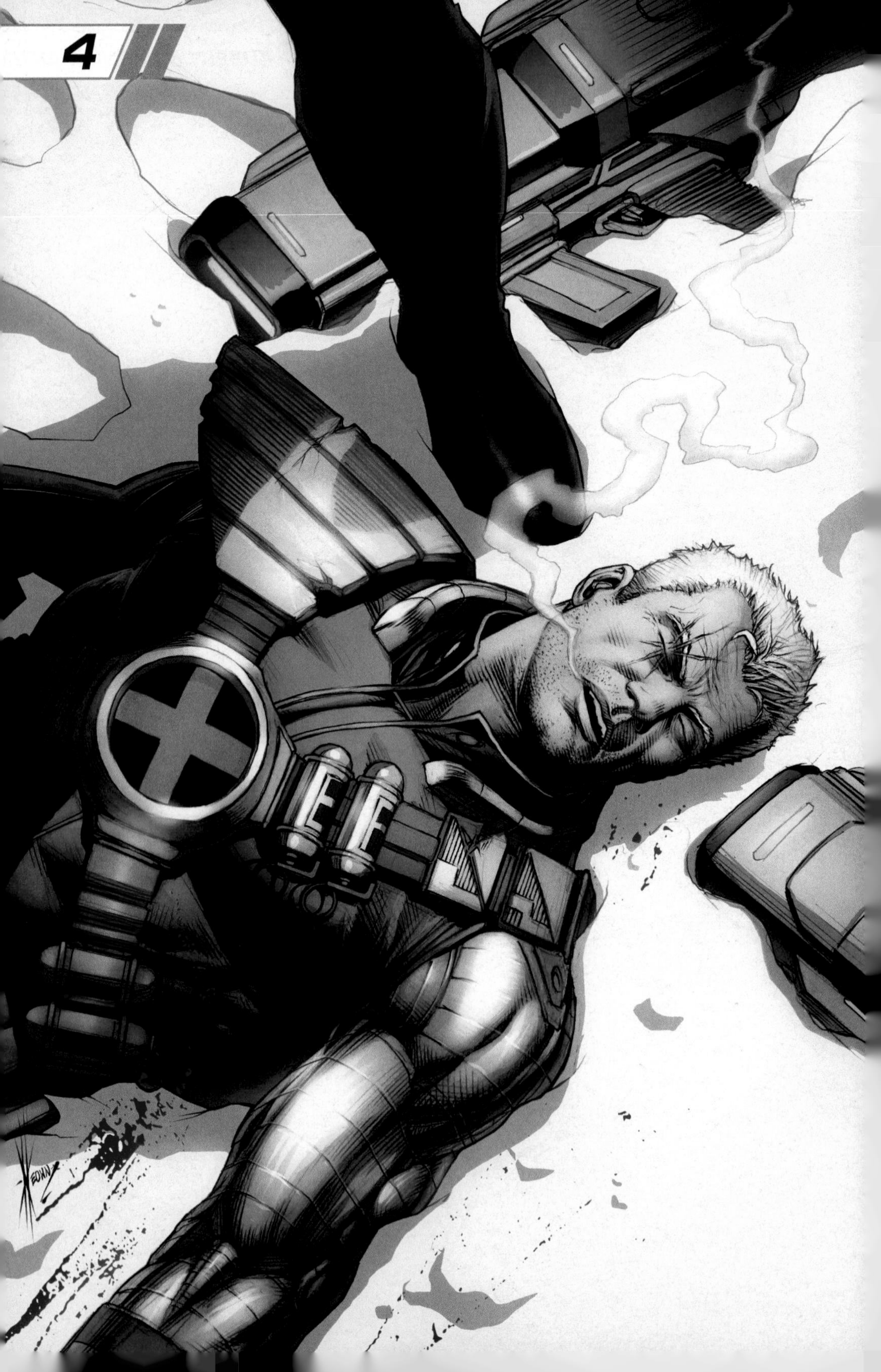
4

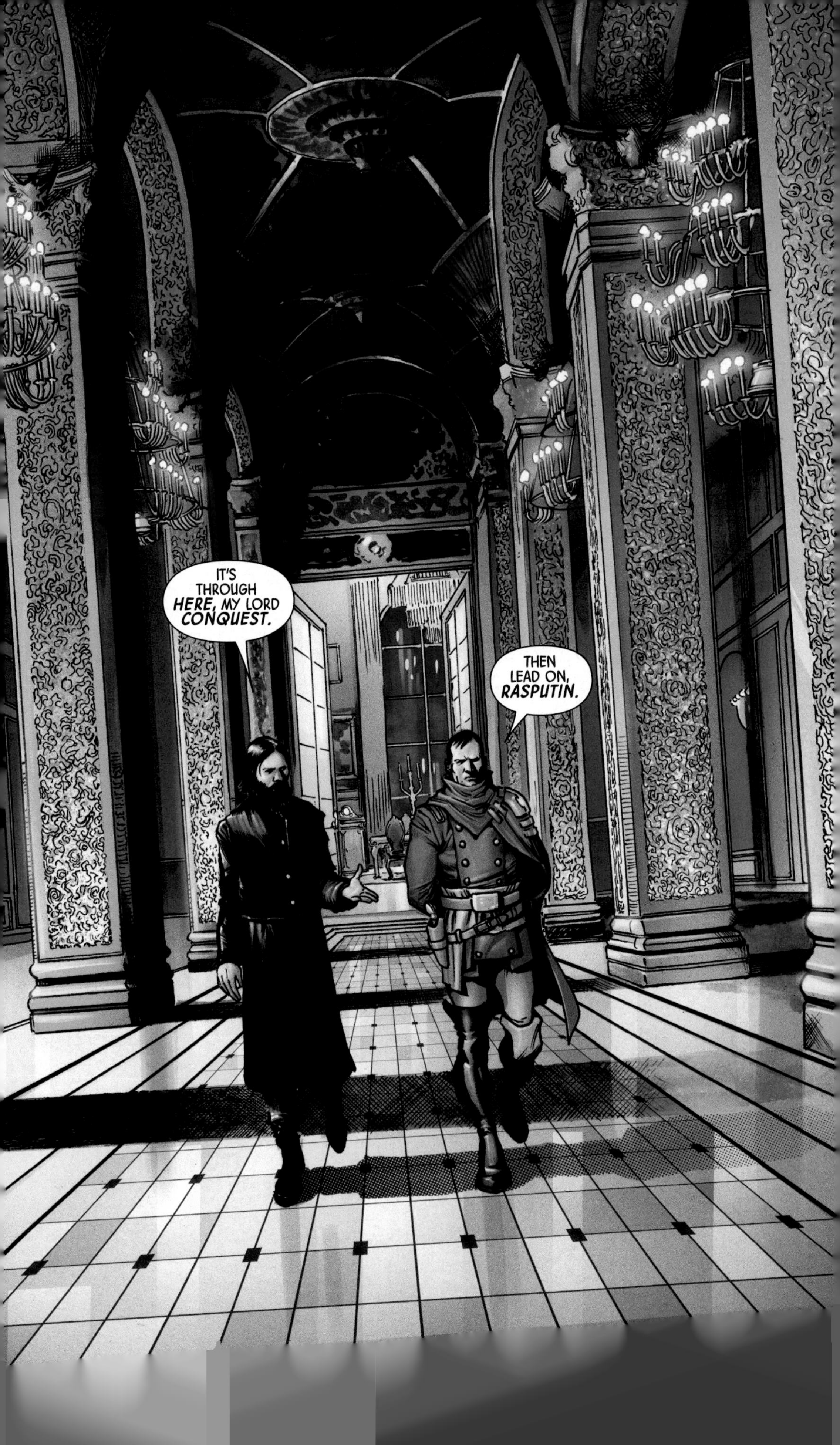
IT'S THROUGH HERE, MY LORD CONQUEST.
THEN LEAD ON, RASPUTIN.

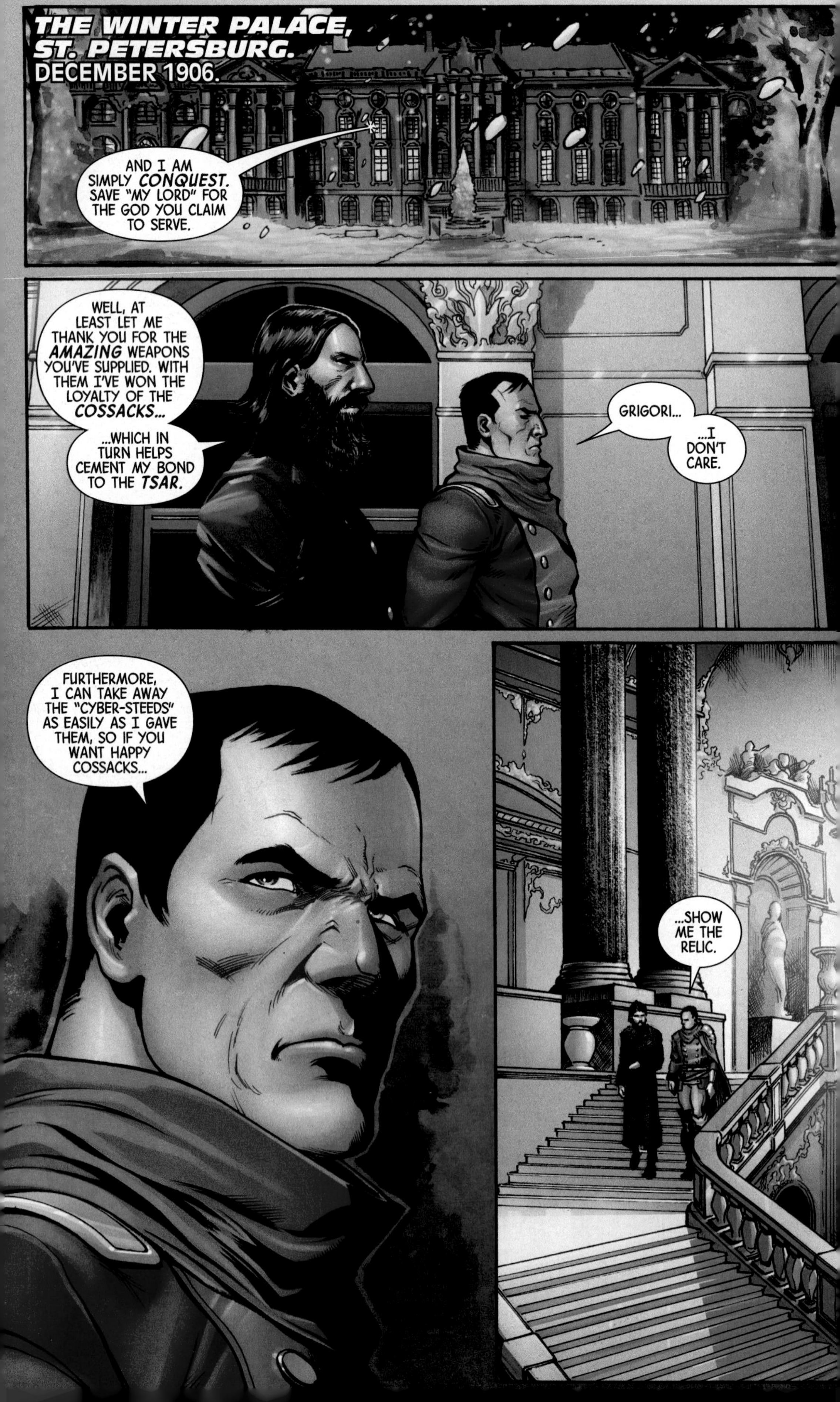
THE WINTER PALACE, ST. PETERSBURG. DECEMBER 1906.
AND I AM SIMPLY CONQUEST. SAVE "MY LORD" FOR THE GOD YOU CLAIM TO SERVE.
WELL, AT LEAST LET ME THANK YOU FOR THE AMAZING WEAPONS YOU'VE SUPPLIED. WITH THEM I'VE WON THE LOYALTY OF THE COSSACKS...
...WHICH IN TURN HELPS CEMENT MY BOND TO THE TSAR.
GRIGORI...
...I DON'T CARE.
FURTHERMORE, I CAN TAKE AWAY THE "CYBER-STEEDS" AS EASILY AS I GAVE THEM, SO IF YOU WANT HAPPY COSSACKS...
...SHOW ME THE RELIC.

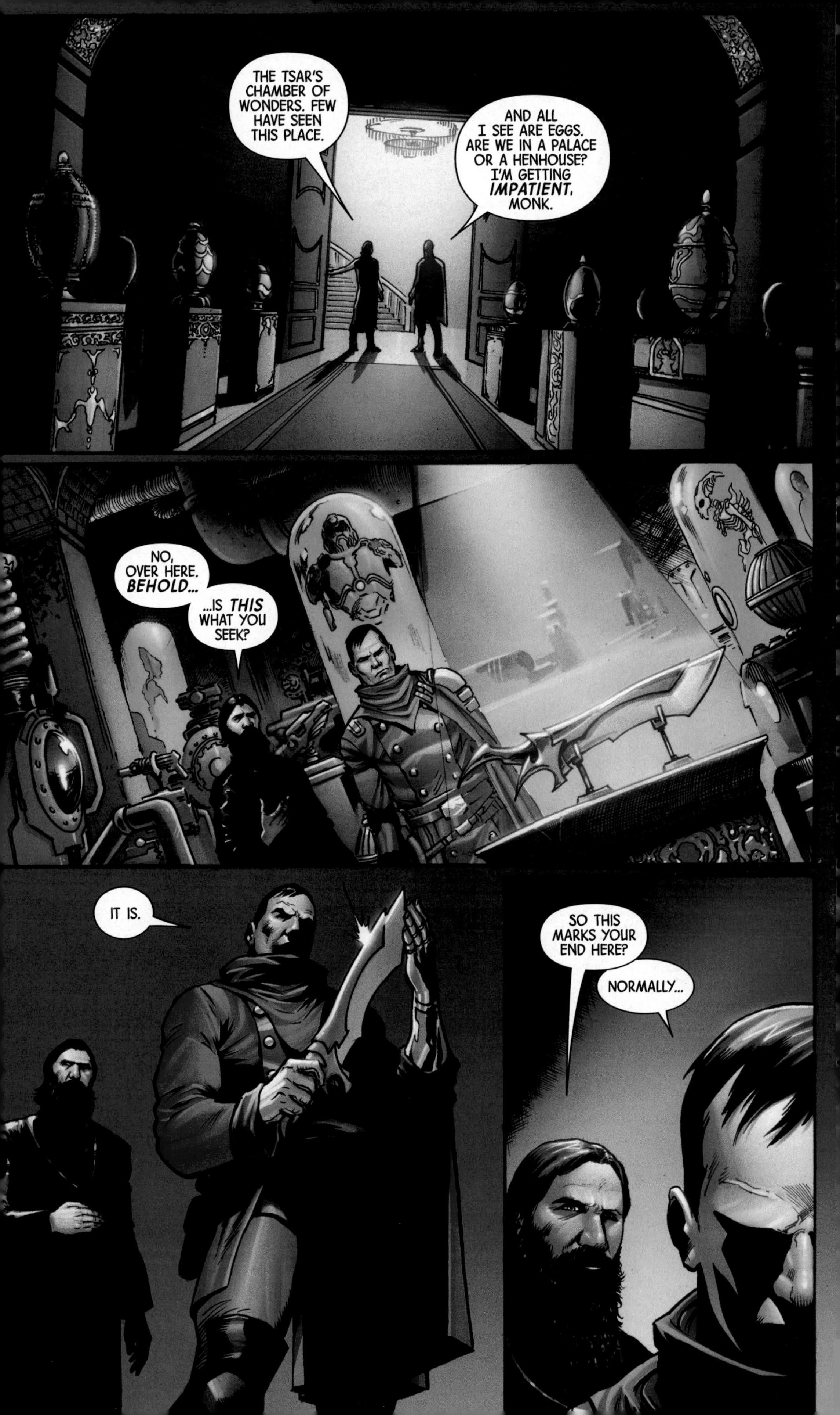
THE TSAR'S CHAMBER OF WONDERS. FEW HAVE SEEN THIS PLACE.
AND ALL I SEE ARE EGGS. ARE WE IN A PALACE OR A HENHOUSE? I'M GETTING *IMPATIENT*, MONK.
NO, OVER HERE. *BEHOLD...*
...IS *THIS* WHAT YOU SEEK?
IT IS.
SO THIS MARKS YOUR END HERE?
NORMALLY...

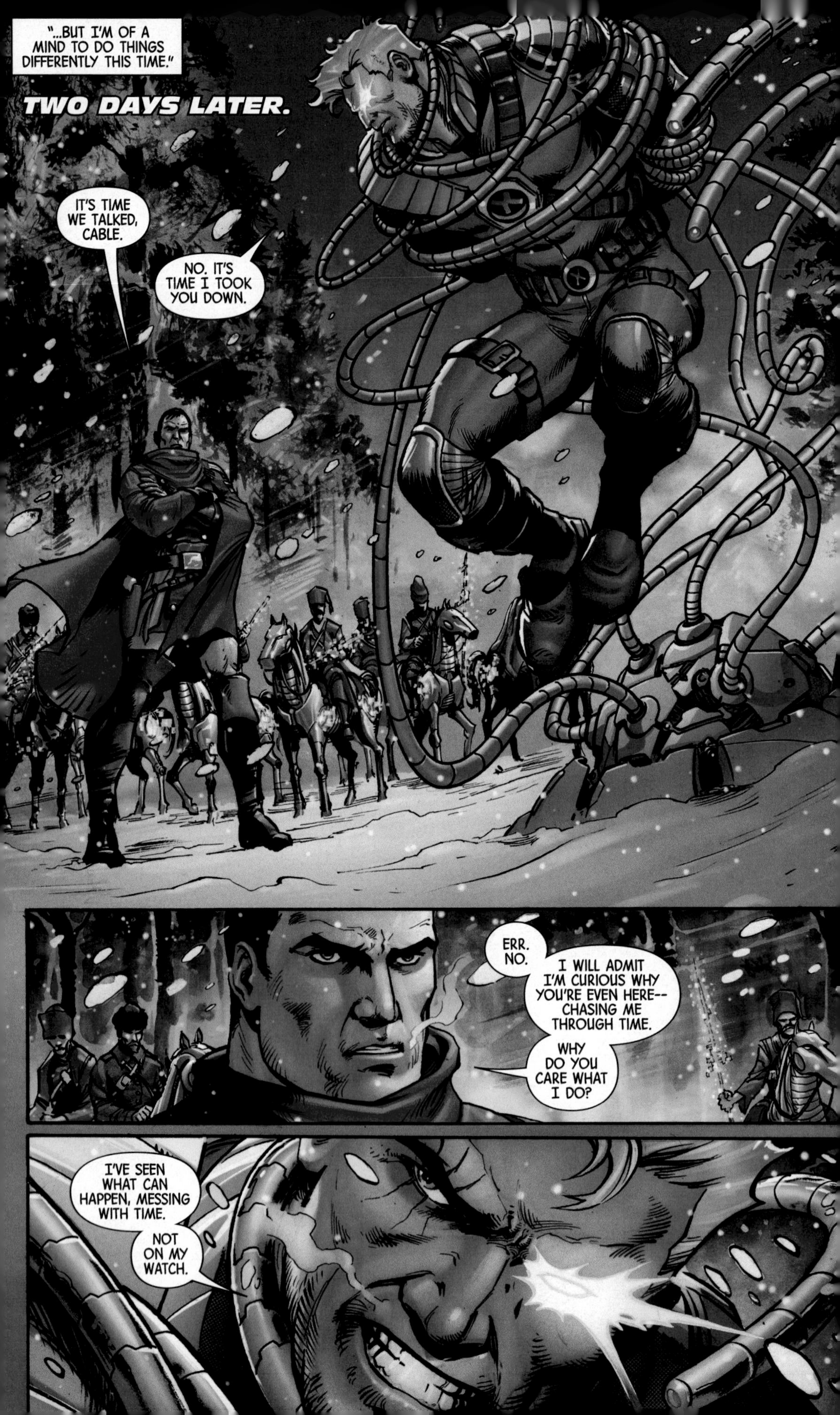

"...BUT I'M OF A MIND TO DO THINGS DIFFERENTLY THIS TIME."
TWO DAYS LATER.
IT'S TIME WE TALKED, CABLE.
NO. IT'S TIME I TOOK YOU DOWN.
ERR. NO.
I WILL ADMIT I'M CURIOUS WHY YOU'RE EVEN HERE-- CHASING ME THROUGH TIME.
WHY DO YOU CARE WHAT I DO?
I'VE SEEN WHAT CAN HAPPEN, MESSING WITH TIME.
NOT ON MY WATCH.

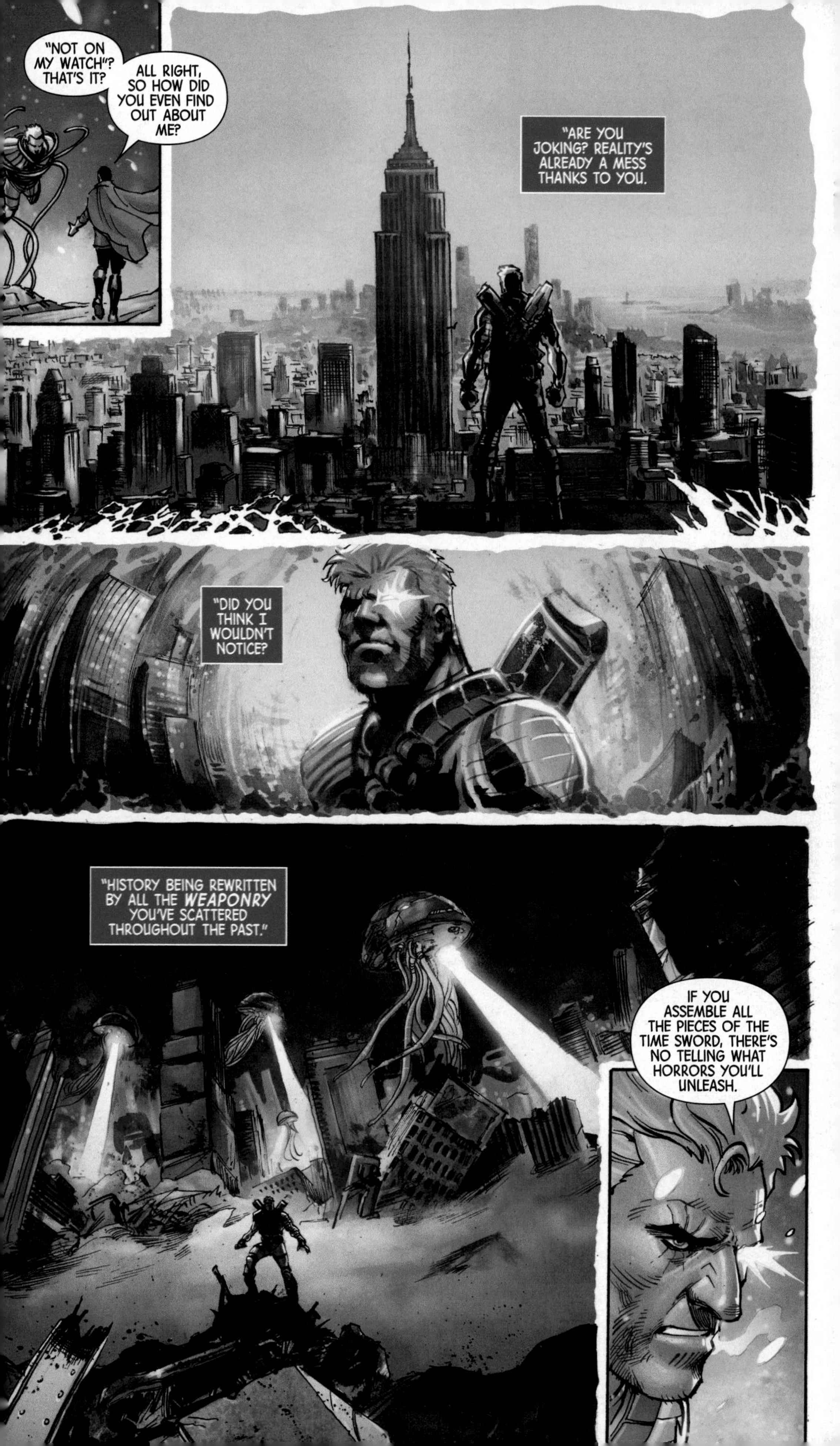
"NOT ON MY WATCH"? THAT'S IT?
ALL RIGHT, SO HOW DID YOU EVEN FIND OUT ABOUT ME?
"ARE YOU JOKING? REALITY'S ALREADY A MESS THANKS TO YOU.
"DID YOU THINK I WOULDN'T NOTICE?
"HISTORY BEING REWRITTEN BY ALL THE *WEAPONRY* YOU'VE SCATTERED THROUGHOUT THE PAST."
IF YOU ASSEMBLE ALL THE PIECES OF THE TIME SWORD, THERE'S NO TELLING WHAT HORRORS YOU'LL UNLEASH.

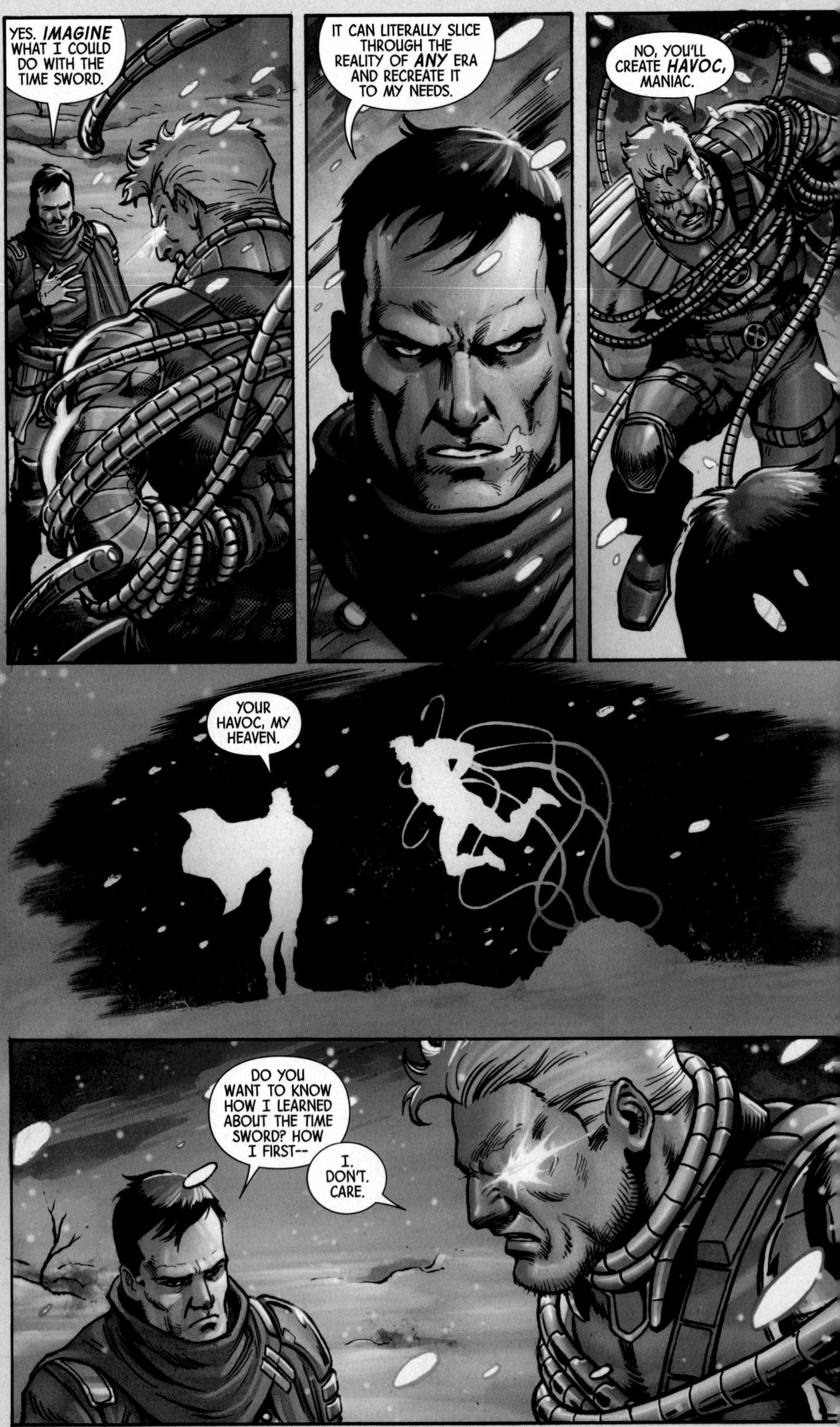
YES. IMAGINE WHAT I COULD DO WITH THE TIME SWORD.
IT CAN LITERALLY SLICE THROUGH THE REALITY OF ANY ERA AND RECREATE IT TO MY NEEDS.
NO, YOU'LL CREATE HAVOC, MANIAC.
YOUR HAVOC, MY HEAVEN.
DO YOU WANT TO KNOW HOW I LEARNED ABOUT THE TIME SWORD? HOW I FIRST--
I. DON'T. CARE.

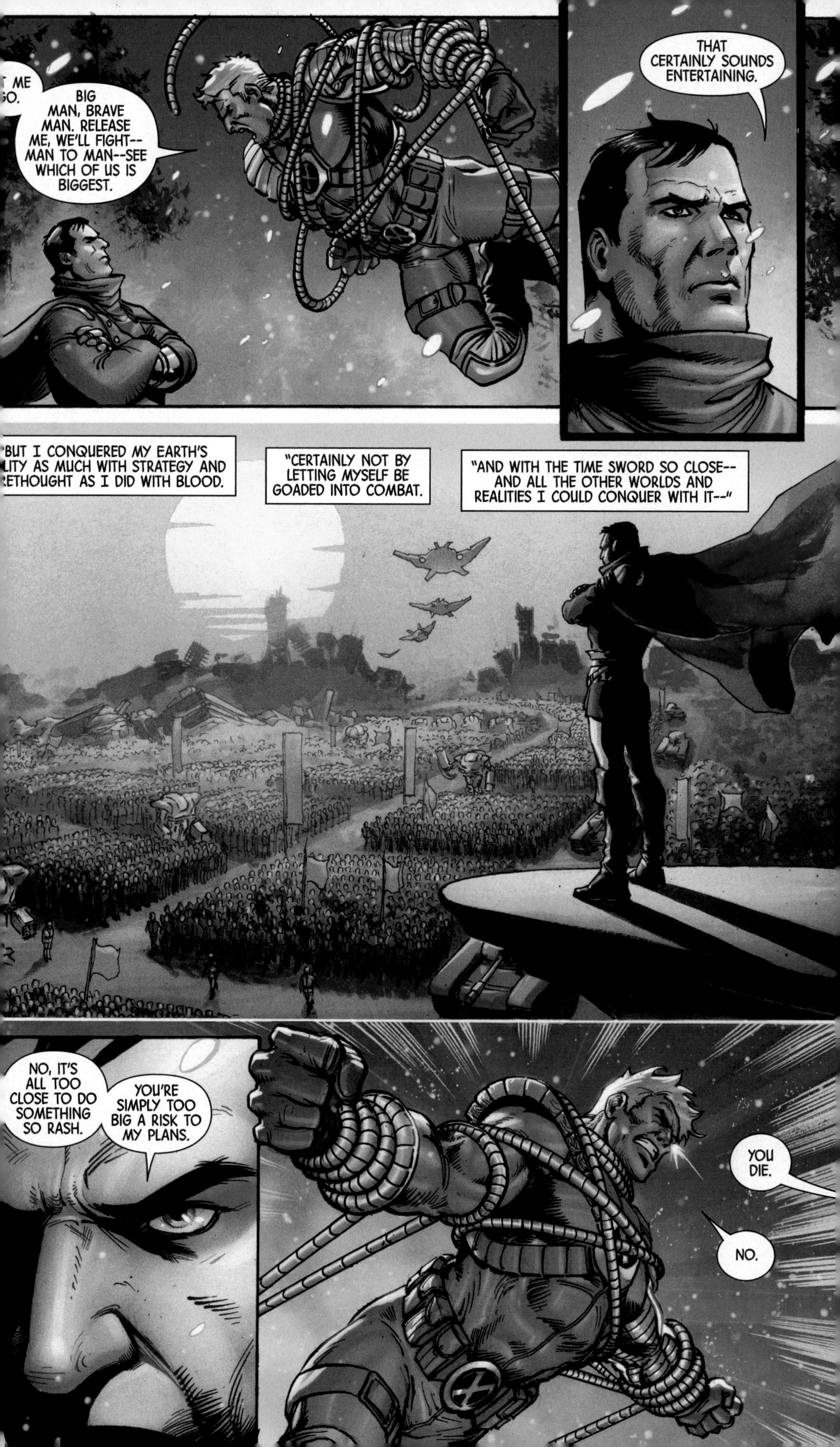

T ME
GO.
BIG MAN, BRAVE MAN. RELEASE ME, WE'LL FIGHT-- MAN TO MAN--SEE WHICH OF US IS BIGGEST.
THAT CERTAINLY SOUNDS ENTERTAINING.
"BUT I CONQUERED MY EARTH'S
LITY AS MUCH WITH STRATEGY AND
ETHOUGHT AS I DID WITH BLOOD.
"CERTAINLY NOT BY LETTING MYSELF BE GOADED INTO COMBAT.
"AND WITH THE TIME SWORD SO CLOSE-- AND ALL THE OTHER WORLDS AND REALITIES I COULD CONQUER WITH IT--"
NO, IT'S ALL TOO CLOSE TO DO SOMETHING SO RASH.
YOU'RE SIMPLY TOO BIG A RISK TO MY PLANS.
YOU DIE.
NO.

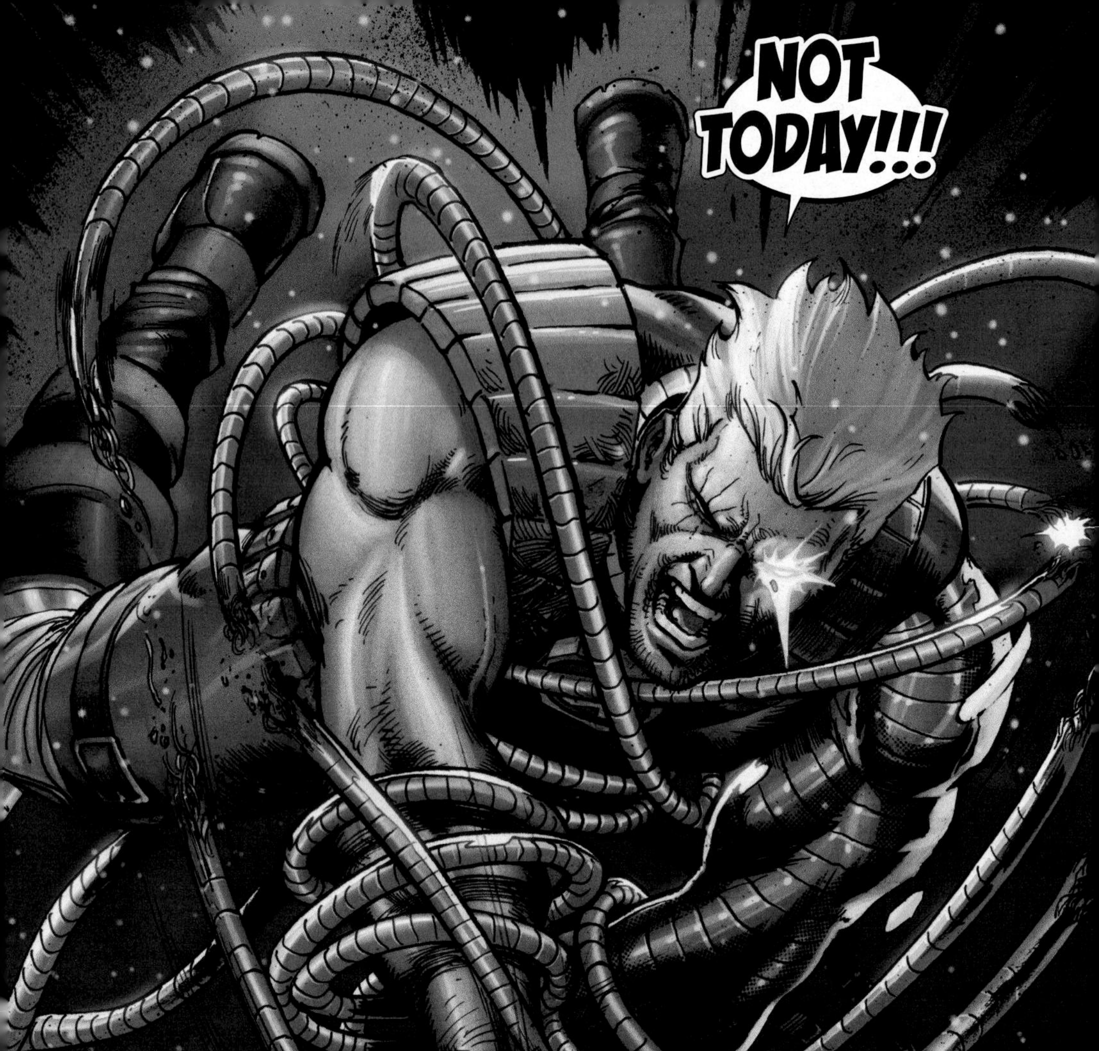
NOT TODAY!!!

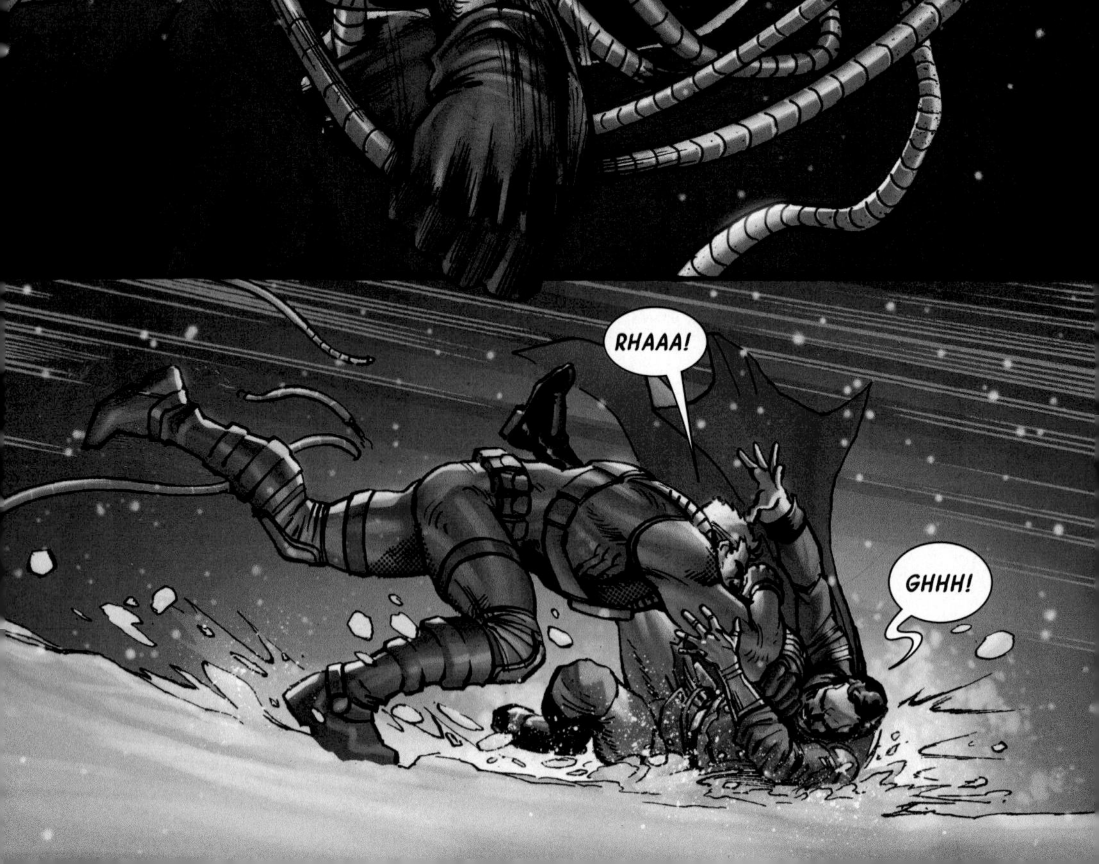
RHAAA!
GHHH!

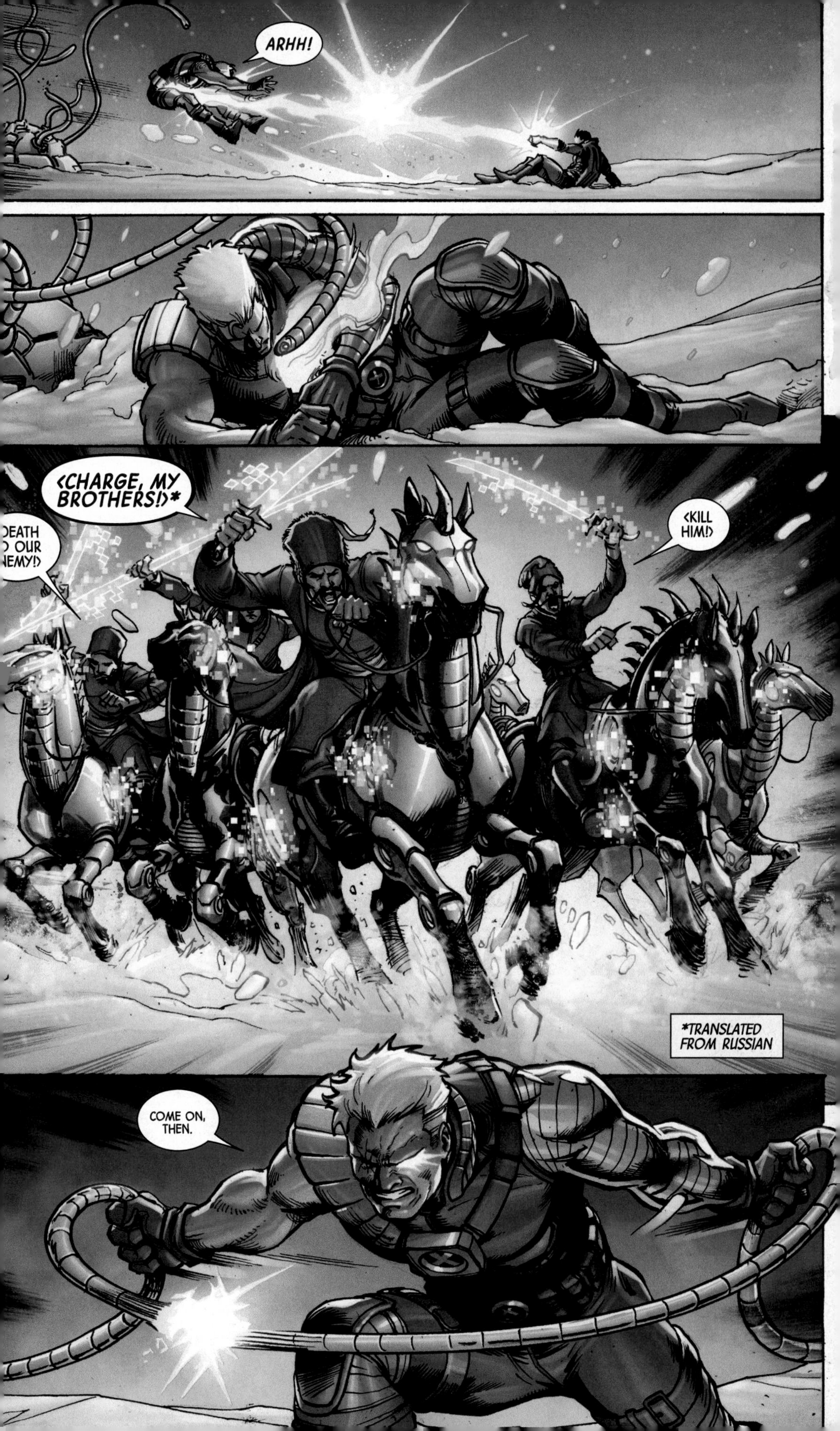
ARHH!
<CHARGE, MY BROTHERS!>*
EATH
O OUR
NEMY!>
<KILL HIM!>
*TRANSLATED FROM RUSSIAN
COME ON, THEN.

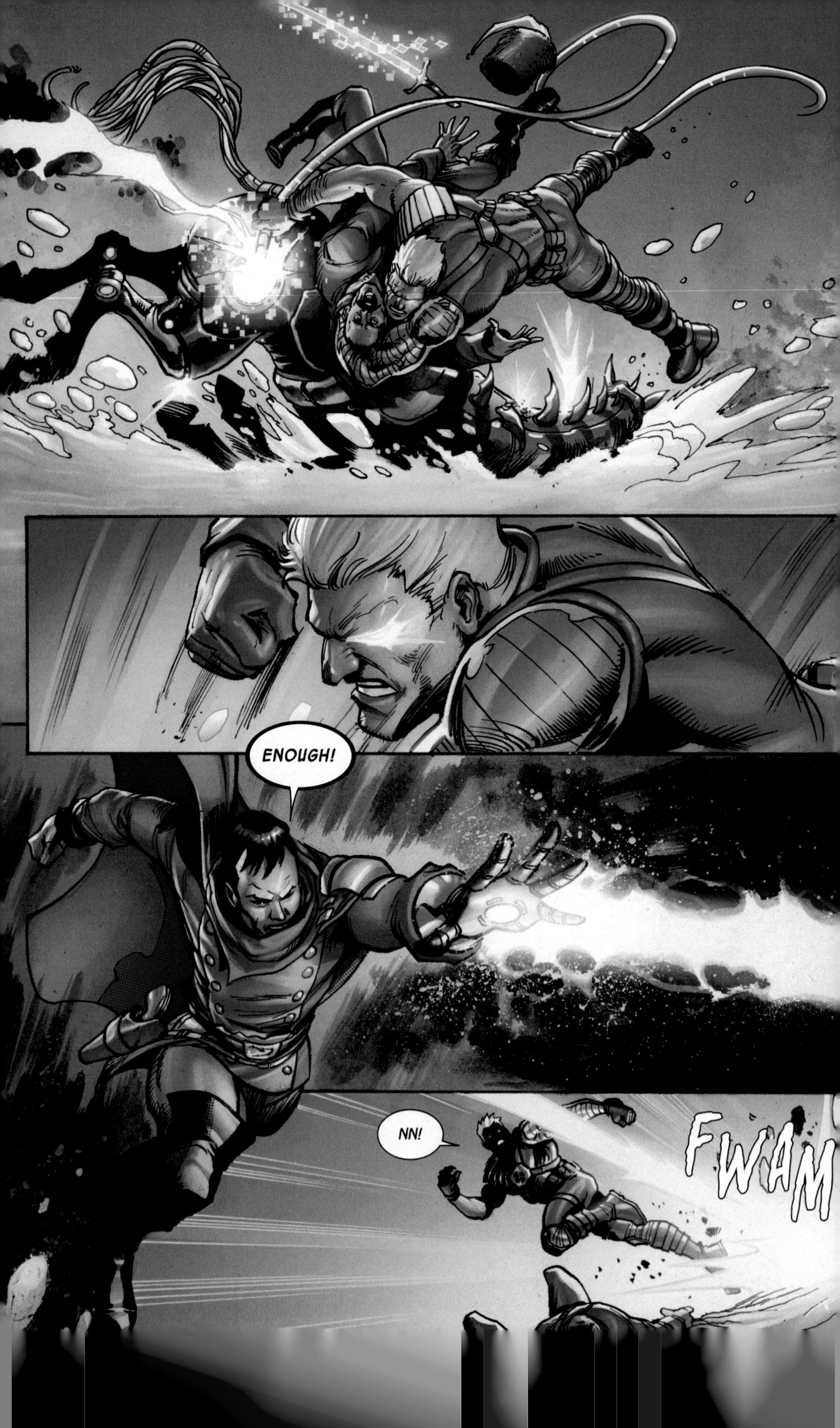
ENOUGH!
NN!
FWAM

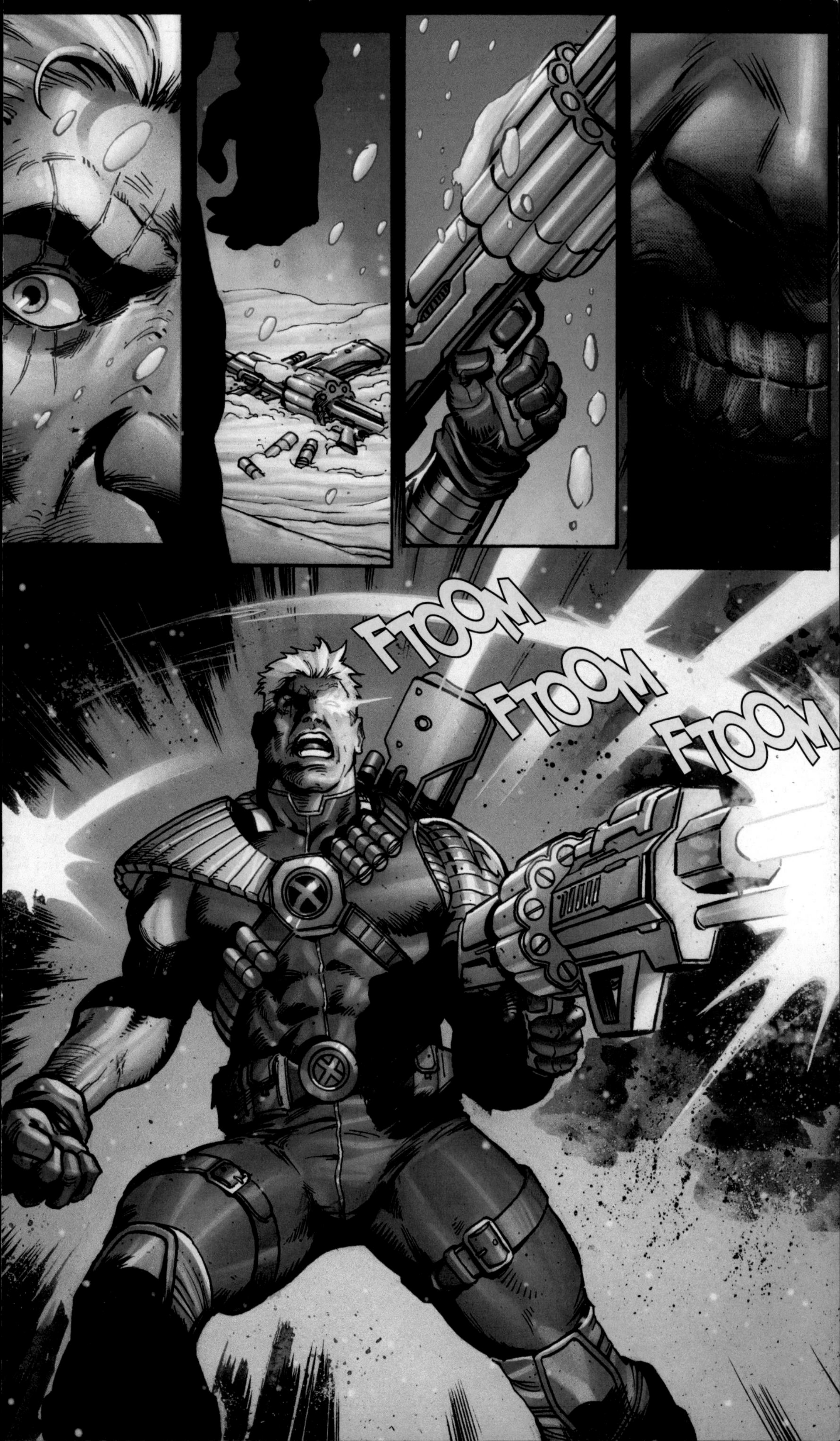
FTOOM
FTOOM
FTOOM

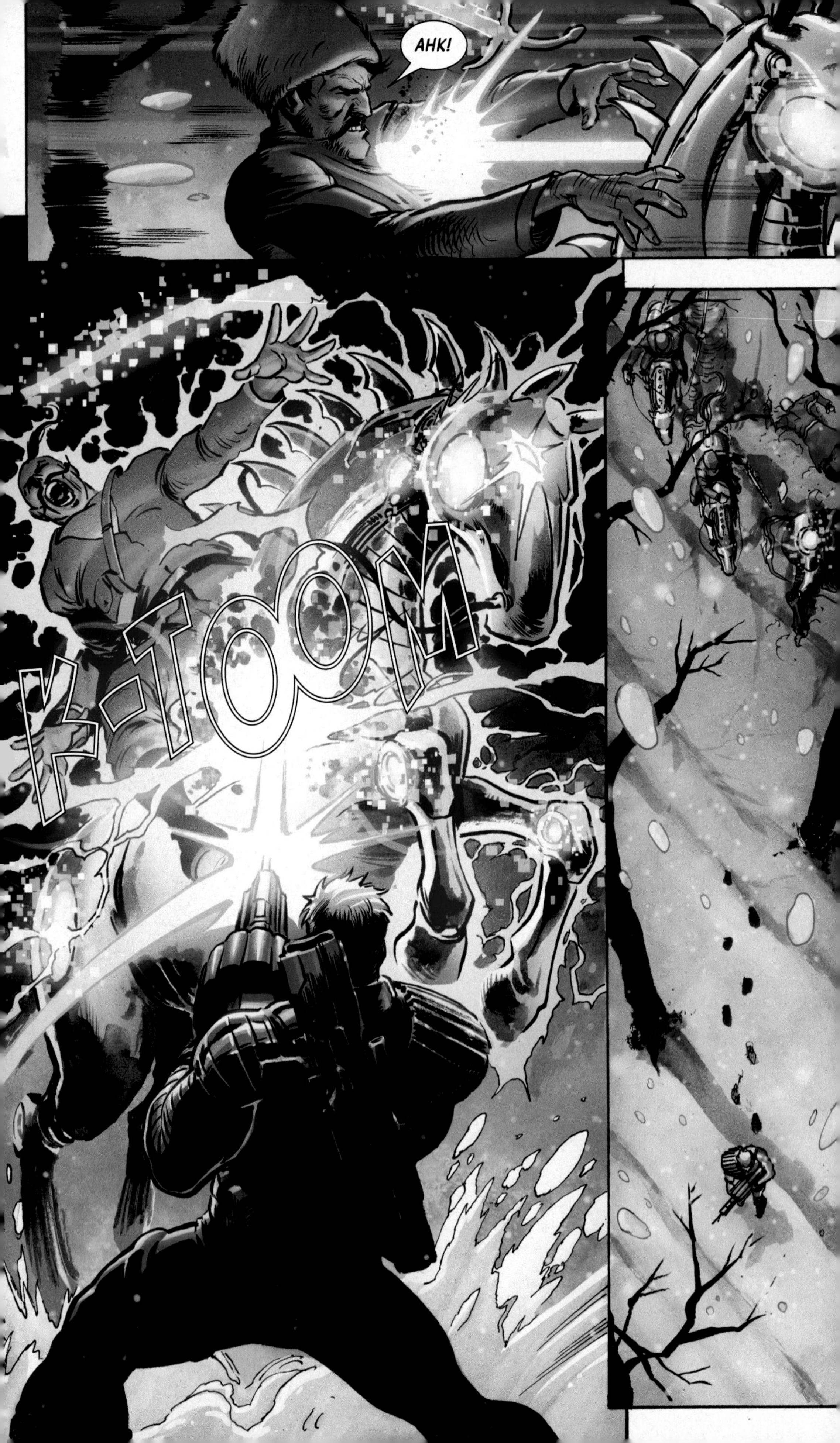
AHK!
K-TOOM

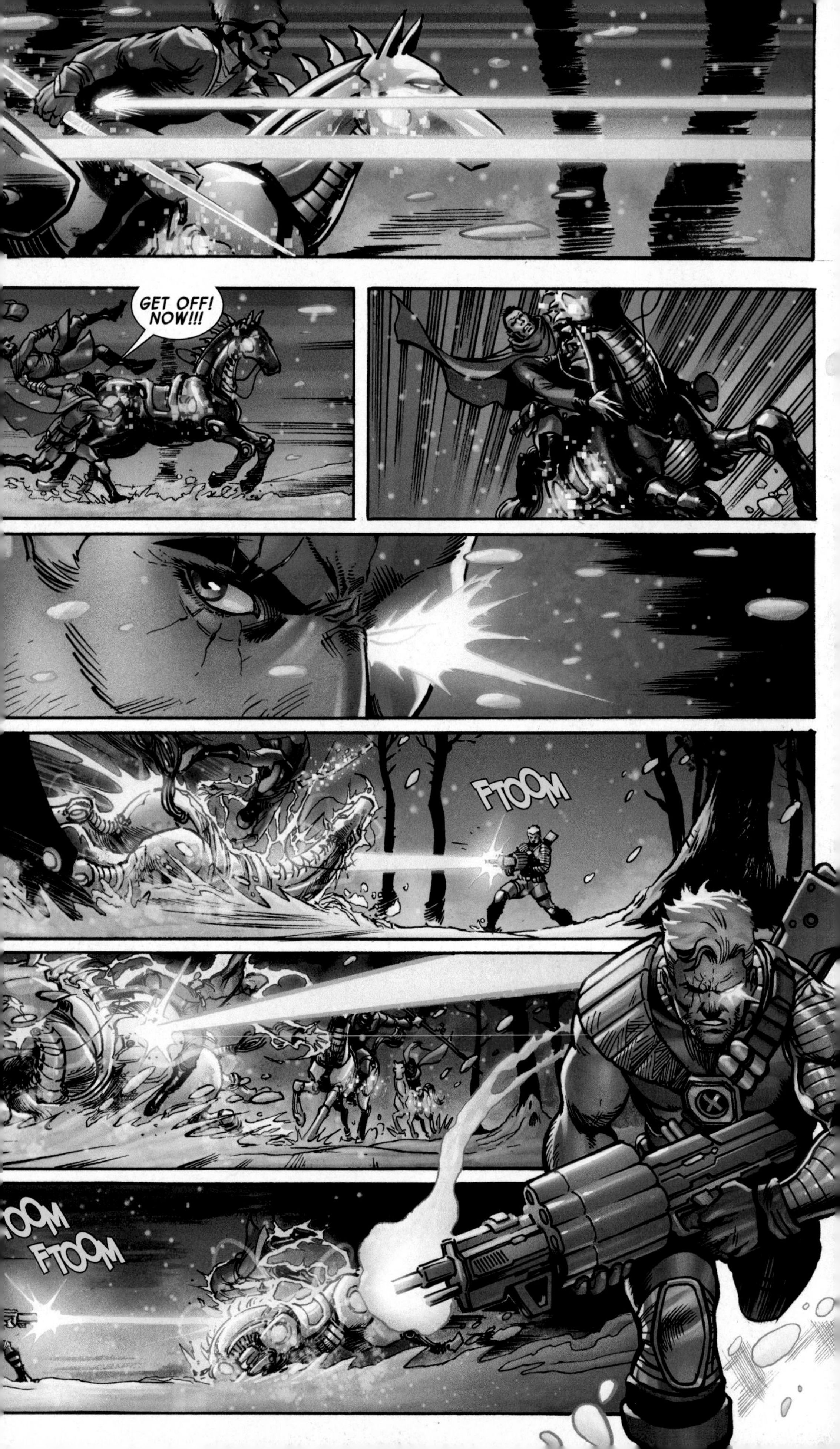
GET OFF! NOW!!!
FTOOM
FTOOM
FTOOM

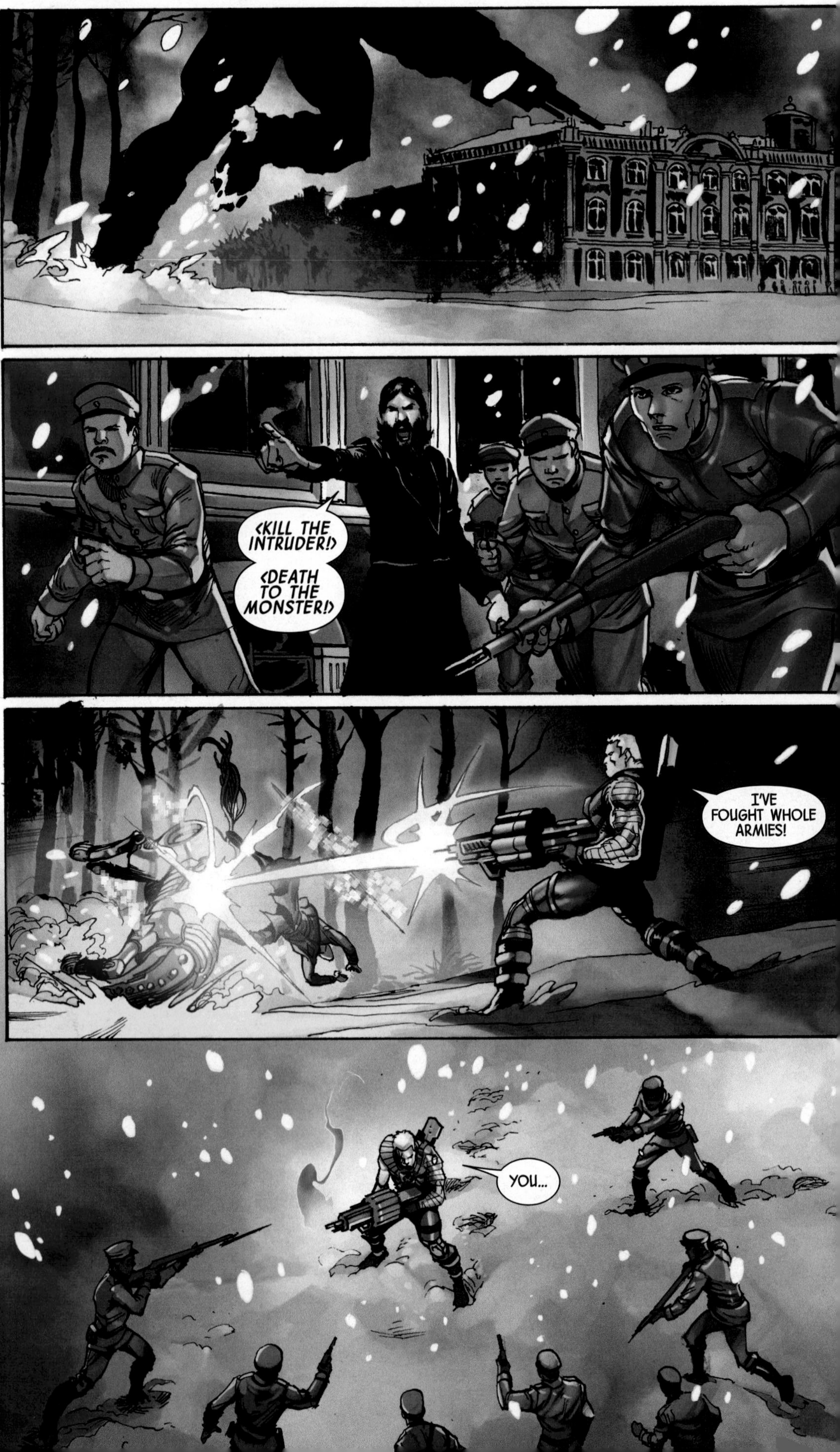
<KILL THE INTRUDER!>
<DEATH TO THE MONSTER!>
I'VE FOUGHT WHOLE ARMIES!
YOU...

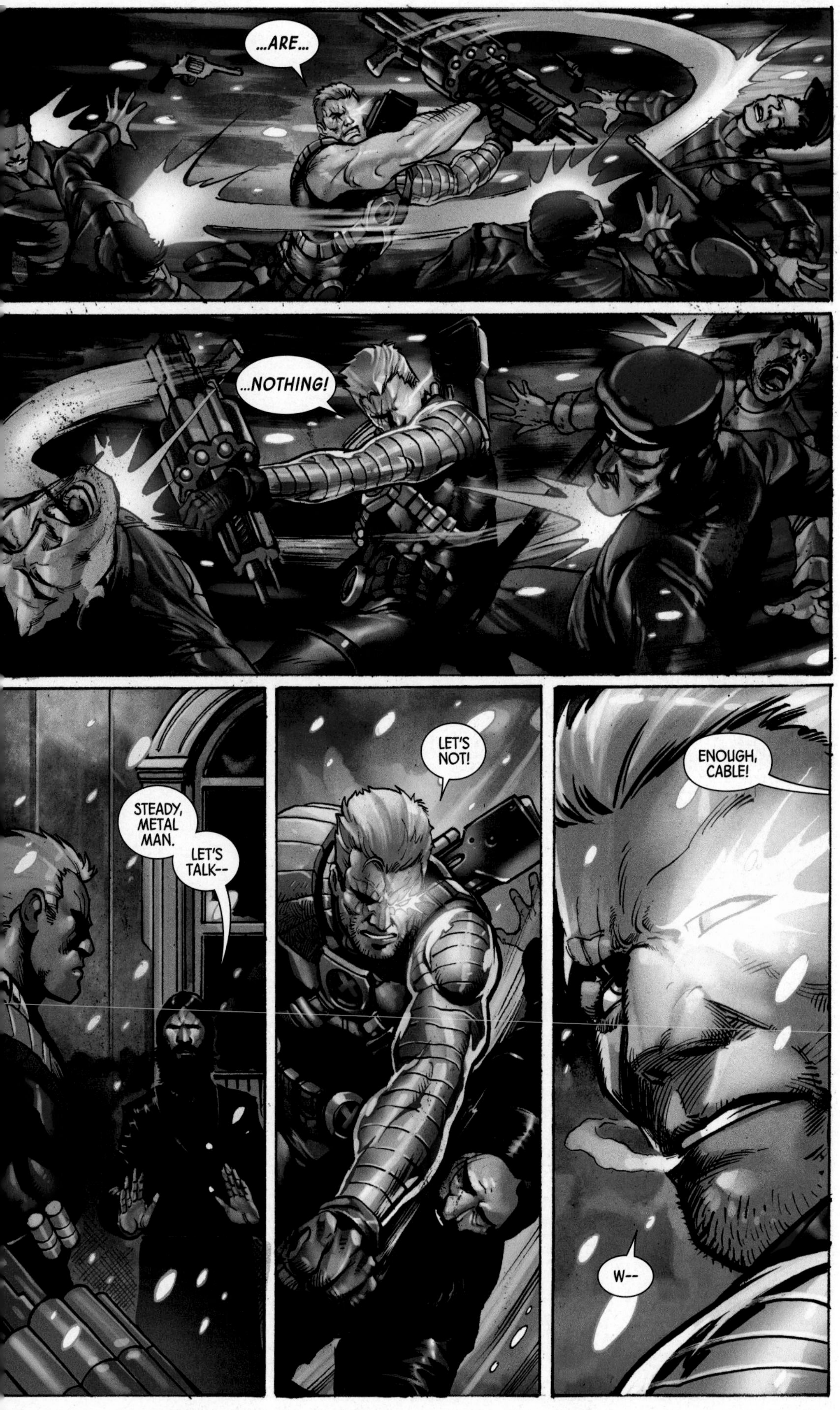
...ARE...
...NOTHING!
STEADY, METAL MAN.
LET'S TALK--
LET'S NOT!
ENOUGH, CABLE!
W--

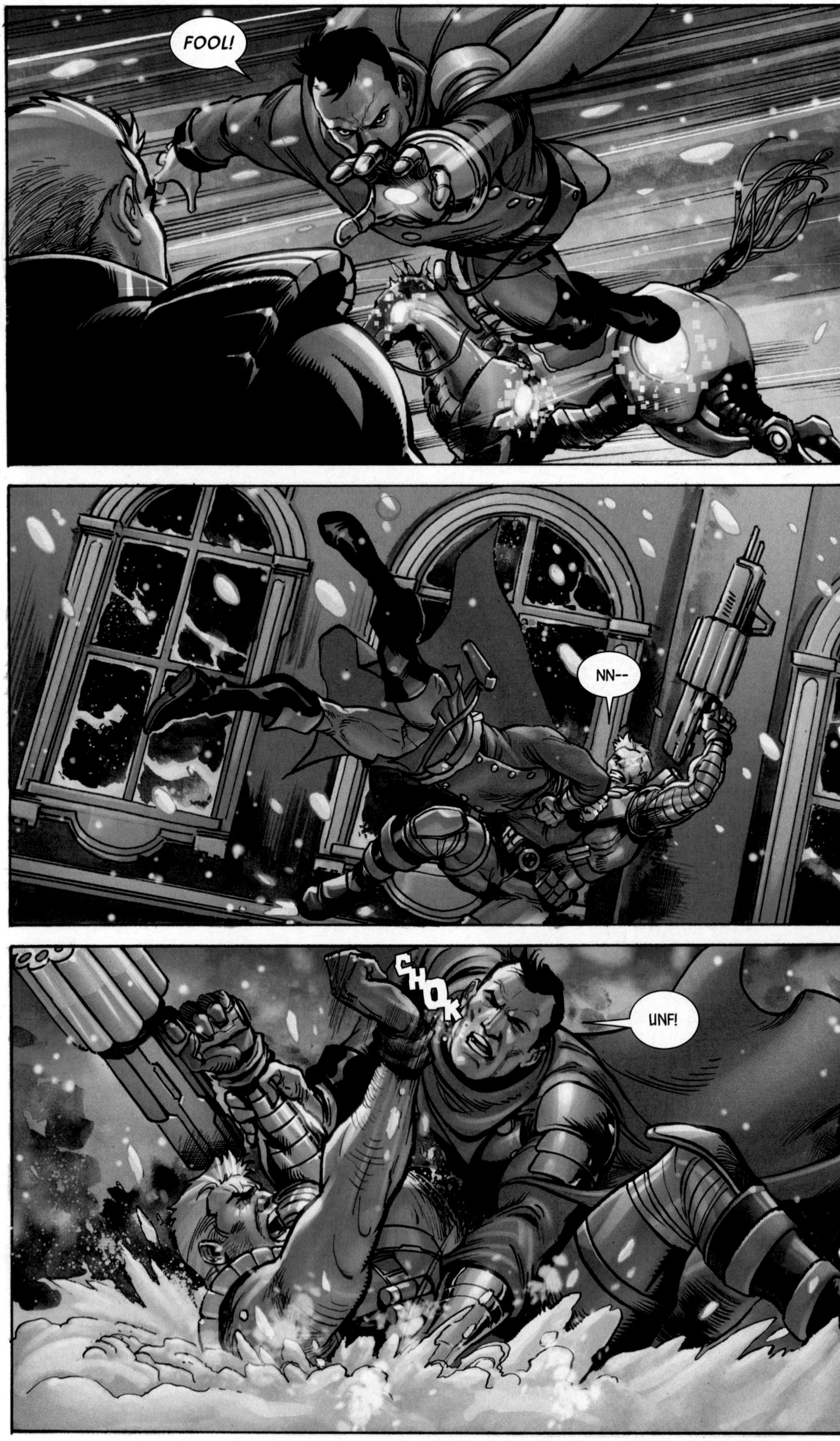
FOOL!
NN--
SHOK
UNF!

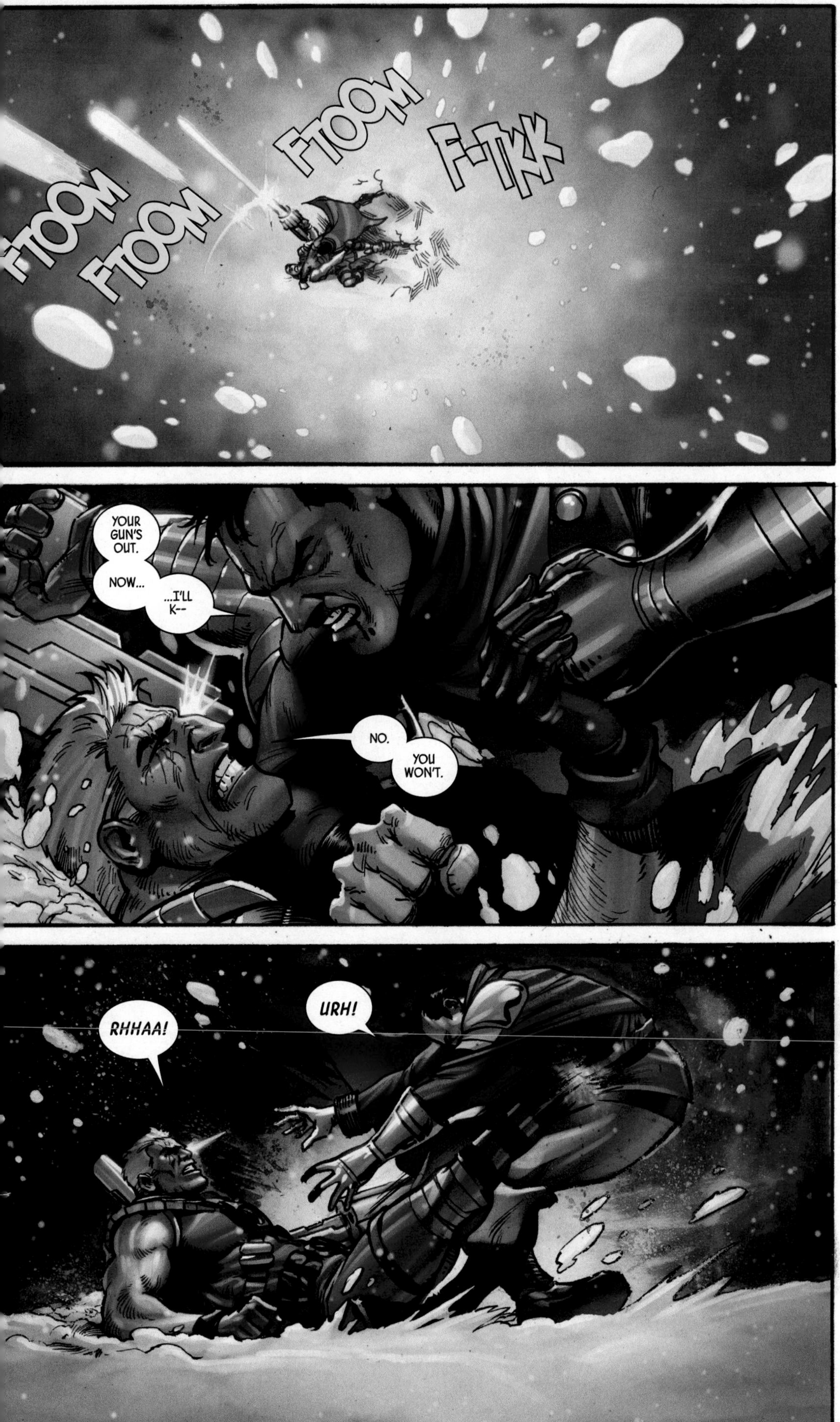
FTOOM
FTOOM
FTOOM
F-TKK
YOUR GUN'S OUT.
NOW...
...I'LL K--
NO.
YOU WON'T.
RHHAA!
URH!

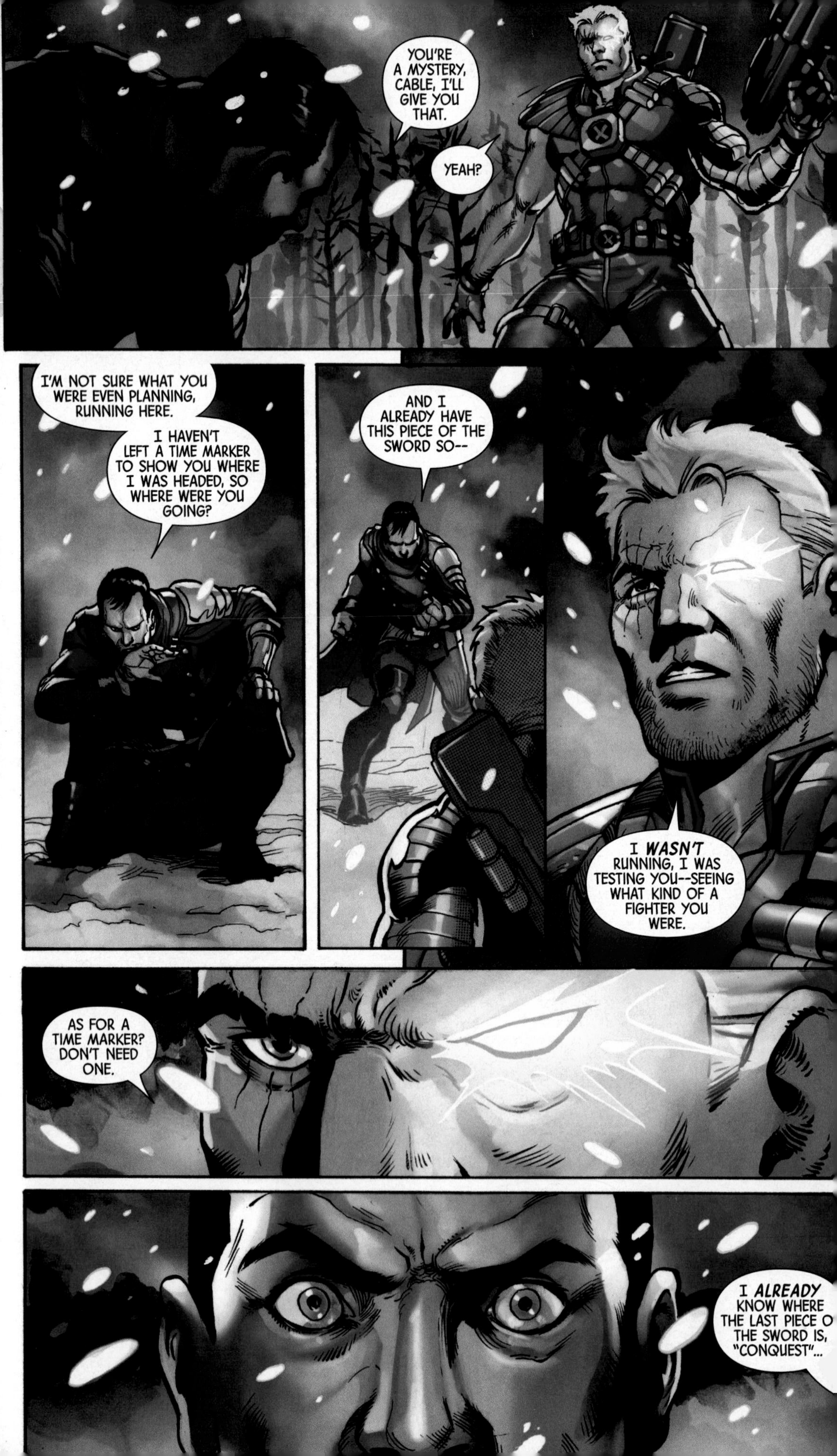
YOU'RE A MYSTERY, CABLE, I'LL GIVE YOU THAT.
YEAH?
I'M NOT SURE WHAT YOU WERE EVEN PLANNING, RUNNING HERE.
I HAVEN'T LEFT A TIME MARKER TO SHOW YOU WHERE I WAS HEADED, SO WHERE WERE YOU GOING?
AND I ALREADY HAVE THIS PIECE OF THE SWORD SO--
I WASN'T RUNNING, I WAS TESTING YOU--SEEING WHAT KIND OF A FIGHTER YOU WERE.
AS FOR A TIME MARKER? DON'T NEED ONE.
I ALREADY KNOW WHERE THE LAST PIECE O THE SWORD IS, "CONQUEST"...

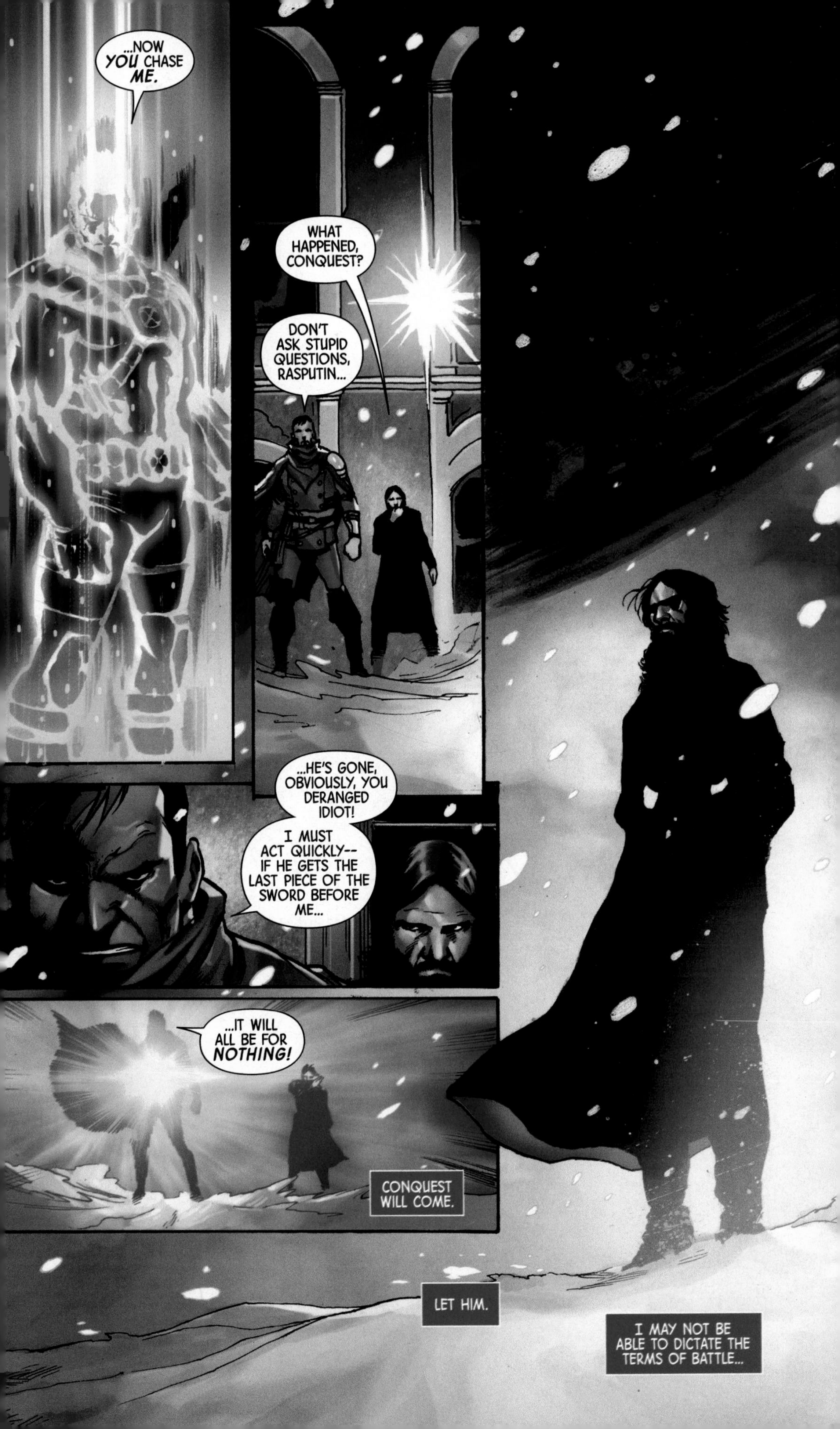
...NOW YOU CHASE ME.
WHAT HAPPENED, CONQUEST?
DON'T ASK STUPID QUESTIONS, RASPUTIN...
...HE'S GONE, OBVIOUSLY, YOU DERANGED IDIOT!
I MUST ACT QUICKLY-- IF HE GETS THE LAST PIECE OF THE SWORD BEFORE ME...
...IT WILL ALL BE FOR NOTHING!
CONQUEST WILL COME.
LET HIM.
I MAY NOT BE ABLE TO DICTATE THE TERMS OF BATTLE...

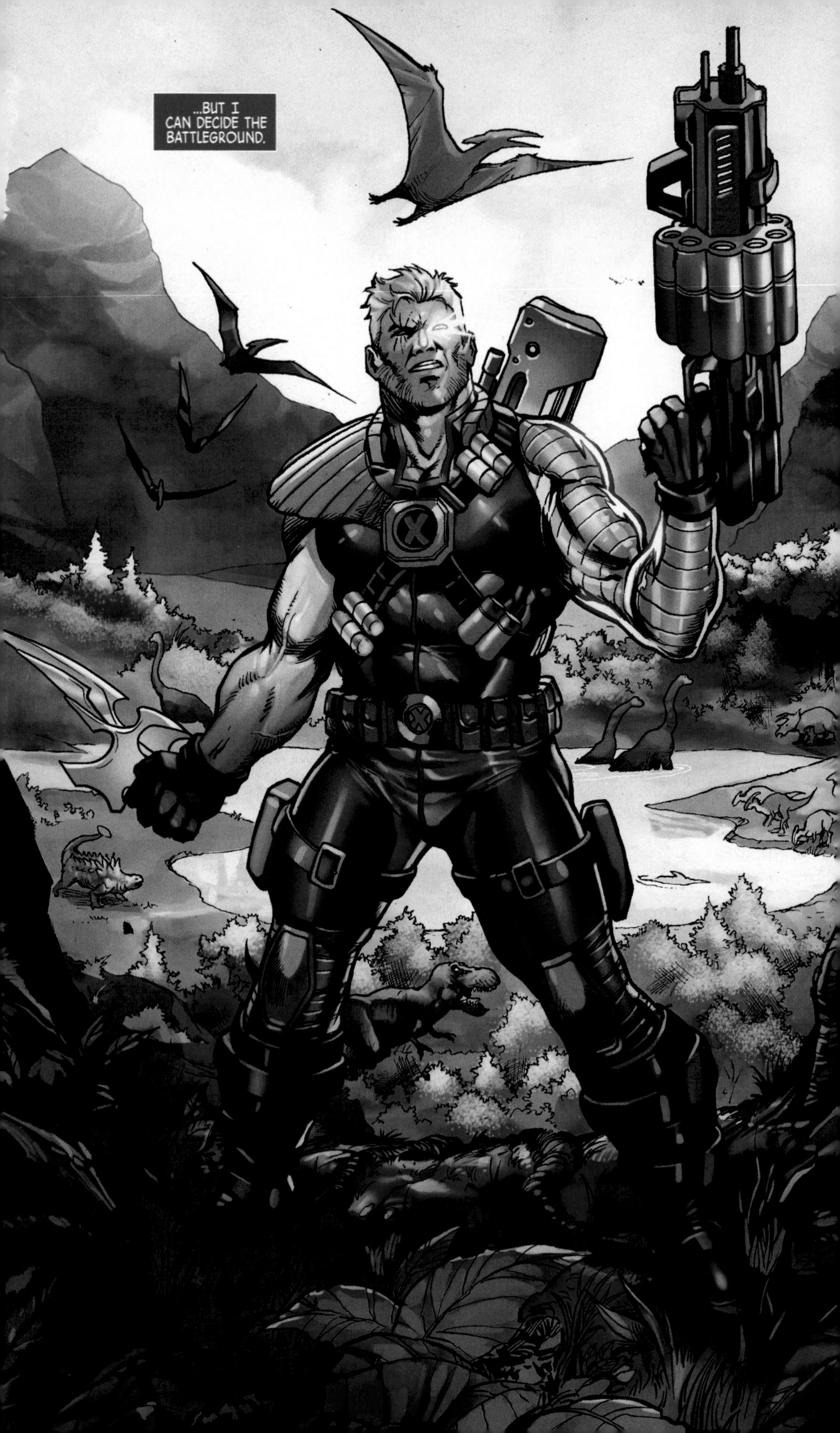
...BUT I CAN DECIDE THE BATTLEGROUND.

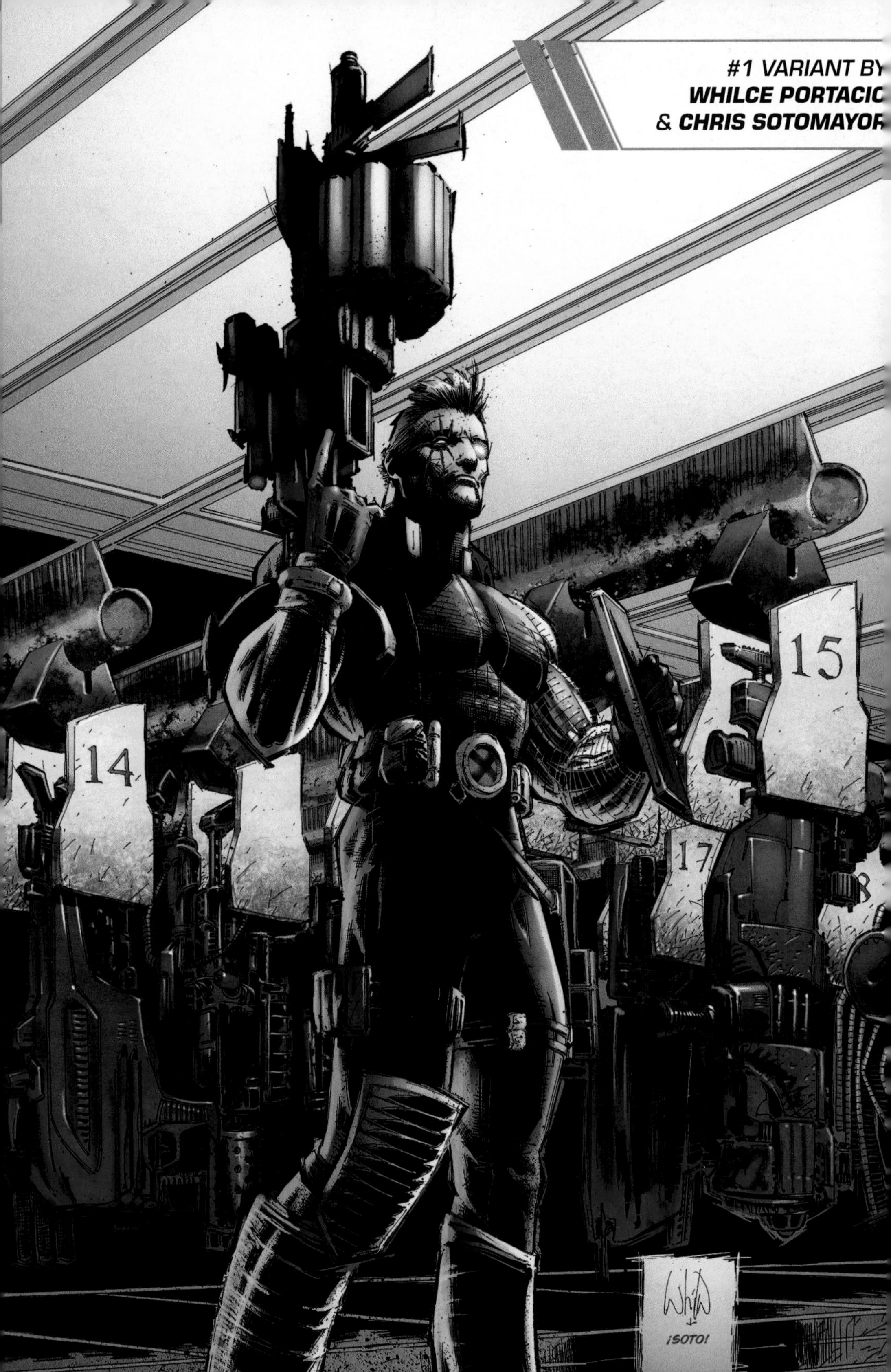
14
15
17
¡SOTO!

#1 VARIANT BY
WHILCE PORTACIO
& **CHRIS SOTOMAYOR**

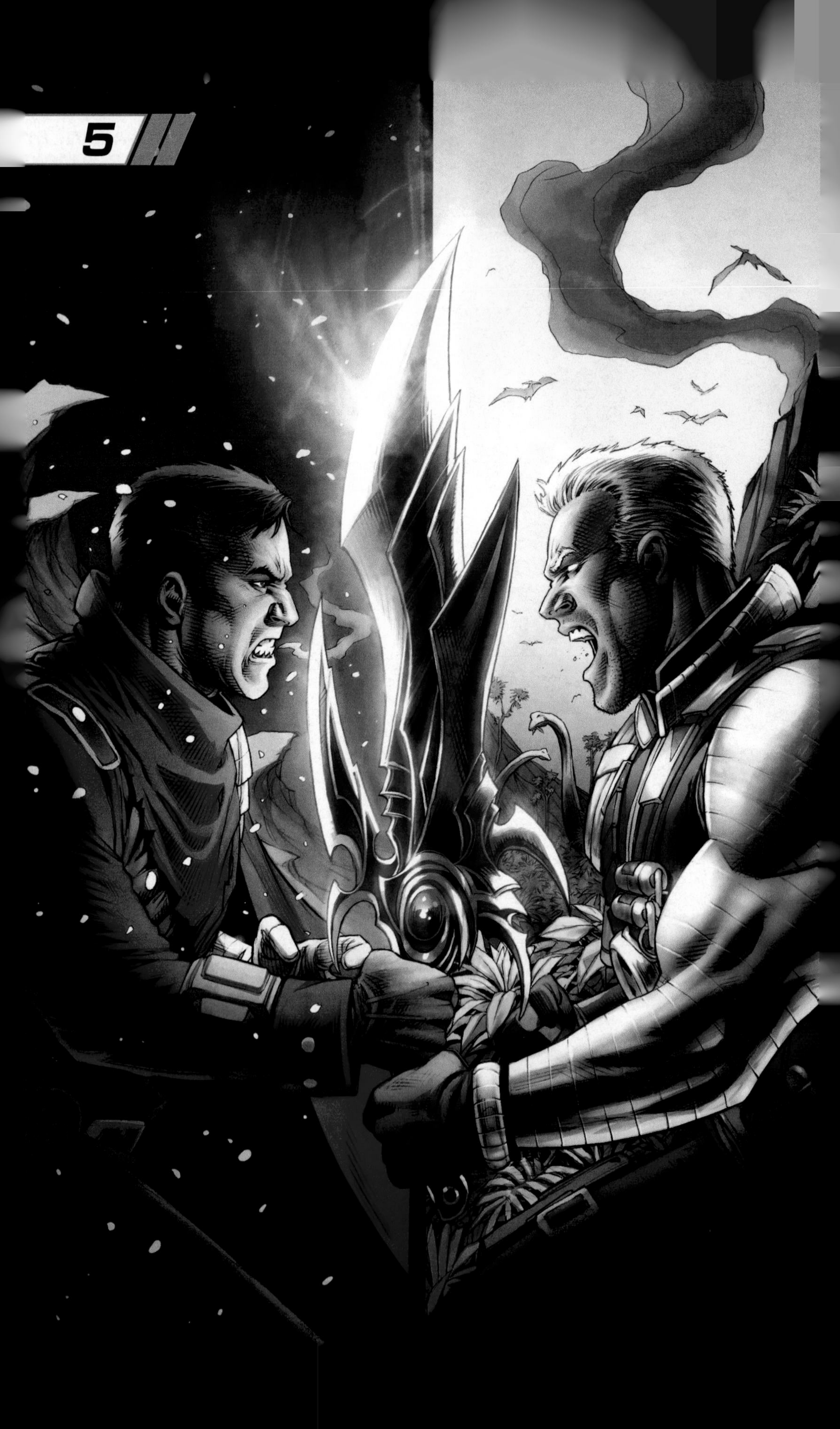
5

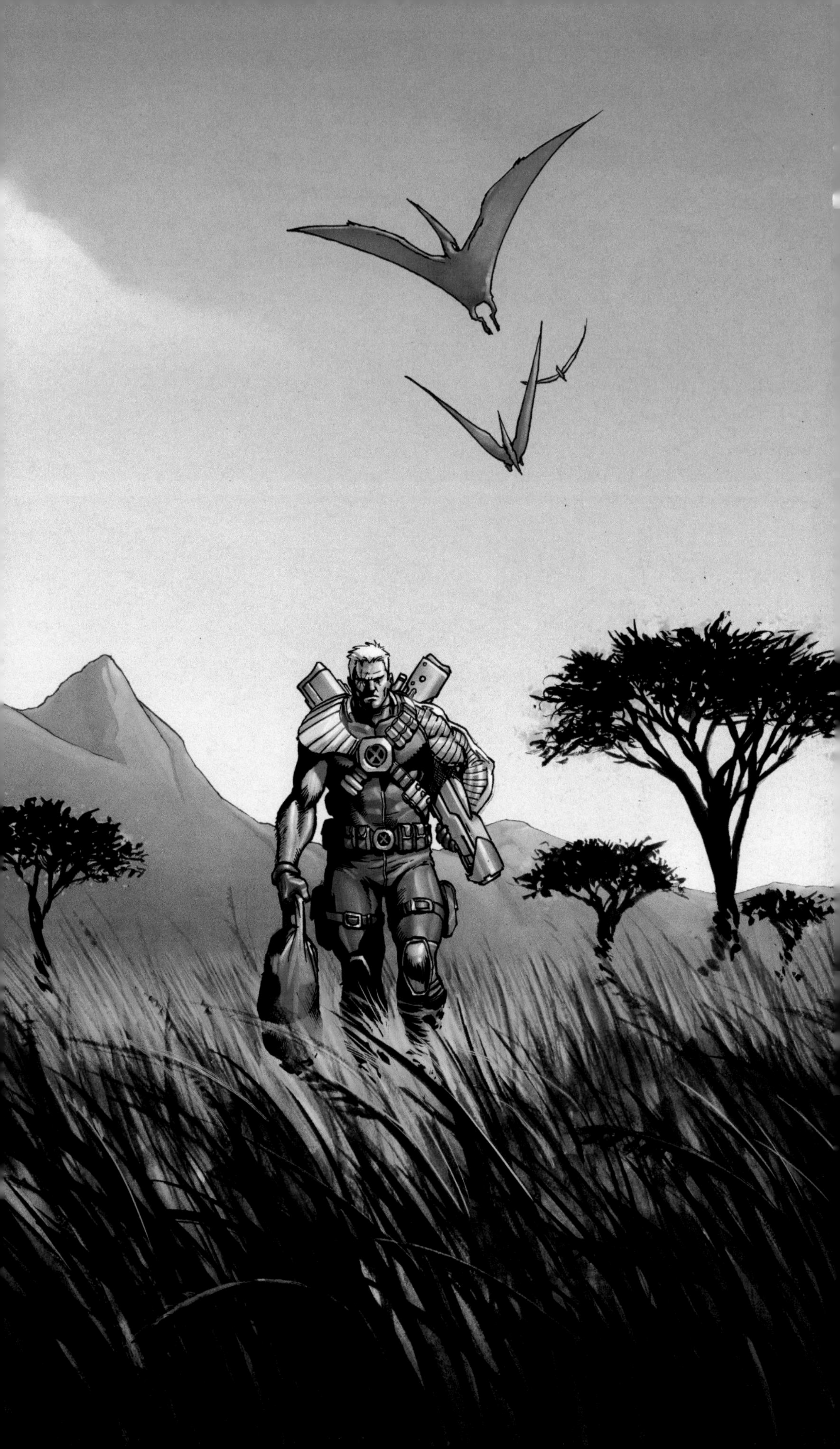

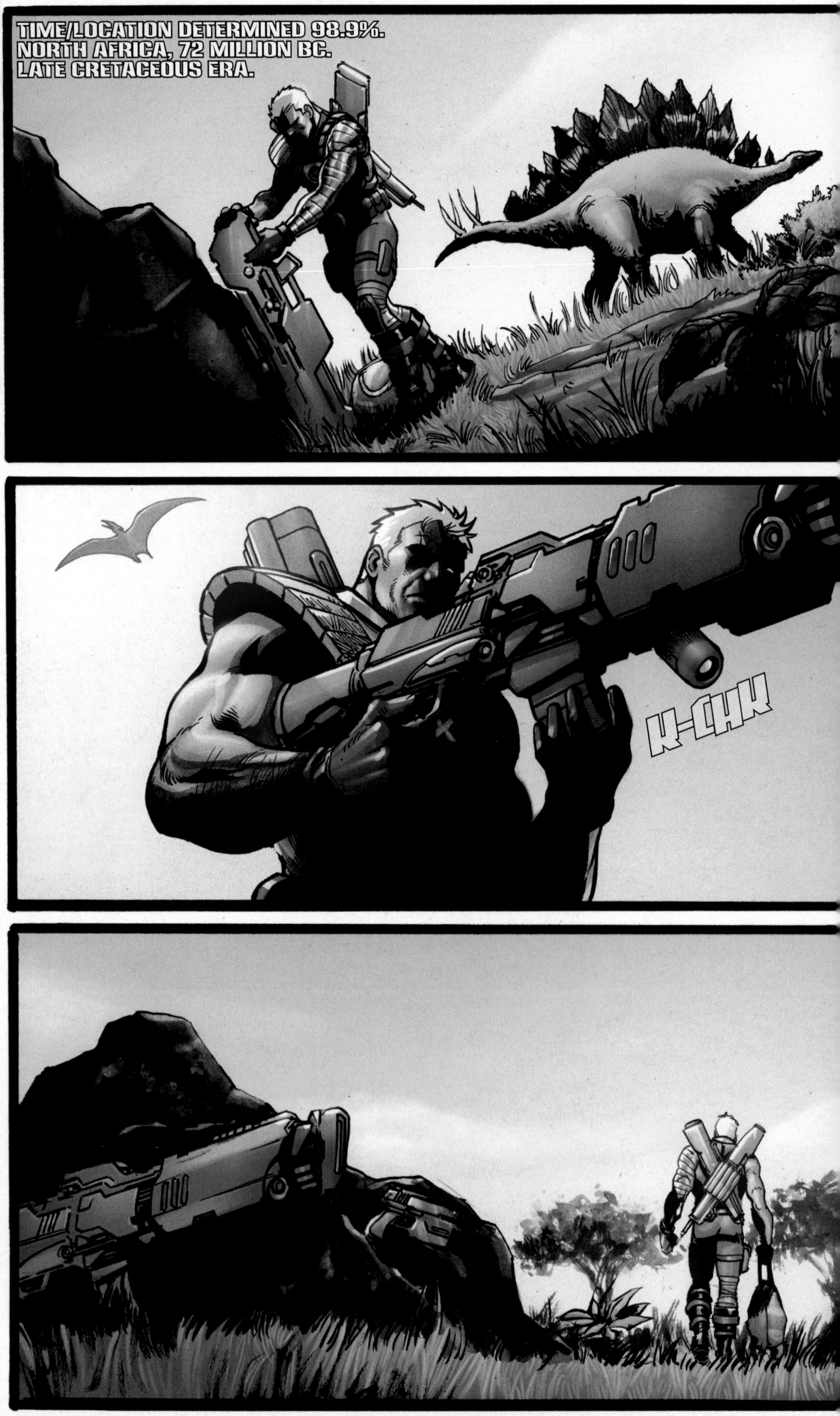
TIME/LOCATION DETERMINED 98.9%.
NORTH AFRICA, 72 MILLION BC.
LATE CRETACEOUS ERA.
K-CHK

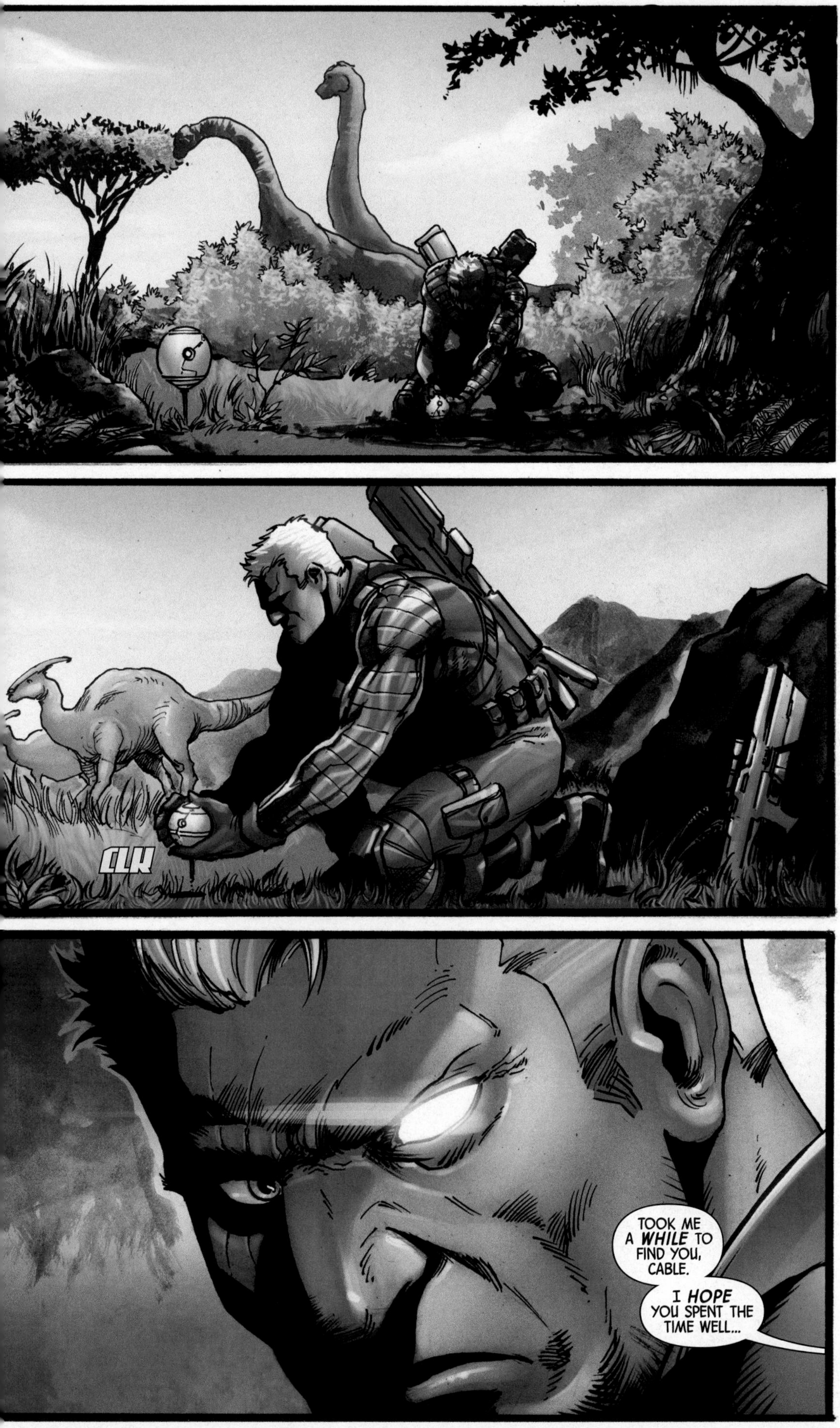
CLK
TOOK ME A WHILE TO FIND YOU, CABLE.
I HOPE YOU SPENT THE TIME WELL...

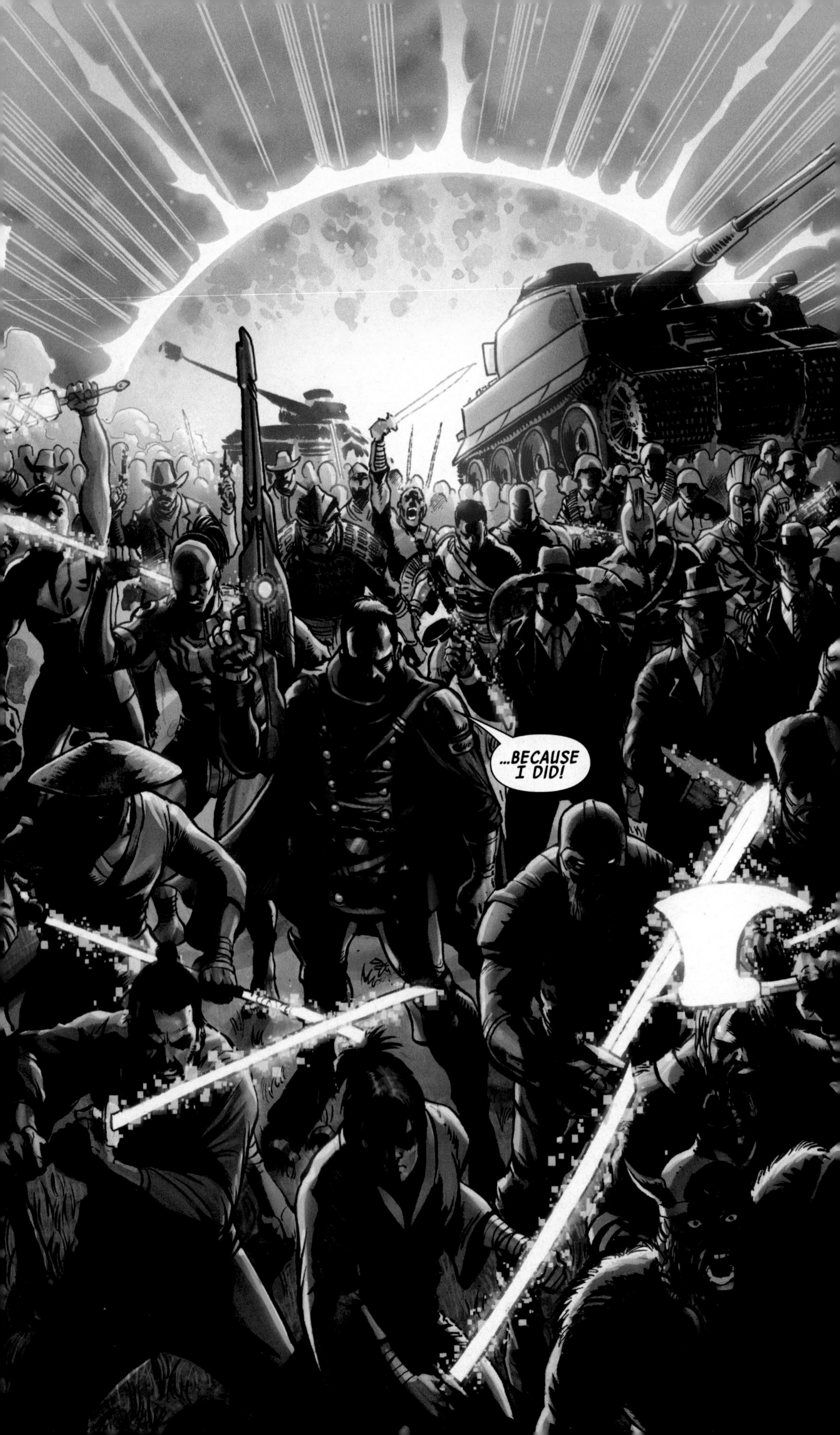
...BECAUSE I DID!

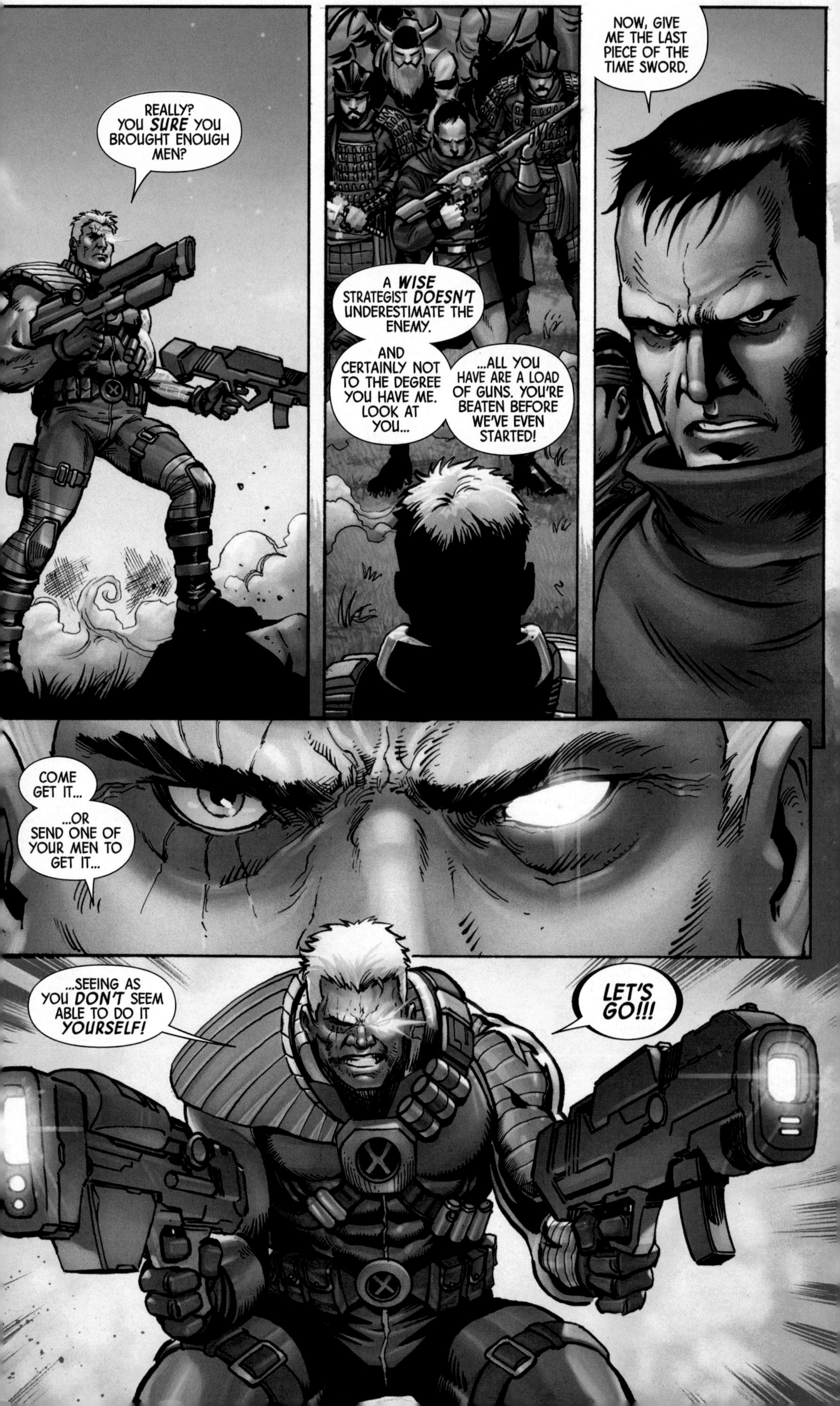
REALLY? YOU SURE YOU BROUGHT ENOUGH MEN?
A WISE STRATEGIST DOESN'T UNDERESTIMATE THE ENEMY.
AND CERTAINLY NOT TO THE DEGREE YOU HAVE ME. LOOK AT YOU...
...ALL YOU HAVE ARE A LOAD OF GUNS. YOU'RE BEATEN BEFORE WE'VE EVEN STARTED!
NOW, GIVE ME THE LAST PIECE OF THE TIME SWORD.
COME GET IT...
...OR SEND ONE OF YOUR MEN TO GET IT...
...SEEING AS YOU DON'T SEEM ABLE TO DO IT YOURSELF!
LET'S GO!!!

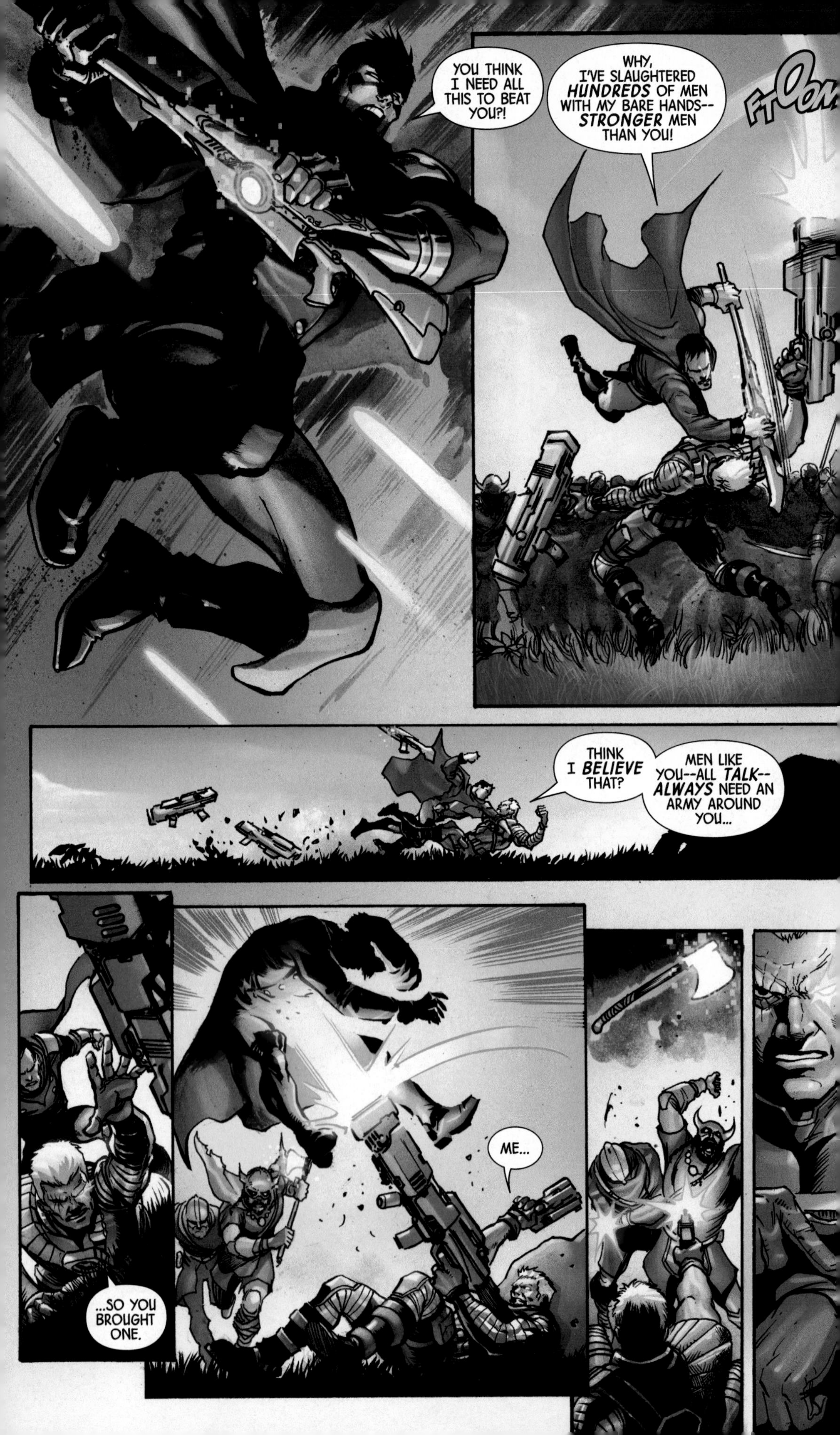
YOU THINK I NEED ALL THIS TO BEAT YOU?!
WHY, I'VE SLAUGHTERED **HUNDREDS** OF MEN WITH MY BARE HANDS-- **STRONGER** MEN THAN YOU!
FTOOM
THINK I **BELIEVE** THAT?
MEN LIKE YOU--ALL **TALK**-- **ALWAYS** NEED AN ARMY AROUND YOU...
...SO YOU BROUGHT ONE.
ME...

"...I HAVE *BEACONS* EVERYWHERE PROGRAMMED-- FREQUENCY ENCODED...

"...TO CORRESPOND TO THE CORTEX AND HYPOTHALAMUS...

"...IN *ANY* ANIMAL.

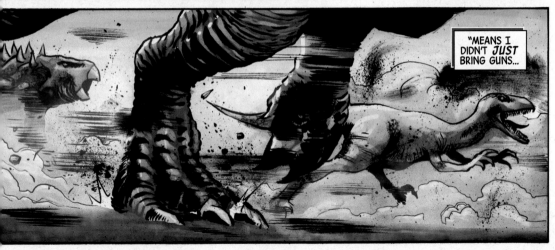

"MEANS I DIDN'T *JUST* BRING GUNS...

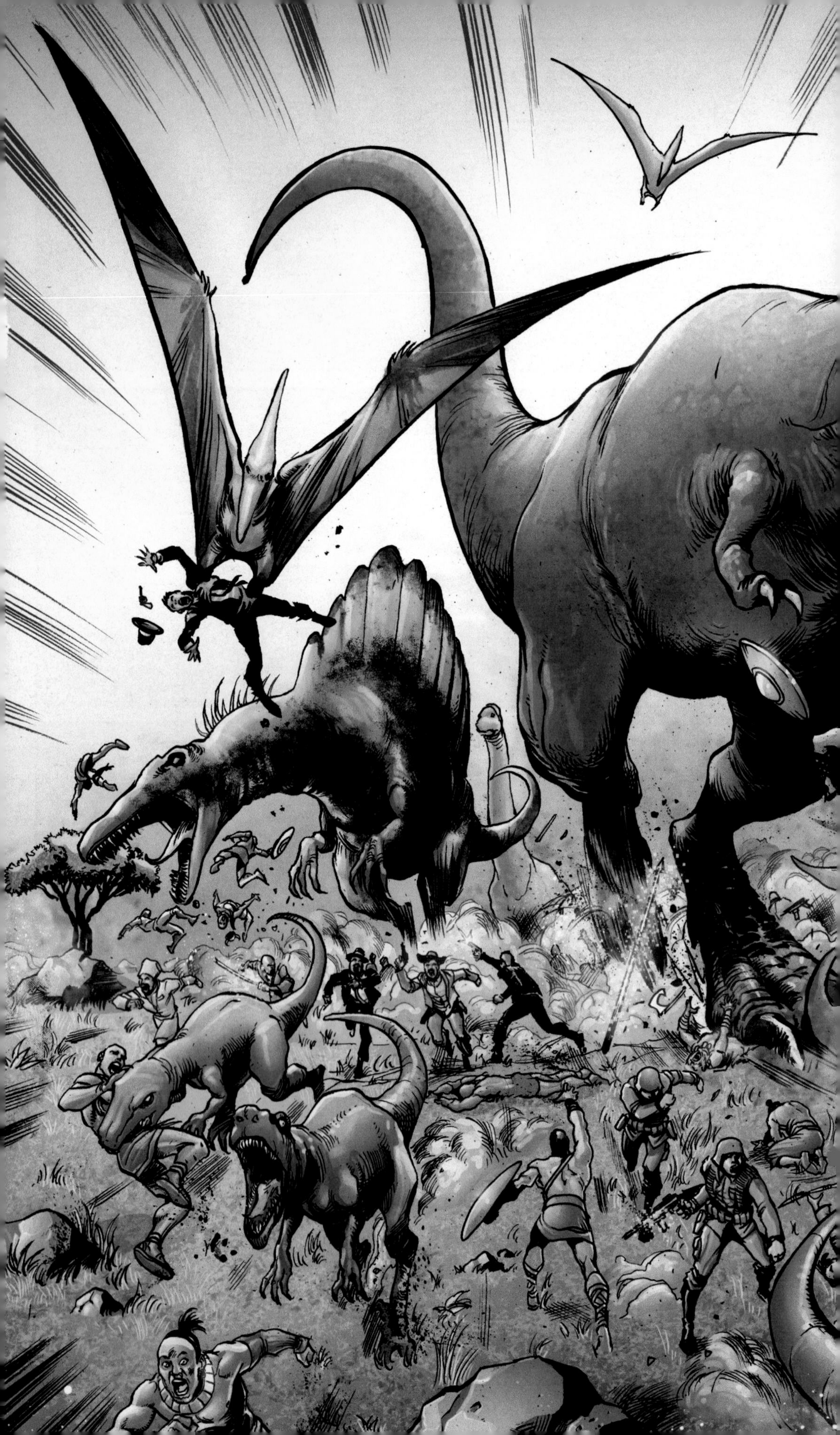

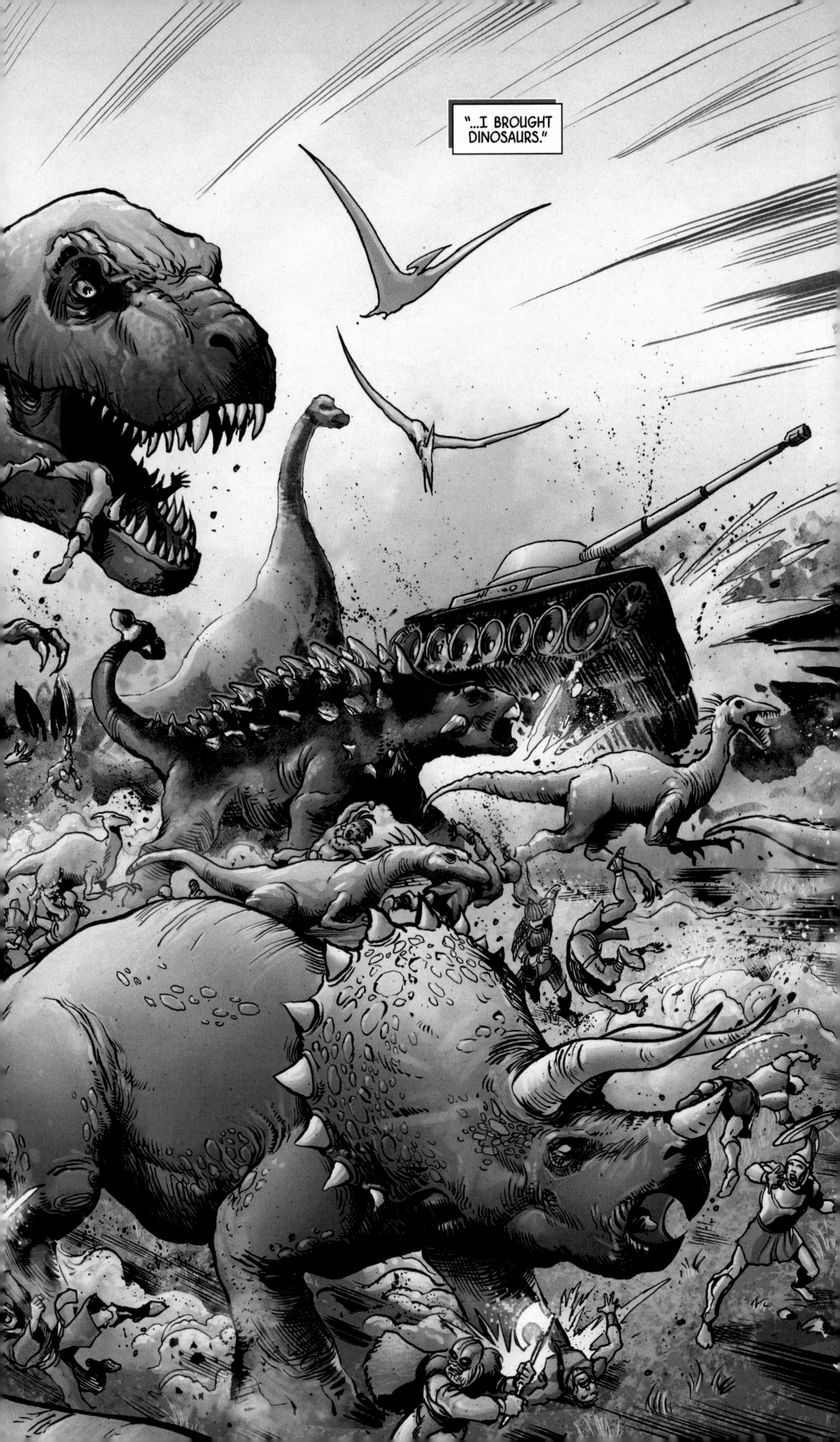
"...I BROUGHT DINOSAURS."

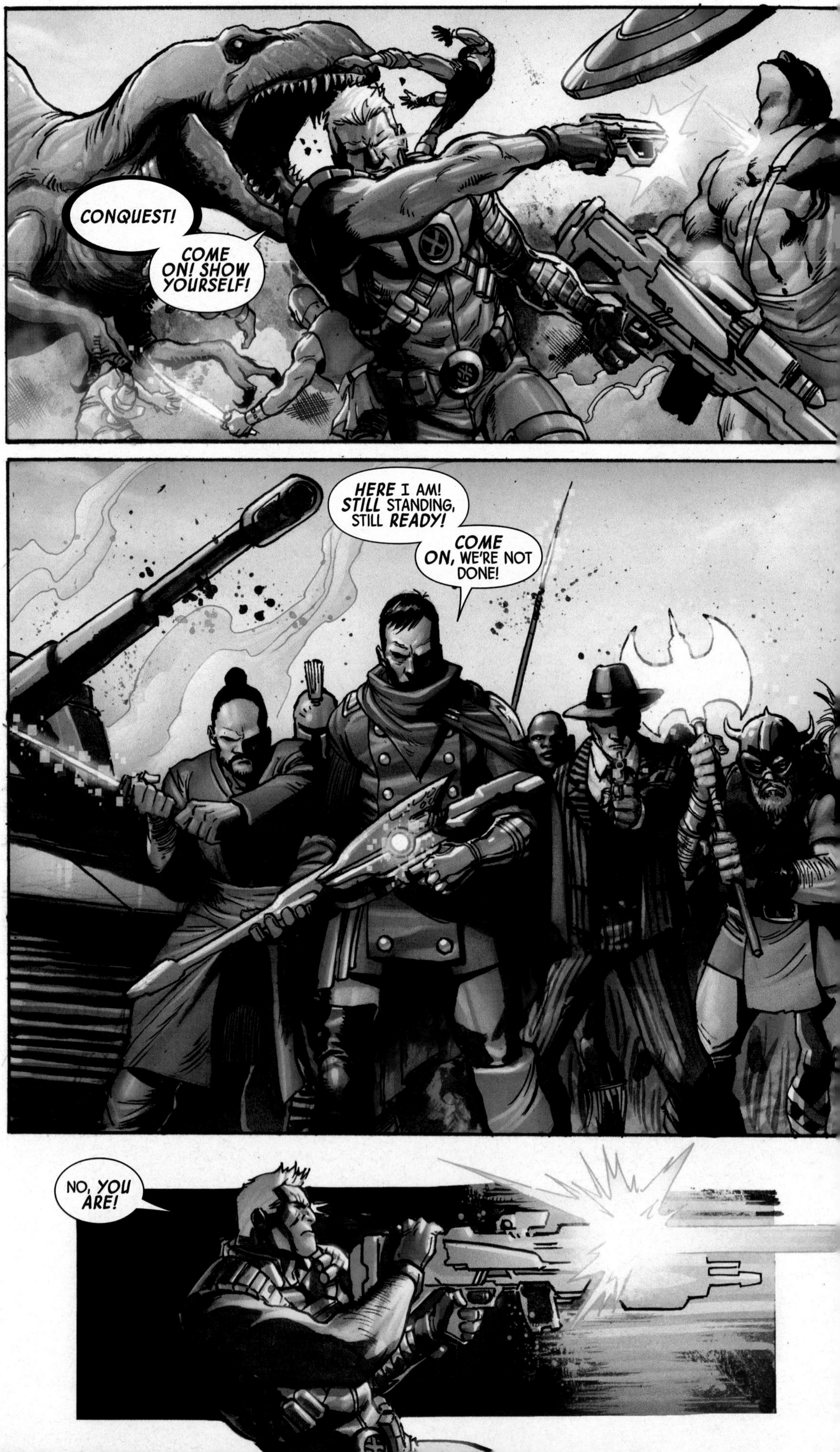
CONQUEST!
COME ON! SHOW YOURSELF!
HERE I AM! STILL STANDING, STILL READY!
COME ON, WE'RE NOT DONE!
NO, YOU ARE!

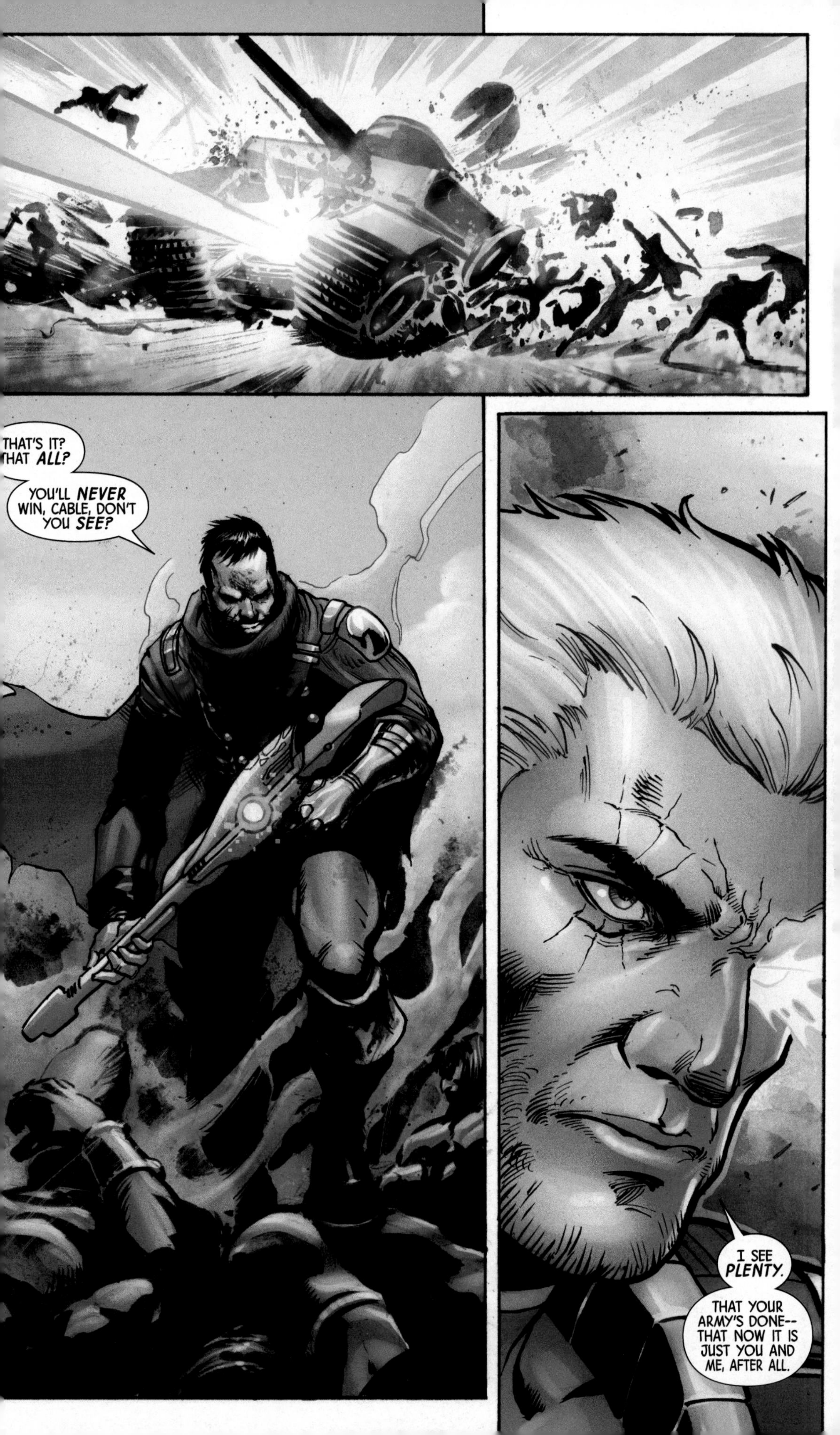
THAT'S IT? THAT ALL?
YOU'LL NEVER WIN, CABLE, DON'T YOU SEE?
I SEE PLENTY.
THAT YOUR ARMY'S DONE-- THAT NOW IT IS JUST YOU AND ME, AFTER ALL.

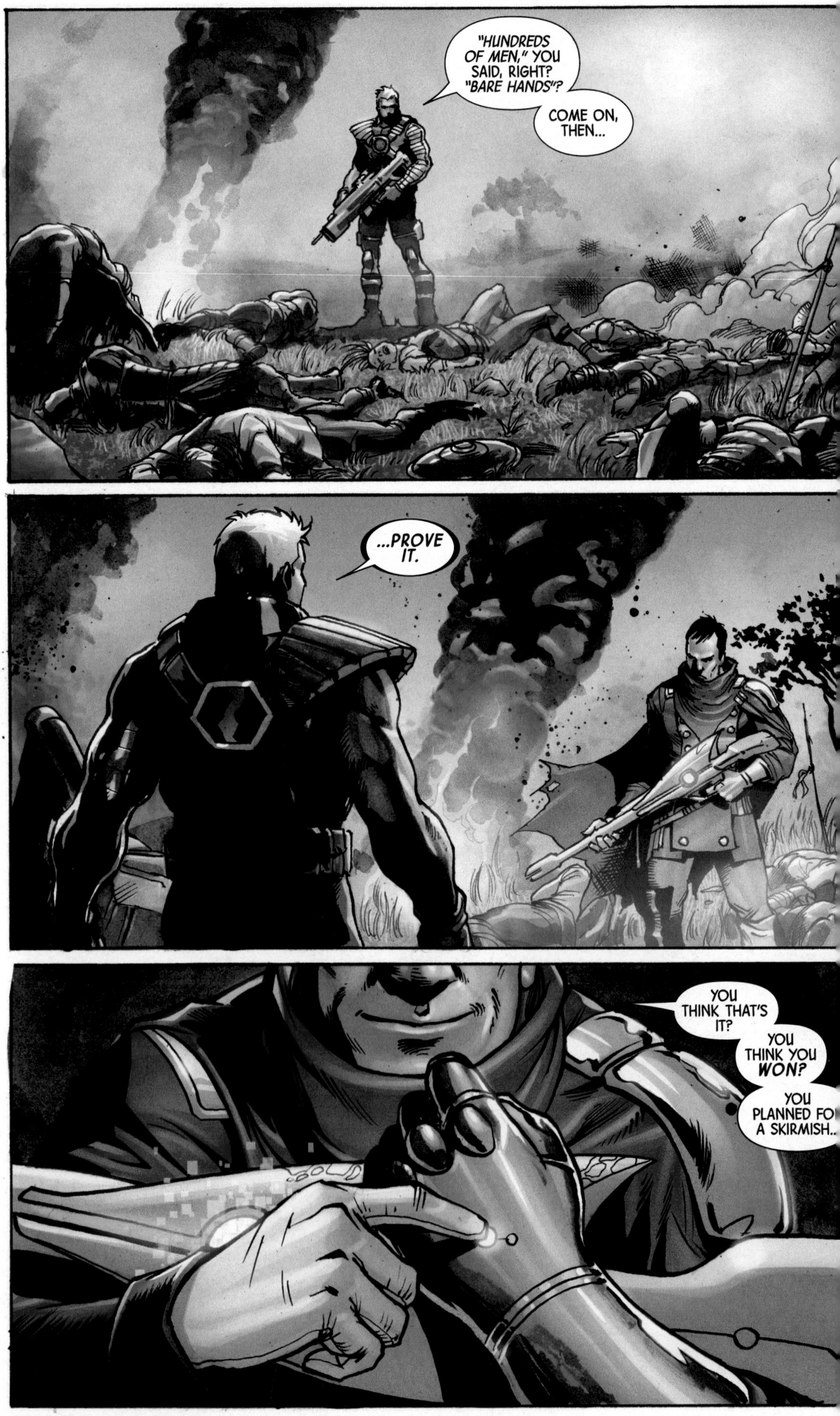
"HUNDREDS OF MEN," YOU SAID, RIGHT? "BARE HANDS"?
COME ON, THEN...
...PROVE IT.
YOU THINK THAT'S IT?
YOU THINK YOU WON?
YOU PLANNED FO A SKIRMISH..

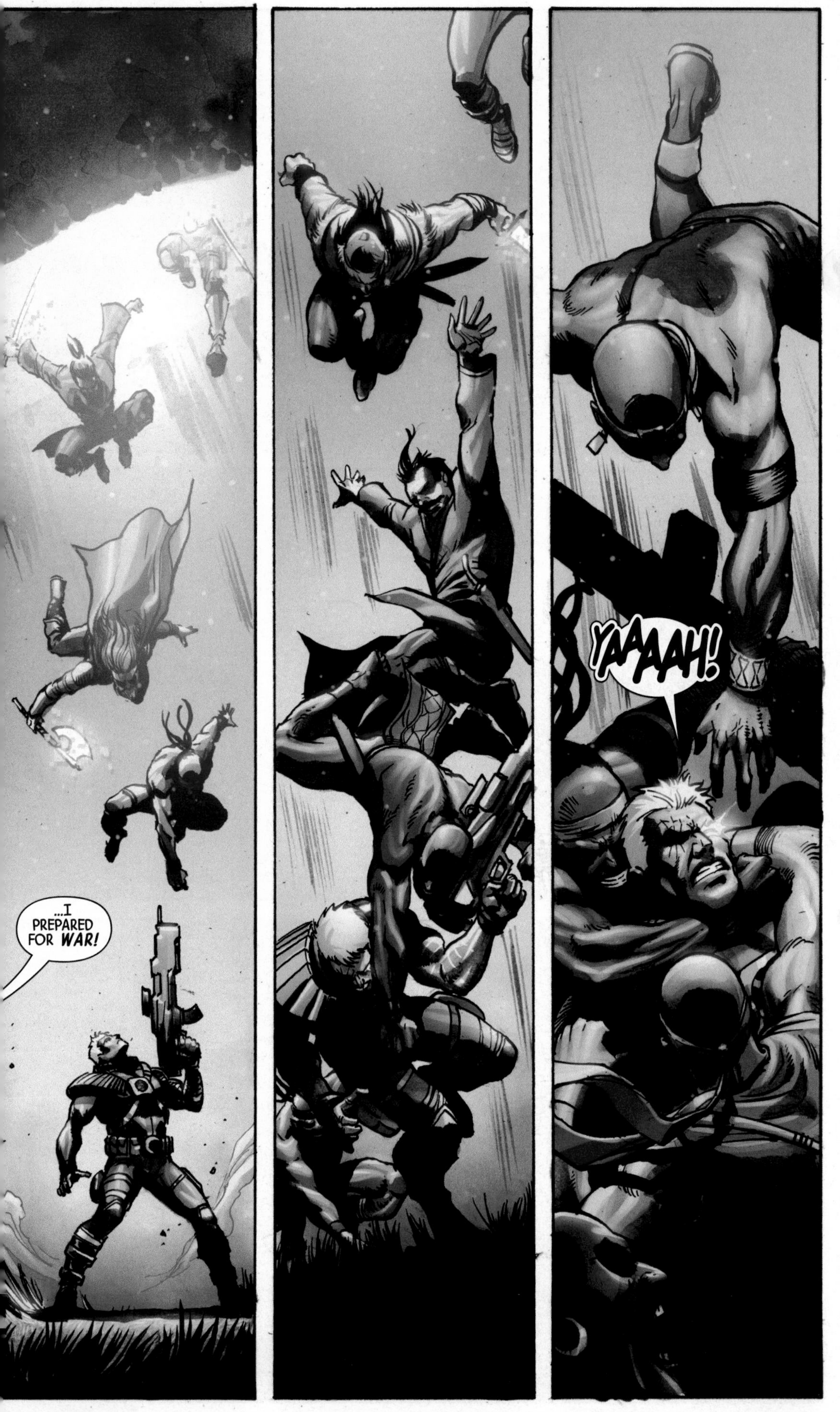
...I PREPARED FOR WAR!
YAAAAH!

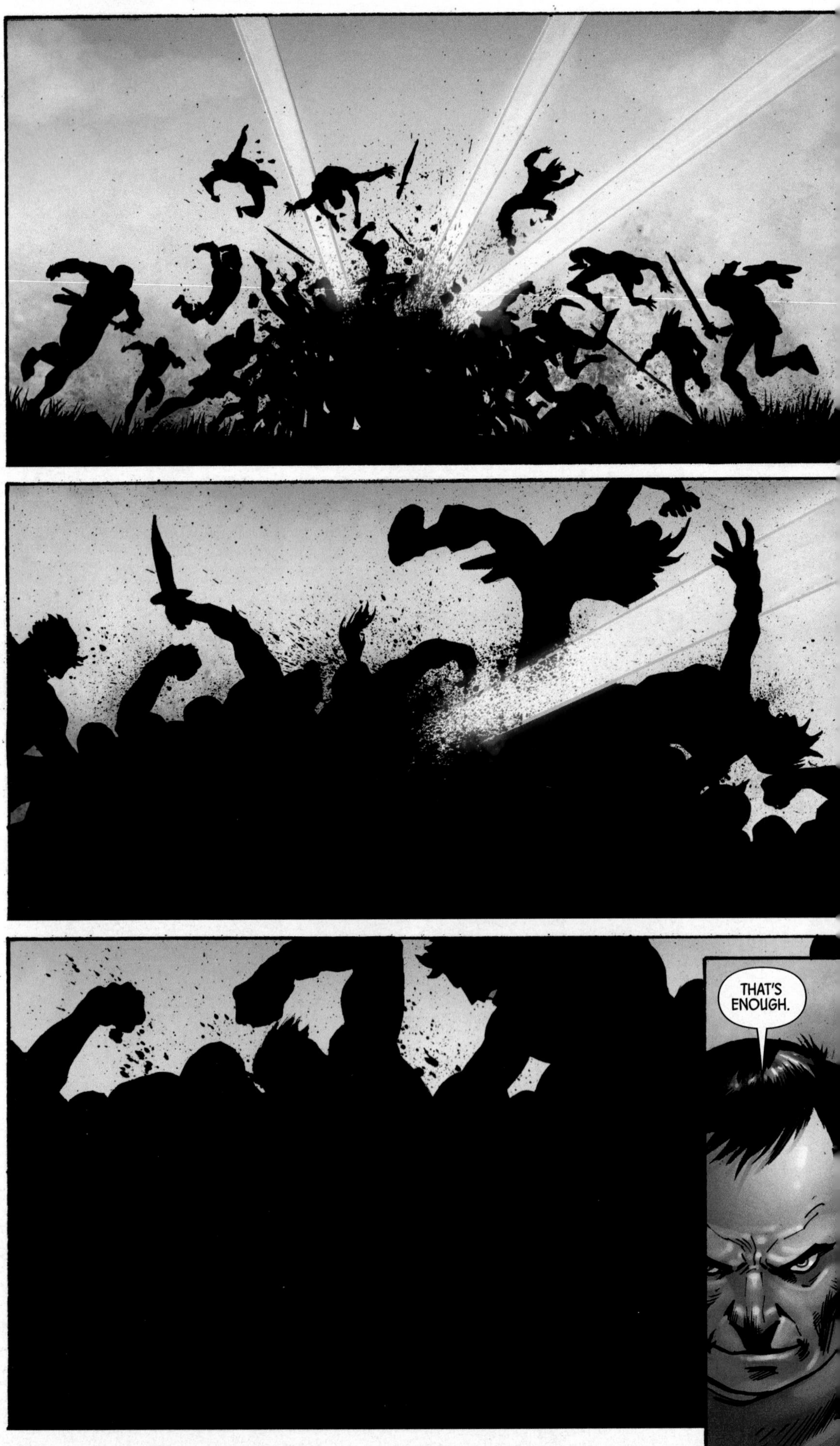
THAT'S ENOUGH.

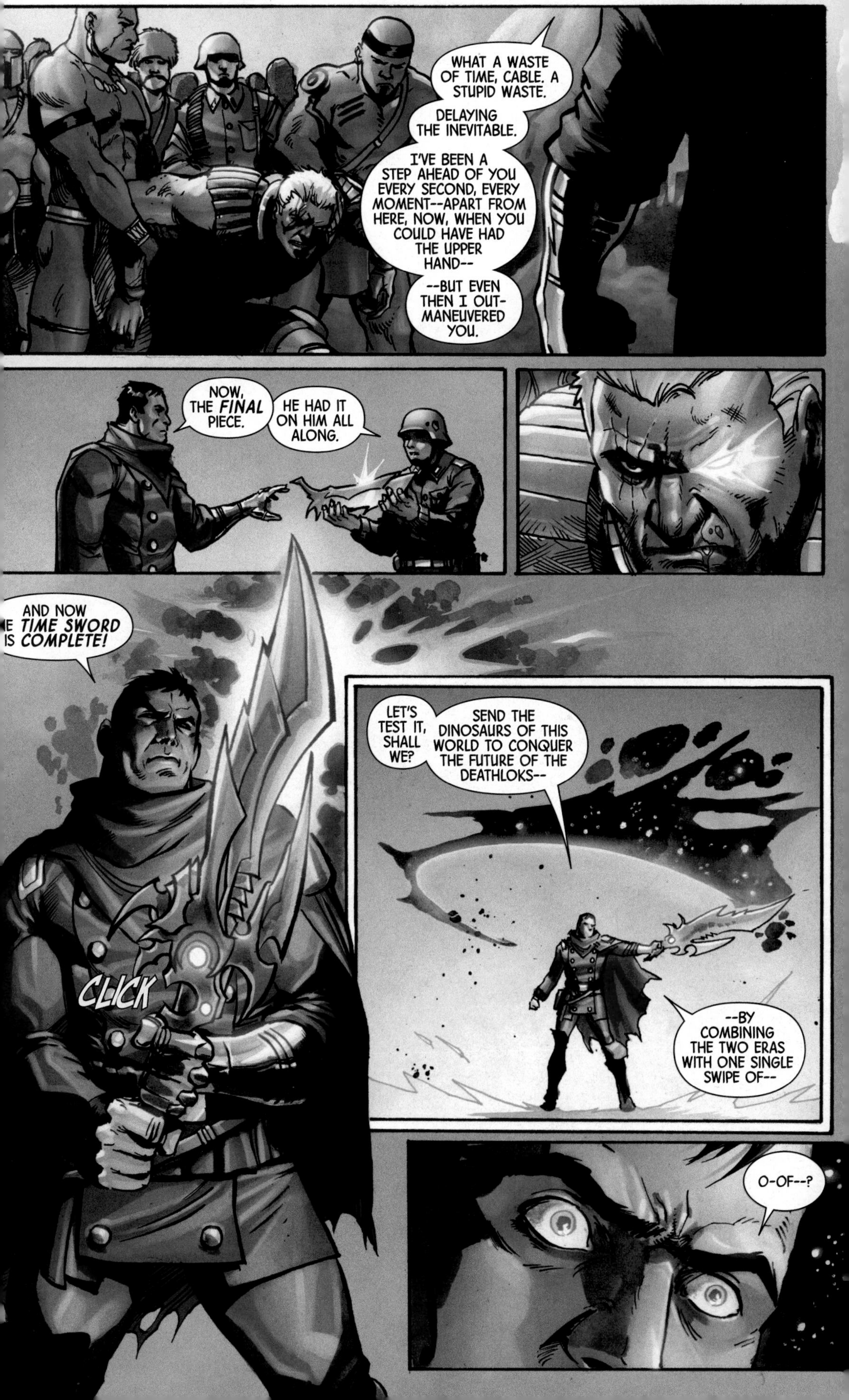
WHAT A WASTE OF TIME, CABLE. A STUPID WASTE.
DELAYING THE INEVITABLE.
I'VE BEEN A STEP AHEAD OF YOU EVERY SECOND, EVERY MOMENT--APART FROM HERE, NOW, WHEN YOU COULD HAVE HAD THE UPPER HAND--
--BUT EVEN THEN I OUT-MANEUVERED YOU.
NOW, THE *FINAL* PIECE.
HE HAD IT ON HIM ALL ALONG.
AND NOW E *TIME SWORD* IS *COMPLETE!*
CLICK
LET'S TEST IT, SHALL WE?
SEND THE DINOSAURS OF THIS WORLD TO CONQUER THE FUTURE OF THE DEATHLOKS--
--BY COMBINING THE TWO ERAS WITH ONE SINGLE SWIPE OF--
O-OF--?

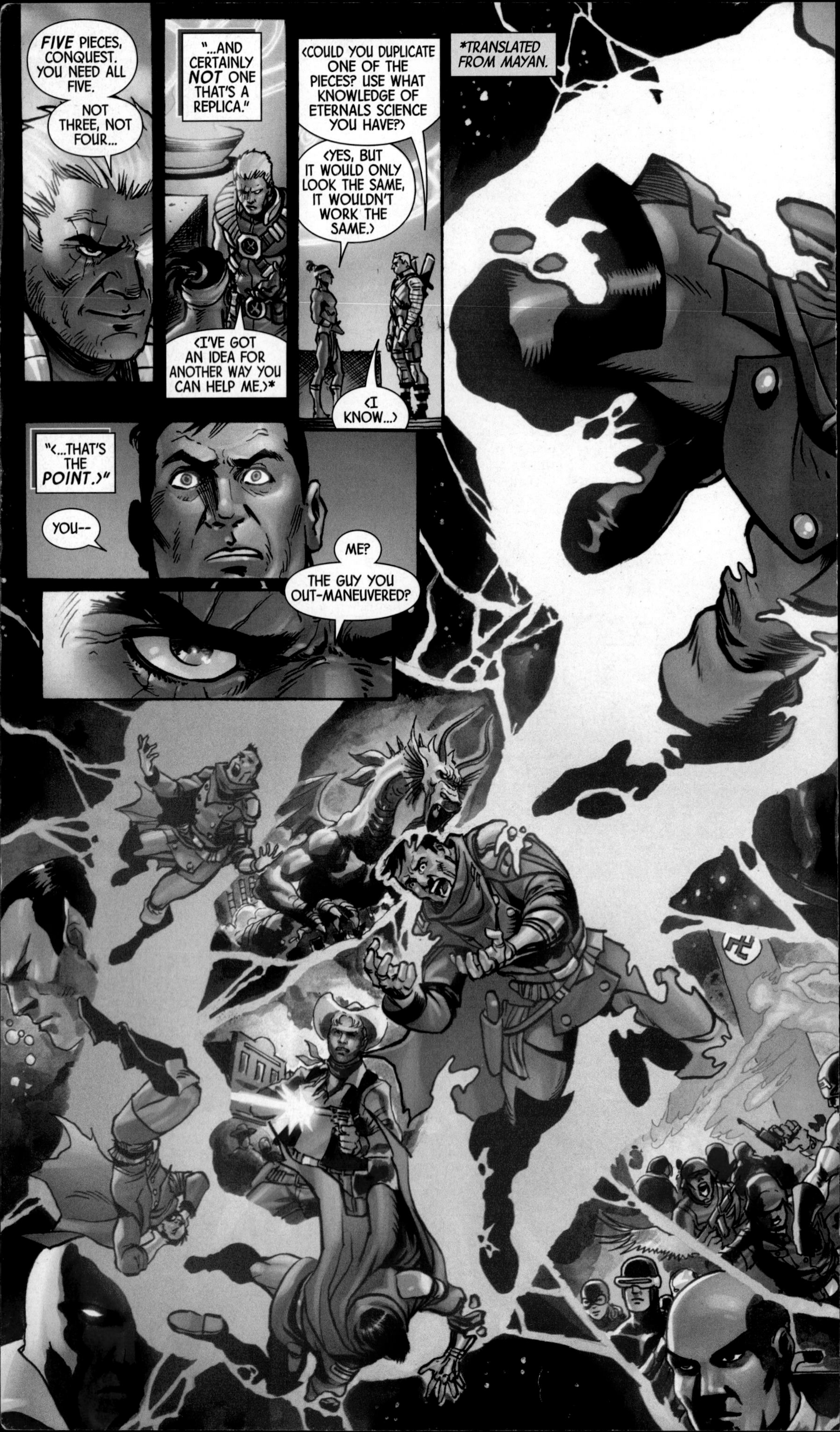
FIVE PIECES, CONQUEST. YOU NEED ALL FIVE.
NOT THREE, NOT FOUR...
"...AND CERTAINLY NOT ONE THAT'S A REPLICA."
<I'VE GOT AN IDEA FOR ANOTHER WAY YOU CAN HELP ME.>*
<COULD YOU DUPLICATE ONE OF THE PIECES? USE WHAT KNOWLEDGE OF ETERNALS SCIENCE YOU HAVE?>
<YES, BUT IT WOULD ONLY LOOK THE SAME, IT WOULDN'T WORK THE SAME.>
<I KNOW...>
*TRANSLATED FROM MAYAN.
"<...THAT'S THE POINT.>"
YOU--
ME?
THE GUY YOU OUT-MANEUVERED?

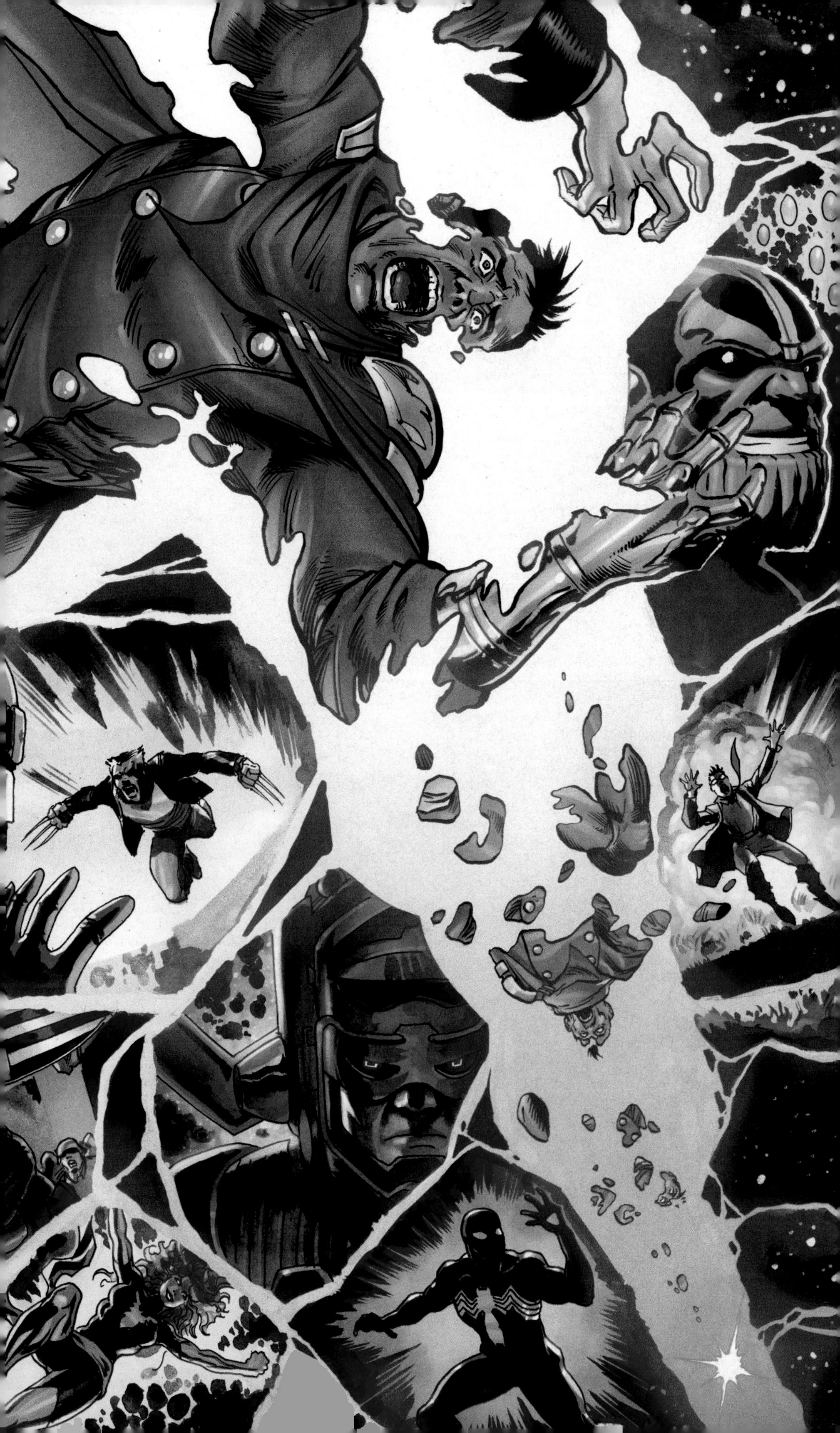

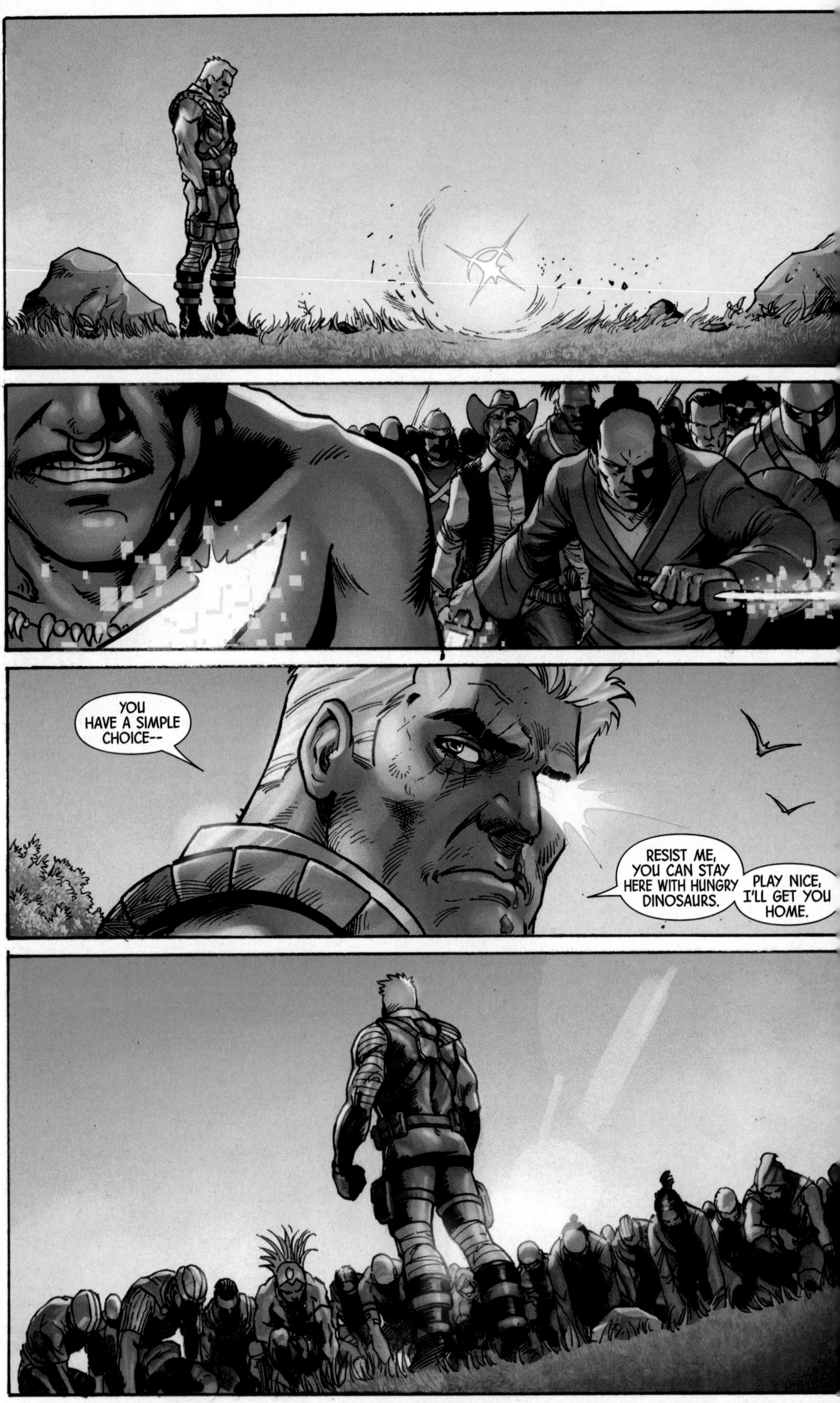
YOU HAVE A SIMPLE CHOICE--
RESIST ME, YOU CAN STAY HERE WITH HUNGRY DINOSAURS.
PLAY NICE, I'LL GET YOU HOME.

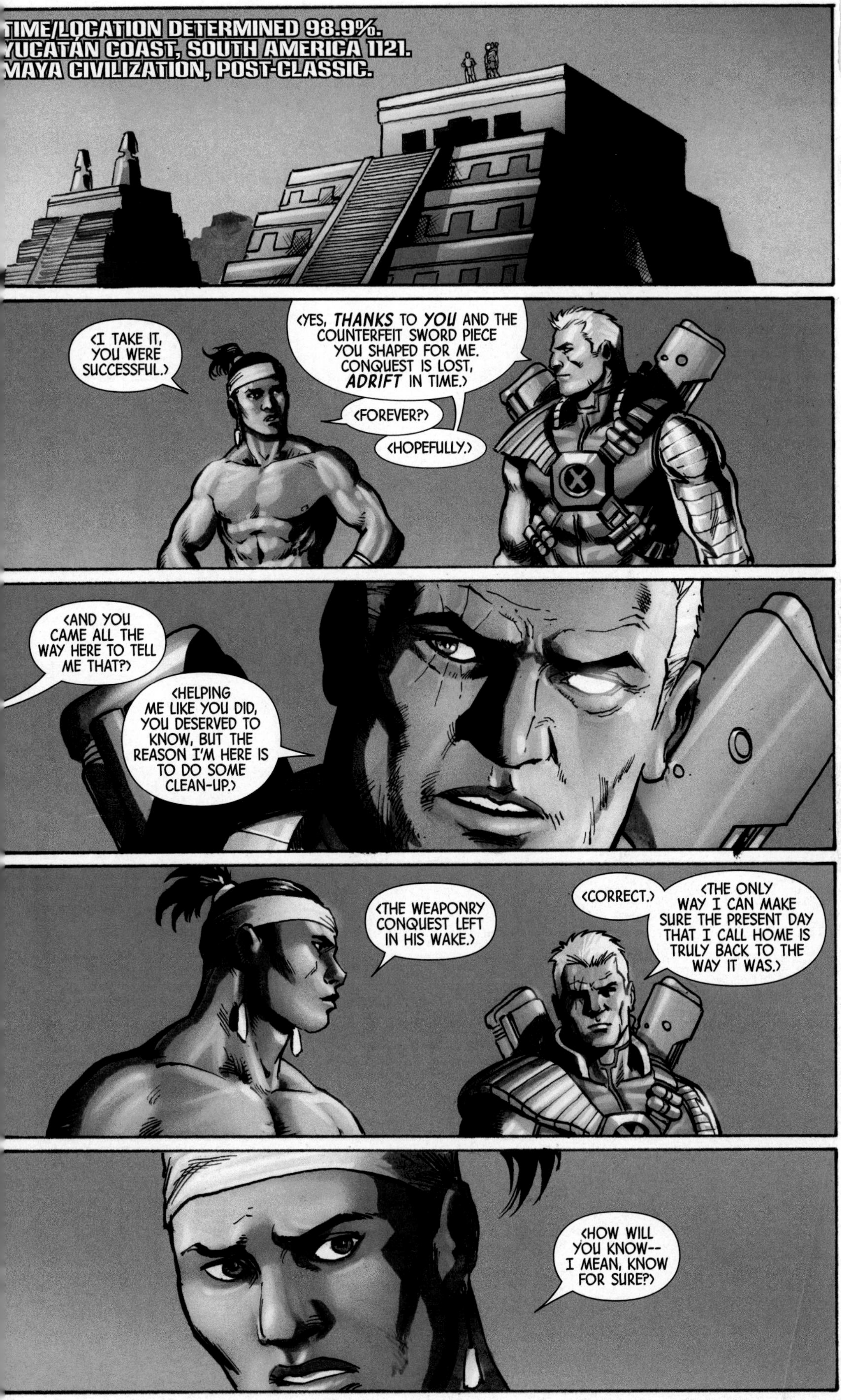
TIME/LOCATION DETERMINED 98.9%. YUCATÁN COAST, SOUTH AMERICA 1121. MAYA CIVILIZATION, POST-CLASSIC.
<I TAKE IT, YOU WERE SUCCESSFUL.>
<YES, THANKS TO YOU AND THE COUNTERFEIT SWORD PIECE YOU SHAPED FOR ME. CONQUEST IS LOST, ADRIFT IN TIME.>
<FOREVER?>
<HOPEFULLY.>
<AND YOU CAME ALL THE WAY HERE TO TELL ME THAT?>
<HELPING ME LIKE YOU DID, YOU DESERVED TO KNOW, BUT THE REASON I'M HERE IS TO DO SOME CLEAN-UP.>
<THE WEAPONRY CONQUEST LEFT IN HIS WAKE.>
<CORRECT.>
<THE ONLY WAY I CAN MAKE SURE THE PRESENT DAY THAT I CALL HOME IS TRULY BACK TO THE WAY IT WAS.>
<HOW WILL YOU KNOW-- I MEAN, KNOW FOR SURE?>

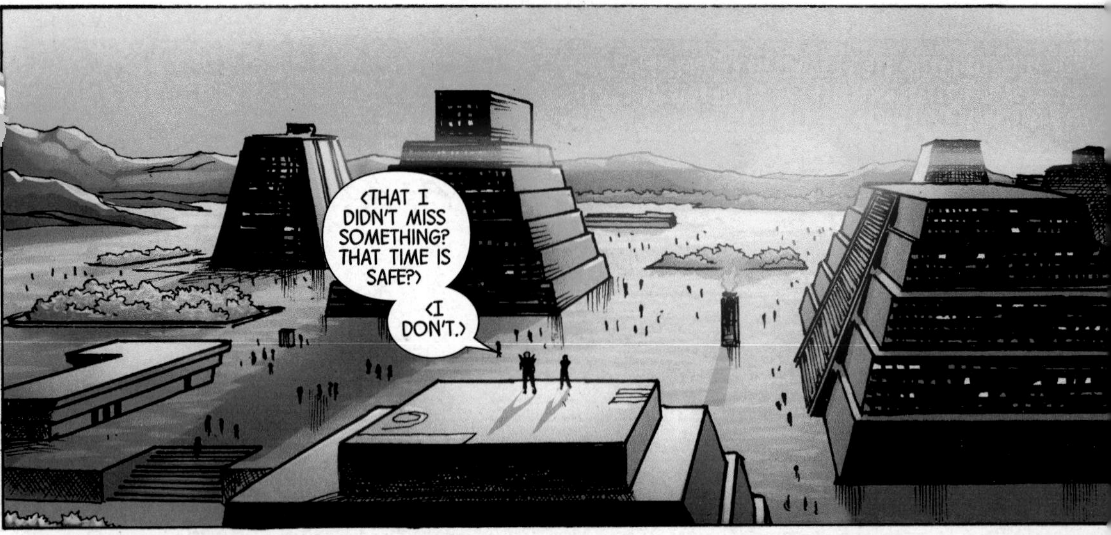
<THAT I DIDN'T MISS SOMETHING? THAT TIME IS SAFE?>
<I DON'T.>

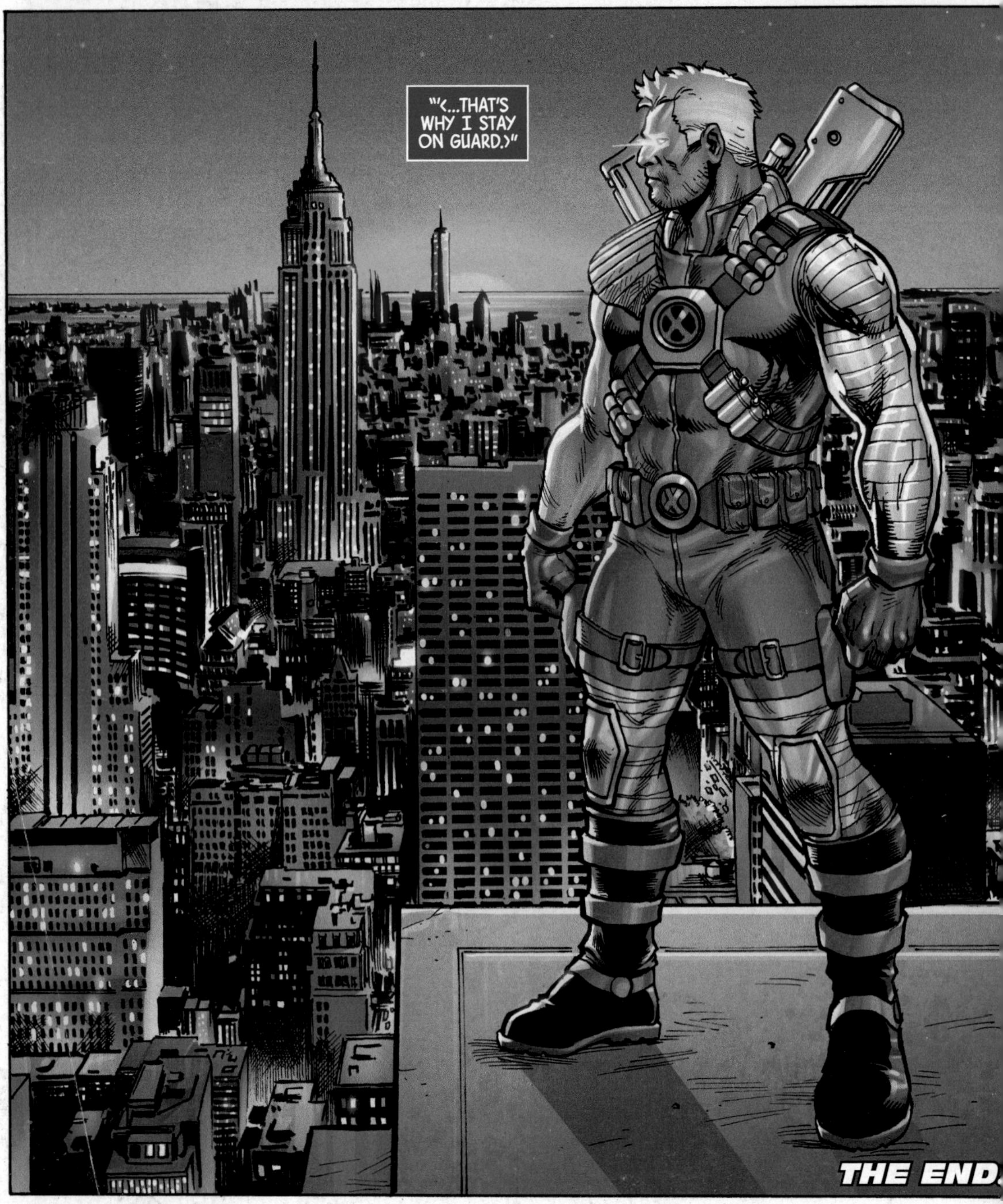
"<...THAT'S WHY I STAY ON GUARD.>"
THE END.